MUSIC IN THE HORROR FILMS
OF VAL LEWTON

Music and the Moving Image

Series Editors
Kevin J. Donnelly, University of Southampton
Beth Carroll, University of Southampton

Titles in the series include:

Film's Musical Moments
by Ian Conrich and Estella Tincknell (eds)

Music, Sound and Multimedia
by Jamie Sexton (ed.)

Music Video and the Politics of Representation
by Diane Railton and Paul Watson

Contemporary Musical Film
by Kevin J. Donnelly and Beth Carroll (eds)

British Music Videos 1966–2016: Genre, Authenticity and Art
by Emily Caston

The Auditory Setting: Environmental Sounds in Film and Media Arts
by Budhaditya Chattopadhyay

Music in the Horror Films of Val Lewton
by Michael Lee

www.edinburghuniversitypress.com/series/MAMI

MUSIC IN THE HORROR FILMS OF VAL LEWTON

Michael Lee

EDINBURGH
University Press

To Bart Aikens

Edinburgh University Press is one of the leading university presses in the UK. We publish academic books and journals in our selected subject areas across the humanities and social sciences, combining cutting-edge scholarship with high editorial and production values to produce academic works of lasting importance. For more information visit our website: edinburghuniversitypress.com

© Michael Lee, 2022, 2024

Edinburgh University Press Ltd
The Tun – Holyrood Road
12(2f) Jackson's Entry
Edinburgh EH8 8PJ

First published in hardback by Edinburgh University Press 2022

Typeset in 10/12.5 Adobe Sabon by
IDSUK (DataConnection) Ltd

A CIP record for this book is available from the British Library

ISBN 978 1 4744 9702 2 (hardback)
ISBN 978 1 4744 9703 9 (paperback)
ISBN 978 1 4744 9704 6 (webready PDF)
ISBN 978 1 4744 9705 3 (epub)

The right of Michael Lee to be identified as the author of this work has been asserted in accordance with the Copyright, Designs and Patents Act 1988, and the Copyright and Related Rights Regulations 2003 (SI No. 2498).

CONTENTS

List of Figures	vi
Acknowledgments	vii
Introduction	1
1 "Happy Mood Over This, Roy": Webb's Score for *Cat People* as Film Analysis	20
2 Fractured Reasons and Fractured Reason in *I Walked with a Zombie*	39
3 *The Leopard Man* as Penitential Horror Film	58
4 Searching for Meaning in *The Seventh Victim*	71
5 A Wartime Fable in the Sounds of *The Ghost Ship*	86
6 Music for Amy and Her Friend: Webb's Score for *The Curse of the Cat People*	105
7 Boris Karloff and the Soundtrack of *The Body Snatcher*	119
8 Validating Uncertainty on the *Isle of the Dead*	143
9 "Dainty Little Notes, Ain't They?": Roy Webb's Age of Reason in *Bedlam*	169
10 A Closing Argument	191
References	200
List of Films Cited	205
Index	208

FIGURES

1.1	Roy Webb, "Victory Signature"	21
1.2	Roy Webb, "Needful Help," mm. 10–11	31
1.3	Roy Webb, "First Quarrel" from *Cat People*	36
2.1	Roy Webb, "Fort Holland"	47
3.1	Roy Webb, "Theresa's Death" from *The Leopard Man*, m. 22	65
3.2	Roy Webb, "Chant"	67
4.1	Roy Webb, "Main Title" from *The Seventh Victim*, melody mm. 3–8	75
4.2	Roy Webb, "Love Theme" from *The Seventh Victim*	77
5.1	Roy Webb, "Finn" from *The Ghost Ship*	100
7.1	Roy Webb, "Introducing Meg" from *The Body Snatcher*, mm. 15–27	132
7.2	Roy Webb, "Danger Ahead" from *The Body Snatcher*, m. 71	133
7.3	Roy Webb, "End Title" from *The Body Snatcher*, mm. 1–12	134
7.4	Roy Webb, "Gray Kills Joseph" from *The Body Snatcher*, mm. 61–84	135–136
8.1	Leigh Harline, "Main Title" from *Isle of the Dead*	155–157
8.2	Leigh Harline, "The Battlefield" from *Isle of the Dead*, mm. 12–29	161–162
8.3	Leigh Harline, "*Vorvolaka*" from *Isle of the Dead*, mm. 15–19	164
8.4	Leigh Harline, "The Coffin" from *Isle of the Dead*, mm. 63–66	165
9.1	Roy Webb, "Main Title" from *Bedlam*, mm. 1–9	178
9.2	Roy Webb, "Main Title" from *Bedlam*, mm. 10–18	179
9.3	Roy Webb, "Main Title" from *Bedlam*, mm. 30–37	180
9.4	Roy Webb, "Main Title" from *Bedlam*, mm. 59–62	180
9.5	Roy Webb, "Main Title" from *Bedlam*, mm. 63–70	181
9.6	Roy Webb, "Nell's Visit to the Asylum" from *Bedlam*, mm. 31–41	183

ACKNOWLEDGMENTS

This book benefitted from the contributions of a great many people. I would like to thank them in a roughly chronological order for their kindness and expertise. This places Bart Aikens at both the beginning and end of these acknowledgments. He was and to some extent remains the consummate "monster kid" whose passion for horror films rubbed off on me somewhere around third grade. The name Val Lewton may well have never meant anything to me had he not drawn my attention to the nine films discussed in this book. When I would visit Los Angeles, sometimes for extended periods of time, Bart put me up on his hide-away bed ungraciously dubbed by me "The Crippler." That ungrateful joke looks all the worse when you consider that he would later edit multiple drafts of the manuscript for me, in his career as a professional editor. His editorial insights and comprehensive knowledge of Lewton's horror films improved the book enormously. We spent dozens (more likely hundreds) of hours discussing Lewton's films in minute detail.

Bart also gave me a birthday gift that changed the trajectory of my life and informed this book, a copy of J. P. Telotte's *Dreams of Darkness: Fantasy and the Films of Val Lewton*. That book, along with Hiett Cooper's Film Studies class at Spencer's Butte Junior High, opened my eyes to the possibility that films could be meaningfully studied.

My mentor first in graduate school and then in life, Robert Moore, spent long hours discussing film with me in ways that inform my thinking about not only film but literally everything. He and his wife, Jaehee Choi, made my return visits to Los Angeles for research possible. They put me up for long periods, but mostly they're dear friends.

In addition to Telotte, I am deeply indebted to Alexander Nemerov whose brilliant book *Icons of Grief: Val Lewton's Home Front Pictures*, his timely visit to the University of Oklahoma, and subsequent correspondence helped this project get on track. In addition to Alexander Nemerov's inspirational book and helpful advice, he put me in touch with Val Lewton, Jr., whose generous correspondence yielded the most important insights into his father's relationship with music. I am grateful to both Nemerov and Lewton for their generosity.

Three other authors invested in Val Lewton's films proved extremely helpful beyond their writings. Edmund Bansak's biography of the producer remains a great favorite of mine. He led me to useful archival materials in his generous correspondence. Clive Dawson, author of a forthcoming book on *I Walked with a Zombie*, offered useful materials on Lewton and censorship as well as much encouragement. Meeting Catherine Haworth at the Music and the Moving Image conference at New York University aided me enormously in rethinking the scholarly value of my hero worship of Roy Webb. I am grateful to her for sharing her wonderful dissertation with me and for correcting my course through her celebration not of heroes, but of entire music departments. That her work so skillfully considers the Music Department at RKO during the exact period Lewton was there renders her an invaluable colleague. My gratitude most certainly extends to James Buhler not only for his having shaped my thinking about film music and hermeneutics through his own work, but also for his helpful reading of my manuscript and excellent professional advice.

Research on this book led to many happy hours spent in archives. The following librarians and institutions were crucial to the fruition of this project. Without UCLA's supremely professional handling of the RKO Music Archive this book would not exist. The staff at UCLA is entirely wonderful, but I want to single out Steven Davison who stepped out of his usual role in UCLA's digital archive to help me gain full advantage of these materials.

USC's Ned Comstock deserves enormous thanks. People often joke that his name appears in the acknowledgment section of virtually every cinema history book, so I am not unique in thanking him. But I felt unique as he gave me what he calls "his Trojan treatment" for my having earned my PhD at USC. This treatment entailed keeping a look out for every piece of paper pertaining to Roy Webb that came to his attention. Several times over the last ten years, a package from him would arrive unannounced full of astonishingly useful materials on Webb and on the Lewton films.

Brigham Young University is home to a large and growing archive on film music, most notably the Max Steiner Collection. Insofar as Webb worked closely with Steiner, my path found its way to the BYU library's Special Collections. Music theorist Brent Yorgason and librarian Jeff Lyon have been hugely helpful during my visits. So has my friend and colleague Christian Asplund, who is a model host and a heroic conversationalist. His friendship and support means a lot to me and to this book.

My debt of gratitude for help with archival research goes out to the library staff at Syracuse University Library Special Collections, The National Security Archive at George Washington University, The University of Cincinnati Archives and Rare Books Leigh Harline Collection, The Library of Congress, and the Margaret Herrick Library of the Academy of Motion Picture Arts and Sciences. The University of Oklahoma Library with its superb interlibrary loan department and terrific Music Librarian, Matt Stock, deserves a huge thank you from me for innumerable helpful acts.

Several colleagues performed heavy lifting on my behalf during the later stages of this project. My friend and colleague Sarah Reichardt Ellis co-authored parts of my chapter on *I Walked with a Zombie* for an earlier article. She also read drafts of certain chapters, offering much useful advice. Brooke McCorkle edited the entire book at one crucial stage and pointed me toward many crucial sources. Her kindness and command of the literature on film music made this book possible. Gary Rhodes patiently heard me talk about this project for over a decade (during which he completed dozens of his own). Gary's help cannot be overstated. He is a friend and a source of inspiration. He pointed me toward Edinburgh University Press.

Edinburgh University Press proved an ideal partner for bringing this project to fruition. Again, I must thank Gary Rhodes for sending me there. Leslie Gillian's encouragement and professionalism guided me through the proposal process. Sam Johnson, Geraldine Lyons, Fiona Conn, Bekah Day, and Caitlin Murphy all contributed enormously to the realization of this project through their various and important expertise. K. J. Donnelly, the planet's leading authority on horror film music and series editor at Edinburgh University Press, and his colleague, Beth Carroll, provided crucial feedback drastically improving this book. I also want to thank the anonymous peer reviewers Donnelly and Carroll selected for their helpful critiques.

Family and friends proved instrumental in this project by listening to me talk about it at extraordinary length over many years. Notable in this role were Sanna Pederson (a scholar's scholar who gave great advice), Jonathan Havercroft, Roger Rideout, Armand Ambrosini, Dolores Leffingwell (who heard the dialogue in *The Body Snatcher* as music long before I did), Eugene Enrico, Jake Johnson, and Kyle Miller. Among my family Karen Lee and Barb Lee did heavy lifting listening to my ranting about Roy Webb and Val Lewton. Jodi Wenzel read the whole manuscript and gave some excellent suggestions. Chris Lee and Patty Williams indulged multiple yuletide viewings of *The Curse of the Cat People* and kept me on task by asking periodically how things were going, sometimes rousing me to fresh labor. Cathy Peacock served this project as a benefactress on many levels with a luxurious guest room in striking distance of New York archives and conferences. The kindness of family and friends made this work possible.

INTRODUCTION

From 1942–1946, Val Lewton produced nine low-budget horror films for RKO Pictures. To varying degrees they achieved commercial success and favorable critical notice. In subsequent decades, they came to enjoy a positive reputation among scholars, critics, filmmakers, and fans of the horror genre disproportionate to their modest means, earning for Lewton the rare status of auteur producer.

Taken as a whole, the Lewton horror films rub against the grain of the horror genre by banishing explicit monsters and exploring the anxieties and potentials for violence that dwell inside relatable people in familiar contemporary settings. The unseen would serve as the source of horror in these films, prompting a new and much studied visual style emphasizing shadows and absences.

The paragraph above summarizes the conclusions of the sixth chapter of the first comprehensive history of horror films, Carlos Clarens's 1967 *An Illustrated History of Horror Film*.[1] Clarens's few pages on Lewton's films did much to codify the scholarly reception of Lewton's output as his tone is rapturous. His metaphors for Lewton's films begin and end with music and just a splash of water in between.

> Taken in their original context – the Hollywood of the early forties – the movies of Val Lewton stand out as chamber music against the seedy bombast of the claw-and-fang epics of the day. Brief, precisely constructed, and neatly executed, they continue to generate an effective secret music of their own. Lewton swimming against the current, could

not hope to turn the tide; he was a modest, lone virtuoso in a period which thrived on marching songs, maudlin themes, and the worn-out misteriosi of a genre already too tired to pick up its coffin and go.²

The most recent book on Lewton, Alexander Nemerov's *Icons of Grief: Val Lewton's Home Front Pictures*, rehearses a more precise litany of Lewton's contribution to the horror genre in equal measures weary and wary.

> By now an ironclad set of accounts explains [Lewton's] work: he made the most of small budgets; he emphasized the unconscious motivations of human beings; he favored darkness and the unseen generally so his audiences could imagine horror rather than see it. None of this is wrong; the trouble at this point is that it is *too* correct. The standard view of Lewton, with its informative but ready-made explanations, forestalls other ways of looking, consigning the best moments of this strange and difficult filmmaker to the hallowed and dusty spaces of "Art," where all the wisdom is clear and one need only recite a set of truisms in order to see – really, *not* to see – the most powerful qualities of these films.³

Both Clarens's enthusiasm for first describing the general qualities of Lewton's films and Nemerov's delight in revealing the specific qualities of ignored details within them inform this book. The conventional wisdom outlined by Clarens and regretted by Nemerov will not be minutely rehearsed here. Readers have a vast literature to draw upon for just such rehearsals as Nemerov points out.⁴

This book examines the music in Lewton's horror films, not the metaphoric music heard by Clarens, but the actual music heard within them. Methods used in this examination include hermeneutic readings of original score composed for the films; archival research embracing drafts of screenplays, interdepartmental memoranda, spotting sheets, and even marginalia scrawled on orchestral scores; and careful study of the films themselves often informed by the large and growing literature on them. The book considers both original underscore generated for each film and all instances of diegetic music. The musical nature of certain dialogue and sound effects presented in ways resembling *musique concrète* also informs this study. Every effort has been made to account for how music collaborates with the image track, dialogue, and sound effects not merely to reinforce the action and clarify each film's "inner truth" as Hollywood film scores usually do,⁵ but also to clarify thematic content, subvert generic conventions, and engage in critique. If there is an originality to this book, it is simply this: the music in these films is treated as though it were a gateway to analyze the films as a whole.

While the approach described here resembles any number of earlier discussions of studio-era Hollywood film scores and certainly falls easily within Peter

Franklin's stated goal of a "film musicology" of the sort widely practiced at least since Claudia Gorbman published her groundbreaking study,[6] this book does offer a few new elements differentiating it from earlier work.

At a surface level, this book most closely resembles Nathan Platte's history *Making Music in Selznick's Hollywood*.[7] Both examine music produced for films created by a hands-on producer working within the Hollywood studio system. This study shares many methods with Platte's work, most notably a love of archival research, but while Platte is centrally concerned with his role as historian of Hollywood film music, this study concerns itself more with the generation of meaning within the films. Musicology here is a tool of Film Studies and pure history is not the goal.

Where our studies surely reach accord is in illustrating how musicians – in this case almost the entire RKO Music Department – worked as collaborators with the larger vision of the filmmakers and often moved beyond the role of collaborators by exhibiting clear and important independence. Time and again, this book will illustrate how screenplays were ignored in terms of their musical suggestions or spotting sheets were subverted toward advancing the independent vision of RKO musicians concerning how best to serve the meaning of scenes and entire films.

One key aim of my approach focuses on illustrating how close analytical readings of music in films reveal that the music in these films facilitates filmic analysis by pointing toward non-obvious conclusions. As production practices prior to the advent of digital technology saved the composition, orchestration, and recording of film music for post-production, the creative forces behind the generation of music for films became the first audience for these incomplete texts. This posture of last creative personnel to contribute allowed studio musicians to function as first analysts of the larger film's meaning, albeit informally as the discipline of film analysis had not yet been born when these films were made.

Similarly, the original orchestral underscore for each film also provides opportunities to consider how the music "adds value" to the image, to use a phrase introduced by Michel Chion.[8] Chion identifies two ways that music adds value. First, "Music can directly express its participation in the feeling of the scene, by taking the scene's rhythm, tone, and phrasing," thus it "participates in the cultural codes for things like sadness, happiness, and movement."[9] Second, "Music can also exhibit conspicuous indifference to the situation, by progressing in a steady, undaunted and ineluctable manner."[10]

In many instances, the scores created for the Lewton horror films offer a third way of "adding value" by serving to comment upon the action of the film and even the thematic organization lurking just below the consciousness of casual observers. At times, the music in the Lewton films suggests analytical insights into the films themselves. While I cannot argue this was the intent of the RKO Music Department, my task in the chapters to follow is to persuade readers that this possibility of film music as film analysis is worth entertaining.

Roy Webb, who composed the scores for eight of the nine horror films Lewton produced, offers a rationale for examining his scores for Lewton as a distinct corpus worthy of such consideration by hinting at a third mode of "adding value" to a film. In an essay for *Film Music Notes*, Webb provides this typically self-effacing introduction to his work with Lewton:

> The officials of FILM MUSIC NOTES have been kind enough to ask me to explain my approach to mystery pictures. I have been told that I have been fairly successful in this field, and feel honored in the assignment of writing this paper. In the first place, I was lucky to be working on the artistic melodramas of producer Val Lewton, and felt that they deserved a deeper and more thoughtful treatment than the usual picture of this category.[11]

That last line motivates this book despite its lack of specificity, or maybe because of it. My aim here is to explore the contours of what that statement might mean by treating the music in Lewton's films with the sort of care Webb claims to have deployed in them.

All of Lewton's films have benefitted from multiple published analyses and one of these films, *Cat People* (1942), has received more than a dozen thoughtful published analyses starting with Robin Wood's very early foray in "The Shadow Worlds of Jacques Tourneur: *Cat People* and *I Walked with a Zombie*" (1976),[12] through numerous psychoanalytic and feminist readings of the film published over the last forty years.[13] My aim is to disavow nothing of the literature on Lewton's films of an analytical nature. This book strives to demonstrate how examination of music within these films contributes to the mosaic of understandings *Cat People* has inspired.

In some cases, the conclusions I draw resemble earlier analyses, yet my methods of arriving at these conclusions are quite distinct. For example, Kim Newman's reading of *Cat People*, at least in terms of the claim that the film sympathizes entirely with the film's apparent monster while criticizing its normal couple, draws a conclusion very similar to my music-based analysis.[14] Newman makes no reference to the film's music other than the lullaby sung within the film in his slim volume, so his path to a conclusion clearly differs from mine.

Val Lewton: Auteur

Focusing on the work of artisans in the RKO Music Department on the films of a producer admired as an auteur offers the sort of challenge that "film musicology" should undertake. The auteur theory has historically devalued such artisans, so musicology has a role to play in revaluing them.

The specifically auteurist literature on Lewton emerged in the 1960s with screenwriter-turned-film-historian DeWitt Bodeen's essay "Val Lewton Proved that Even Low-Budget Films Can Have Artistic Integrity" (1963).[15] In this essay, Bodeen provides an intimate history of the Lewton unit for which he provided three screenplays. Bodeen propels Lewton's auteur image to the forefront, merging biographical insight about the man with analytical commentary on both his stylistic and structural approach to filmmaking.

Joel Siegel wrote the first book-length study of Lewton's career in 1973 when he contributed *Val Lewton: The Reality of Terror* to the prestigious Cinema One series that had previously published work on auteurist darlings Jean-Luc Godard, Jean-Pierre Melville, François Truffaut, Orson Welles, Douglas Sirk, George Cukor, Samuel Fuller, and John Ford. The series only published twenty-eight titles, placing Lewton in rare company, especially as the series' only non-director.

As for Siegel's book itself, he provides a detailed biography and thoughtful analysis of every one of Lewton's fourteen productions including the lightly regarded later works at studios other than RKO. Siegel takes special care to emphasize Lewton's role in crafting the final draft of the screenplay of each of his films. Siegel approaches Lewton as an auteur fully in command of the meaning of his work and committed to a personal style of cinema summing up his case as follows:

> It is generally nonsensical to speak of producers as creators when, in all but a few cases, they are the enemies of creation. One of the exceptions was Lewton who, though credited only as producer, was unarguably the artistic creator and prime mover of his films. Apart from his last, troubled productions, Lewton's films were easily identified by their attention to detail, their unusually literate screenplays, their skillful, suggestive use of shadow and sound. Although his production unit at RKO was fully democratic, with each member having a full say on artistic matters, Lewton's eleven RKO films constitute an uncommonly personal body of work.[16]

The most recent book on Val Lewton may also be the most innovative. In *Icons of Grief: Val Lewton's Home Front Pictures* (2005), art historian Alexander Nemerov offers fine-grained examinations of four nearly immobile images from Lewton's horror films. In each case, Nemerov situates the image within the larger visual culture of wartime America. Nemerov argues that Lewton's work is out of tune with its times for emphasizing grief when the War Department wanted Hollywood to keep things cheerful on the home front. Nemerov's work paints a portrait of Lewton as a rueful figure trapped in the cellar of commercial cinema's lowest genre which he felt certain would ruin him, yet a man wholly invested in the dignity of minorness and thus superbly situated to thrive in that exact cellar.[17]

Even Nemerov's relatively recent work situates Lewton as an auteur by intermixing his biography with his output in a way that renders that output personal. Nemerov's auteurist leanings are never more fully displayed than in his acknowledgment of Lewton's collaborators. He wrote, "Other creative people naturally made major contributions, and their work is important to my argument."[18] He then lists director Jacques Tourneur, director of photography Nicholas Musuraca, writer DeWitt Bodeen, set designers Albert D'Agostino and Walter Keller, and composer Roy Webb as these "other creative people." Muddying the waters, the middle of this paragraph of tribute to collaborators features film critic Manny Farber's assertion that "each film has a different director and writing crew, but they look enough alike to make you feel that Lewton controlled the work on all of them."[19] Nemerov does not contradict Farber and by including Farber's assessment in his mention of Lewton's collaborators situates his work within an auteurist frame.

Val Lewton's auteur status vexes my project. These films are still largely understood as his. The title of this book offers little help in this regard, and despite my comments above, I may not disagree with Manny Farber either. Yet, I am arguing here that the music in these films contributes enormously to the meaning of these films, even clarifying the films' thematic content.

In an effort to distance this book from the auteurist reception of Lewton's horror films, let me share a biographical anecdote – the only new one about Lewton contained in this book featuring his name in the title – establishing Lewton's inability to attend to the music on the soundtrack with the same degree of detail he exerted on the scripts he rewrote. I asked Val Lewton's son, Val Lewton, Jr., if he had any recollections of his father's views on the music in his films. He replied:

> [My father] must have understood the importance of music to film but didn't have the facility to really appreciate the nuances of a film score. The first thing you must understand is that my father was tone deaf. He identified, and this is no exaggeration, most classical music as Rimsky-Korsakov's *Scheherazade*. His inability to sing 'Annie Laurie' was a family joke, especially with my mother who played piano and came from a musical family. He could hum the theme from *Cat People*, a folk tune he knew that had about three notes. As in other areas of filmmaking my father was fortunate to be able to use the same great RKO professionals that worked with Orson Welles and Alfred Hitchcock.[20]

In the analyses that follow, this anecdote about Lewton's tone deafness will prove useful again and again, for the staff of RKO's Music Department consistently ignored the references to specific source music within the scripts for Lewton's films. Invariably the discrepancies between each screenplay and finished soundtrack reveal the Music Department improving the film as a whole, and at least one notable case within *Cat People* providing a rubric for understanding the film's entire subversion of genre norms. Not only was Val Lewton not the author of these details, but he was ill-suited to grasp them.

Roy Webb: Auteur?

So if Val Lewton was not the auteur behind the music in these films, does that elevate Roy Webb who composed eight of the nine original scores to that stature? Here I want to point to the work of Catherine Haworth. In her study of gender and music in RKO crime films and in subsequent conference papers focused on RKO's Music Department during the 1940s, Haworth steadfastly resists what she calls "the great men/films/scores" model by deflecting focus to the unsung contributions of the entire RKO Music Department staff and by emphasizing feminist critique.[21] Her work strikes a sharp contrast to the early days of film music scholarship, which was most often informed by auteurist sensitivities. The composer emerges as the heroic figure producing miraculous volumes of music the author deems "great" on short notice, often saving this or that film from ignominy.

While the tone of this book is often celebratory as regards the music in Lewton's horror films, my aim is not to elevate Roy Webb – or anyone else who worked on the music in these films – to heroic status. That said, my celebratory tone and focus on a small number of individual texts resembles older approaches to studying film music, ideally not in a way that Haworth or other thoughtful readers would find objectionable.

Most of the book-length work done on film music now is organized around theory and critique rather than films associated with an individual filmmaker or composer although many standout exceptions are still being published and read. I organized the book around a body of texts rather than a theoretical approach or a critique rooted in class or identity for feeling that so much fine work has already been done along those lines that a return to texts might allow for varied theoretical work to inform the discussion on a more ad hoc basis and for preferring a celebratory approach to scholarship. To be sure these films are available for critique. They resulted from corporate models of production anathema to class-based criticism of film music of the sort undertaken by Theodor Adorno and Hanns Eisler.[22] They were produced at a time and place when women, people of color, LGBTQ identities, and the disabled were marginalized both in reality and in the fictions produced to amuse that reality. My aim here is not to deny any of that critique. Indeed, citations of fine examples of critical work find their way into the chapters that follow in order to facilitate understanding these texts. Yet, I find myself still moved and inspired by these films and by the music in them. My hermeneutical approach lacks the skepticism of critique described by Paul Ricoeur when he coined the term "the hermeneutics of skepticism."[23] My faith in these texts and their strivings to make the world a more thoughtful place endured through many viewings. This situation led me to examine postcritique, which does not deny the efficacy of criticism but wonders what would happen if one could set aside Ricoeur's skeptical hermeneutic and its central assumption that texts deceive their reader, forcing excavation deeper into the work to find precisely what is wrong with it.

In their anthology *Critique and Postcritique*, editors Elizabeth Anker and Rita Felski describe the project of critique as having a "diagnostic quality." They write, "To diagnose is to look closely and intently, in the belief that such scrutiny will bring problems to light that can be deciphered by an authoritative interpreter. The stance is one of judicious and knowledgeable detachment."[24]

Like Anker and Felski, my aim is not a rejection of the fruits of critique, but to set aside skepticism for the moment and explore what might be right deep inside a text. As mentioned previously, the film *Cat People* (1942) has prompted numerous readings of the film from a variety of critical perspectives. The literature on gender depiction in the film is especially noteworthy. Naturally my discussion will also look at gender in the film for its unusual female antagonist. I conclude that the film rubs against the grain of the entire horror genre and provides its female lead the status of victim, monster, and her own pursuer. Lewton's next film, *I Walked with a Zombie* (1943) – set on an imaginary Caribbean island – begs for a different sort of critique, which is not to suggest that an entirely gender-based reading of the film would not illuminate the text.[25] The film's depiction of its Caribbean characters in contrast to its colonial ones features an important and multi-faceted role for music that fractures the certainties of Western rationality. Organizing my argument around a skeptical critique would not serve this diverse body of texts. As for the body of texts, they were chosen for having frequently been cited for subverting horror genre conventions and for advancing a humane thematics that is often remarkable for its sophistication and sweep in taking up the cause of the marginalized. This contention is the wellspring of the book's structural conceit around a body of texts and its celebratory tone.

Unlike Anker and Felski, my method does not "bracket" questions central to critique, but rather uses them or sets them aside as they prove useful in understanding each text under discussion. Theories rooted in the depiction of identities inform every chapter of this book, but they do not provide its centrifugal force.

Returning to Roy Webb briefly, the book's closest thing to a "great man," Webb's life has largely escaped attention, and little will be added about it in the pages that follow. There is no book-length study of his life or work, a surprising situation given that most Hollywood composers of his stature have received more than one by now.[26] This is a book about his musical contributions to a cycle of films that enjoy popular and academic admiration, but it is also about the crucial roles played by his fellow composers Leigh Harline, Sir Lancelot, and LeRoy Antoine; his colleagues who orchestrated these films including Leonid Raab, Maurice De Packh, and Gilbert Grau; Norman Bennet's on-set keyboard work and his likely role in selecting the repertory he played; and the work of sound recordists starting with John L. Cass, executor of the first "jump scare" in a horror film. While the prevailing tone of musicology today avoids celebratory discussion of heroic composers, no longer undertaking them unselfconsciously at any rate, this book offers an unapologetic celebration of not only Roy Webb's but the entire RKO Music Department's contribution to Val Lewton's films toward the purpose of understanding this body of films better. The celebration emerges as a by-product of the analysis, but it is there.

Studying Music in Horror Films

Of course, I am not the first author to write about music in horror films, or even the first to write about music in Val Lewton's horror films. I am not even the first to acknowledge that I am not the first.[27] The growing literature on horror film music falls largely into two categories. The first includes discussion of practices mostly at Universal Pictures and in a few seminal horror films at other studios most notably *Dr. Jekyll and Mr. Hyde* (1931) and *King Kong* (1933) produced during the first decade of sound film. The second deals with music in horror films made after the studio system collapsed in the late 1950s.

As Lewton's films are every inch the product of the studio system, the latter vast literature provides little of relevance to this study while doing much to illuminate the last sixty years of music in horror films. Take for example the two most widely cited anthologies of writing on music in horror films, Philip Hayward's *Terror Tracks: Music, Sound and Horror Cinema* (2009) and Neil Lerner's *Music in the Horror Film: Listening to Fear* (2010). Exactly one essay concerns music in a film made prior to Hammer's *Horror of Dracula* (1957), Neil Lerner's important reading of music and sound in *Dr. Jekyll and Mr. Hyde* (1931).

Certainly, some sonic innovations first heard in Lewton's films, like the "jump scare," echo in later horror films, making later theoretical discussion of them highly relevant to this study. But we find music in Lewton's films performing comparatively few of the tasks Stan Link described as key functions performed by later horror film music.[28] For example, there are precious few "stingers" in the Lewton films, and the few that are there are accounted for in Chapter 7. These startling moments of loud, dissonant music coinciding with some horrific image on the screen are a mainstay of the genre's musical conventions probably starting with Max Steiner's score for *The Most Dangerous Game* (1932). K. J. Donnelly describes their function as transcending the usual representational potentials of film music by offering up a sensational potential by literally startling the audience.[29] Such important theoretical discussion – even when ideally applied to recent horror – surely pertains to aspects of the music in Lewton's films and aid this study in proposing a rupture in Lewton's style isolating the final three vehicles for Boris Karloff as distinct from the six earlier films.

Most useful to a theoretical understanding of a common feature of Lewton's soundtracks is the use of sound effects as a sort of *musique concrète*. This practice pre-dates Lewton's efforts as revealed in Neil Lerner's work on *Dr. Jekyll and Mr. Hyde*, and post-dates it gaining intensity as the decades unfold.[30] Irwin Bazelon's theoretical work on what he calls the soundtrack as "proto-*musique concrète*" informs both Lerner and this study.[31] Stan Link provides an excellent summary of this function of sound in horror films.[32]

As for the literature on studio-era horror films, much of it gravitates toward Max Steiner's work on *King Kong* and Franz Waxman's score for *The Bride of Frankenstein* (1935) as two influential approaches to horror film music, while Philip Hayward does a remarkable job with both in his brief history of horror film music introducing his anthology.[33] According to Hayward, Waxman operated in a musical language largely derived from late Romantic composers Richard Wagner and Richard Strauss featuring leitmotifs, advanced tonal harmony, and introducing the stinger into the film music lexicon.[34] His presentation of Max Steiner sees all that and one thing more, "mickey-mousing." This was initially a term of abuse applied to those moments when Steiner would create obvious image track/underscore associations, like ascending scalar figures accompanying Kong's climb up the Empire State Building. How a venerable practice dating from the Italian madrigal became a term of abuse when transferred to a Hollywood film score provides an interesting mystery. Much of the work of Roy Webb "paints" the text of Lewton's films vividly, as the book that follows tries to demonstrate, most notably in *The Seventh Victim* (1943) where "mickey-mousing" arises frequently.

I would add to Hayward, that Steiner was rather more willing than Waxman to allow his harmonies to overflow the conventions of late Romanticism and drift over the nebulous boundary into atonality. In their important theoretical work on film music, David Neumeyer and James Buhler cast atonality in a central role within music for horror films juxtaposing it to "the preference for closed classical dramatic forms in Hollywood's studio era no doubt underwrote a corresponding preference for tonal composition." They continue, "It is surely not a coincidence that atonality makes its deepest inroads in suspense, horror, and science fiction films."[35] In horror, they argue that atonality serves the dystopian projection of the monster.

Returning to Hayward, he sees a fusion of Waxman and Steiner's accomplishments in Roy Webb's scores for the Lewton films, and here we transition into the literature specifically on music in the horror films of Val Lewton. Apart from Catherine Haworth's work on *The Leopard Man* (1943), that literature is little more than a paragraph here and there. Hayward cites *Cat People* and *The Body Snatcher* (1945) as places where Webb "combined the scoring techniques pioneered by Waxman and Steiner with a distinctive use of songs woven into the narratives and incorporated into the score."[36] The two films Hayward mentions by name, *Cat People* and *The Body Snatcher*, exist, according to my argument, on two sides of a divide in the sonic style employed by the Lewton unit. The lullaby sung in the diegesis of *Cat People* and woven into the film's score undergoes drastic transformations to illustrate the main character's mental deterioration, while the Scottish folk songs, some authentic some ersatz, woven into the score of *The Body Snatcher* serve the convention of placing the audience in Scotland while watching a film shot entirely in Hollywood. Pointing this out stems from the privilege of writing a book-length study of one body of films while Hayward must account for a full history of music in horror films. Hayward deserves credit for elevating Webb into Waxman's and Steiner's company, for including him as an exemplar of horror film music from the 1940s, and for noting the role of songs as differentiating Webb from both Waxman and Steiner. Hayward was right. My job is to explore in greater detail all the facets of his rightness.

Even before Hayward included Webb's work with Lewton in an historical overview emphasizing only highlights, K. J. Donnelly laid out a superb overview of horror film music in his fifth chapter of *The Spectre of Sound: Music in Film and Television*.[37] After a brief survey of music in the horror cycle at Universal Pictures during the 1930s, Donnelly observes the quality of Universal's horror films deteriorating in the 1940s. He characterizes Webb's music for Lewton's films as exemplifying the undervalued quality of subtlety, while claiming that the music within them "broadly followed the Hollywood norm of the time."[38] I think it would be unfair in a monograph specifically about a small body of film music to criticize Donnelly for writing too generally about that same body of film music when he is surveying the entire "historical vista" of horror film music in under ten pages. Instead, I want to admire how Donnelly's emphasis on Webb's subtlety captures an important difference between Webb's work and the work of his better-known peers at other studios. Donnelly attributes Webb's subtlety to "the films themselves."[39] I agree wholeheartedly with Donnelly and want to draw readers' attention to moments of subtlety in all of Webb's scores – and in Leigh Harline's too – created for Lewton's horror films. The mission of this book is to bring the claims of both Donnelly and Hayward regarding Roy Webb's music for Val Lewton's horror films into sharper focus just as other authors have brought the music in *Dr. Jekyll and Mr. Hyde*, *King Kong*, the Universal horror cycle of the 1930s, and so many horror films made after the studio era collapsed into sharper focus. I hope others will write detailed analyses of all the other bodies of horror film music deemed important by Hayward and Donnelly. This book, in some ways the first of its kind insofar as it places a magnifying glass on the particulars of one body of horror texts, proposes to handle the Lewton films.

An Overview of the Book's Nine Chapters

Each chapter that follows discusses the music in a single film. The films are presented chronologically. While efforts have been made to present a coherent whole arranged around the book's central contention that analysis of the music in these films provides insights into the creation of meaning within the films themselves, insights that have sometimes eluded previous analysts or that reinforce earlier analyses in unexpected ways, each chapter can be viewed as a self-contained argument about the music in that particular film. Here is an overview of the book that follows.

Chapter 1 opens with a meditation on RKO's new "Victory Signature" wondering why Roy Webb provided dissonant and downcast music. As *Cat People* was the first film to feature this music, I offer my analysis of his music for the film as a possible key to understanding why he resisted a request for an upbeat, wartime corporate theme. I argue that the film departs from normative practices of 1940s horror films by situating its main character, Irena (Simone Simon), simultaneously as monster, victim, and pursuer. In doing so, the film de-emphasizes the other characters and implicates them in a tyranny of the normal that drives Irena to suicide.

The music in the film – from its opening corporate signature (a trope on the opening of Beethoven's Fifth Symphony) to a melancholy variation of a French cradlesong as Irena commits suicide – serves to situate the audience in rapport with Irena and only Irena, effectively interpreting the film analytically. In between we find Roy Webb ignoring spotting sheets asking for a "happy mood" and making a canny substitution of quoted material heard on a hand organ that provides an important criticism of the "normal" characters in the film. Webb further criticizes the normal characters by denying them orchestral underscore, even going so far as to twice subvert his instructions on spotting sheets asking for orchestral music. Webb's original material for the film features a network of motivic associations with narrative elements, and all of them concern Irena alone. Claudia Gorbman's and Peter Franklin's discussions of Max Steiner's score for *King Kong* (1933) prove useful here as I model my analysis of music in *Cat People* on their observations revealing both overall similarities and important differences between the two approaches. The conclusion returns to the "Victory Signature" and suggests that Webb shared Lewton's and Irena's inability to join in the hyper-normative celebration of a victory that was many lives and many days away.

The second chapter echoes and amplifies observations in J. P. Telotte's analysis of *I Walked with a Zombie* which sees the film's structural conceit of various narrators troubling the reliability of cinematic narration in a manner extending innovations found in *Citizen Kane* (1941). Through an examination of the film's music, we further see how musical choices in the film fracture the Western side of the film's central dichotomy of colonial/Caribbean. This fracturing is achieved through Roy Webb's seemingly willful use of contradictory modernist structural techniques in crafting underscore for the film's Western characters, through the use of Chopin's E major Étude, Op. 10, No. 3 within the film's diegesis, and most importantly through the juxtaposition of Webb's and Chopin's musical contributions to those of Calypso singer/songwriter Sir Lancelot and Haitian musician LeRoy Antoine both of whom worked on the film's soundtrack and appeared in the film. Rare for a Hollywood film of the 1940s, Caribbean music is represented not by ersatz music with roots in Hollywood, but with music by Caribbeans. More than attention to narrative verisimilitude and local color is at stake for the Lewton unit in this juxtaposition. This chapter argues that the film achieves a rare albeit mild critique of the colonial project.

The discussion of Chopin in this chapter owes a heavy debt to my colleague and co-author Sarah Reichardt Ellis. We published an article on the use of Chopin in horror movies of the 1930s and 1940s and part of that article reappears in this chapter.[40]

My discussion of *The Leopard Man* extends into the musical realm my earlier analysis of the film itself.[41] This chapter hinges on two closely related claims. First, Val Lewton hated making horror films, a fact illustrated in his letters to his mother and sister housed in the Val Lewton Papers in The Library of Congress. My second claim is far more speculative. Having created two successful horror films, Lewton approached the third as a penitential rite. To achieve this unlikely end, he structured this film around its victims rather than its monster or pursuers. This victim-centered structure roots the film's violence in the making of violent imagery as entertainment.

The music in *The Leopard Man* includes a penitential chant as the diegetic soundtrack for the film's climax. The RKO Music Department deployed musical sounds within the film in ways that trouble the audience's relationship with their sources. Catherine Haworth's analysis of the film's castanets and Robynn Stilwell's theory of music from a "fantastical gap" aid in shaping this chapter's approach. The film's music drifts from the diegesis to the underscore and into the "fantastical gaps" between them with fluidity, implicating the creators of this fluid sound world in the film's penitential potential by providing aural analogues for the film's narrative and visual acts of penance.

The Seventh Victim, topic of the fourth chapter, is easily Val Lewton's most complex film. Fittingly it features the series' most complex music. The film presents viewers with the possibility widely examined in modernist philosophy that life offers no meaning, a chilling proposition to entertain in a "B" movie. My analysis examines how Roy Webb's score for the film features three madrigalistic musical elements, each painting an important thematic element of the text: the fruitless striving for happiness, repetition associated with the death impulse, and death itself. Marginalia from Webb and the film's two orchestrators, Maurice De Packh and Leonid Raab, clarify the Music Department's understanding of the meaning of these figures, aiding this analysis enormously. Also helpful is the selection, likely by studio pianist Norman Bennett, of diegetic piano literature heard in the film emphasizing these madrigalisms in ways useful to interpreting the music's contribution to the film's themes.

Chapter 5 examines *The Ghost Ship* (1943) as a wartime fable pitting the ideals of liberal democracy and its faith in the "common man" against the cynicism of authoritarianism. The structure of the chapter looks at how each facet of the film's soundtrack – the original score, sound effects, dialogue, and diegetic music – each serve to illustrate the position of one character in the film. While the film's sound effects as created by first-time sound designer Francis Sarver often hide the criminal conduct of the film's homicidal Captain Stone (Richard Dix), its dialogue promotes the ideals of liberal democracy as championed by the film's protagonist, Tom Merriam (Russell Wade). These two men make claims about the common man as represented by the crew, Tom's optimistic and Stone's pessimistic. The crew itself – often represented by its most musical member, Billy Radd, played by Sir Lancelot who composed two original Calypso numbers for the film – confirms Stone's perspective as they use music to shirk their responsibilities one to another. Roy Webb's orchestral underscore almost exclusively invites the audience into the interiority of a minor character, The Finn (Skelton Knaggs), who proves the film's unlikely hero and Tom's only consistent ally. As liberal democracy's best hope in the film, his privileged relationship with the film's orchestral underscore is noteworthy. The chapter offers an analysis placing the film's wartime context at center stage and drawing on David Bordwell and his associates' structuralist approach to the classical Hollywood Style.

The topic of the sixth chapter, *The Curse of the Cat People* (1944), stands as one of the weirdest sequels in Hollywood history. The film offers neither a curse nor a cat person, but instead explores the inner life of Alice's (Jane

Randolph) and Oliver's (Kent Smith) melancholy child, Amy (Anne Carter). J. P. Telotte argues that the film explores the reality imbedded in fantasy and the fantasies that undergird reality. Roy Webb's orchestral underscore and several examples of diegetic music in the film amplify Telotte's conclusions. This chapter further explores how music serves to clarify the nature of Irena in the film, a nature that has caused past critics much perplexity. Is she a ghost or an imaginary friend? This chapter demonstrates how music answers this question. It also looks at how the film's soundtrack privileges the inner life of a young girl, situating its audience into her aural experiences by having the audience hear what only she can hear, and by illustrating her memories and intensifying her experiences. This special aural treatment afforded Amy echoes the visual treatment of her whereby the audience experiences key moments in the film only through her youthful eyes.

Lewton's final three horror films all star horror veteran Boris Karloff. The seventh chapter examines all the ways in which the presence of Karloff altered the style of Lewton's films, including their sonic style. While the earlier six films departed from genre norms by presenting stories set in the domestic present, the Karloff vehicles are all costume pictures set in the foreign past. *The Body Snatcher* also features far more scenes of overt violence than its suggestive predecessors. The film's physical and temporal setting placed new demands on the RKO Music Department to stretch a thin budget and transport its audience to Edinburgh, 1831 just as its greater emphasis on overt shocks demanded music more typical of the genre as practiced at Universal Pictures where Karloff made his name. The chapter looks at the demands a horror star placed on the music in the film, exploring its unusual use of Scottish topics, its profusion of stingers, and its lurid agitatos. But not all is conventional in the music of *The Body Snatcher* as certain characters perform with the orchestral underscore as might happen in a musical. This situation grants them an otherworldly quality in a tale suggestive of supernatural occurrences. Ghostly voices in the underscore prompt a reminder of Kevin Donnelly's work on the spectral nature of film music. Finally, the chapter considers the musicality of Karloff's voice as his lilting and rhythmic voice presents lines that marginalia in his personal copies of the film's script reveal he had rewritten himself. The chapter strives to model how a star study and film musicology can align to analyze a single film in a manner similar to but a bit more expansively than Claudia Gorbman's groundbreaking work on *The Master* (2012).

Chapter 8 concerns *Isle of the Dead* (1945), the only Lewton horror film scored by Leigh Harline. The chapter opens with a discussion of the film's troubled production and Leigh Harline's move from Disney to freelance composition, and speculates on how Harline came to score this film. The chapter argues that the film centers on a theme of uncertainty vs. certainty in an original analysis. The bulk of the chapter concerns how Harline's scoring foregrounds this theme through its evocation of a Greek topic rooted in a genre of epic song favoring parlando-rubato troubling the temporality of his music and tension between the minor mode and Greek modes generating uncertainty in its pitch language. Examination of how Harline's highly original scoring of the film, his approach to tempo and meter, and his strange harmonic language all reinforce uncertainty in the listener. Insofar as Lewton's celebrated style emphasizes uncertainty through "dark patches," leaving the viewer unable to see what might be lurking nearby, a musical score emphasizing uncertainty in meter, tempo, and harmony serves Lewton's style extremely well.

Lewton's final horror film, *Bedlam* (1946), strives to be three things: a historical costume drama set in 1761 London, a horror film involving the internment of a young reformer in the film's titular insane asylum, and a message picture about the need for compassionate care for the mentally ill. With three generic codes operating simultaneously, inevitably some of them work at cross-purposes. Message pictures of the sort pouring out of Hollywood in the immediate postwar era tend to have contemporary settings for calling on contemporary action. Worse, Lewton confused his message by using the inmates needing compassionate care for most of the film's horrific content, resulting in a film both championing and at times "othering" the mentally ill.

The music in the film ably supports these three conflicting codes. Carefully researched street cries serve as diegetic music transporting the audience to the film's setting. Roy Webb supplies a score mixing a galant musical bustle with Handelian grandeur and a good deal of fully diminished seventh chords and ascending chromatic scales often in tremolo. These confusing elements drawn partly from period drama and partly from horror scores are first presented in a "Main Title" cue that merits a blow-by-blow analysis for laying out Webb's take on The Age of Reason. The message picture part of the complex equation proves the most difficult to represent musically, but Webb strives to do so by supporting his reformers with a "Religioso" disqualified from sounding "in period" for presenting an urgent harmony more typical of his scores for modern dramas, thus providing the contemporary element necessary to a message picture.

Taken together, these nine chapters offer detailed analyses of a sort that the music in these films was not intended to support. While much of what the book claims about the music in these films has apparently eluded viewer/listeners for the seventy-five years they have existed, this is not a claim to some magic insight on my part. All I have going for me is an abundant love of these films, so abundant as to feel sure that there is something good beneath their surfaces, and the luxury of time to consider the music in them in relation to the films they support. The result, I hope, is an example of what Peter Franklin simply dubbed "film musicology," wherein both film and music enjoy, if not equal care, considerable care on the path toward a hermeneutic study.

Notes

1. Carlos Clarens, *An Illustrated History of Horror and Science-Fiction Films* (New York: Putnam, 1967), pp. 111–116.
2. Ibid., p. 111.
3. Alexander Nemerov, *Icons of Grief: Val Lewton's Home Front Pictures* (Berkeley: University of California Press, 2005), p. 9.
4. The best place to start is Joel Siegel, *Val Lewton: The Reality of Terror* (New York: Viking Press, 1973).
5. The phrase comes from Claudia Gorbman, *Unheard Melodies: Narrative Film Music* (Bloomington: University of Indiana Press, 1987), p. 79.
6. Peter Franklin, *Seeing Through Music: Gender and Modernism in Classic Hollywood Film Scores* (Oxford: Oxford University Press, 2011), p. 15. See also Gorbman, *Unheard Melodies*.
7. Nathan Platte, *Making Music in Selznick's Hollywood* (New York: Oxford University Press, 2018).
8. Michel Chion, *Audio-Vision: Sound on Screen*, Claudia Gorbman, translator (New York: Columbia University Press, 1994), pp. 5–9.
9. Chion, *Audio-Vision*, p. 8.
10. Ibid.
11. Roy Webb, "Pattern for Mystery," *Film Music Notes* (March 1945).
12. Robin Wood, "The Shadow Worlds of Jacques Tourneur: *Cat People* and *I Walked with a Zombie*," in *Personal Views: Explorations in Film, Revised Edition* (Detroit, MI: Wayne State University Press, 2006), pp. 252–272.
13. Here are a few examples of psychoanalytic and feminist readings of *Cat People*. There are many more. J. P. Telotte, "Structures of Absence: *Cat People*," *Dreams of Darkness: Fantasy and the Films of Val Lewton* (Urbana: University of Illinois Press, 1985), pp. 21–39; Karen Hollinger, "The Monster as Woman: Two Generations of *Cat People*," *Film Criticism*, Volume 13, No. 2 (Winter, 1989), pp. 36–46; John Berks, "What Alice Does: Looking Otherwise at *The Cat People*," *Cinema Journal* (Fall, 1992), pp. 26–42; Linda Rohrer Paige, "The Transformation of Woman: The 'Curse' of the Cat Woman in Val Lewton/Jacques Tourneur's *Cat People*, its Sequel, and Remake," *Literature Film Quarterly* (Fall, 1997), pp. 291–299; and William Paul, "What Does Dr. Judd Want? Transformation, Transference, and Divided Selves in *Cat People*," in *Horror Film and Psychoanalysis: Freud's Worst Nightmare*, ed. Steven Jay Schneider (Cambridge: Cambridge University Press, 2004) pp. 159–176.
14. Kim Newman, *Cat People* (London: BFI Publishing, 1999).
15. DeWitt Bodeen, "Val Lewton Proved that Even Low-Budget Films Can Have Artistic Integrity," *Films in Review* (Fall, 1963), pp. 210–224.
16. Siegel, *Val Lewton*, p. 23.
17. Nemerov, pp. 5–7.
18. Nemerov, pp. 10–11.
19. Manny Farber, "Against the Grain," *The New Republic* (September 11, 1944), p. 339.
20. Correspondence between the author and Val Lewton, Jr., January 19, 2006.

21. Catherine Haworth, "Dames, Darlings, and Detectives: Women, Agency, and the Soundtrack in RKO Radio Pictures Crime Films," PhD dissertation, University of Leeds, 2010, p. 61.
22. Hanns Eisler and Theodor Adorno, *Composing for the Films* (New York: Oxford University Press, 1947).
23. Paul Ricoeur, *Freud and Philosophy*, Denis Savage, translator (New Haven, CT: Yale University Press, 1970), p. 35.
24. Elizabeth Anker and Rita Felski, *Critique and Postcritique* (Durham, NC: Duke University Press, 2017), p. 4.
25. Illustrating my point, I have co-authored an article with Sarah Ellis that discusses one scene of that film through the lens of a gender-based reading of music within it. Elements of that argument find their way into this book. Sarah Reichardt Ellis and Michael Lee, "Monsters, Meaning, and the Music of Chopin in American Horror Films of the 1930s and '40s," *Journal of Musicological Research*, Volume 39, Issue 1 (Winter, 2020), pp. 24–41.
26. I considered writing a "life and works" book about Webb but chose to write this book instead. One reason is that he was private and unassuming to an almost laughable degree. RKO generated a biography for him now housed at the Margaret Herrick Library in Beverly Hills, California titled "Roy Webb: Biography." It reveals very little about him other than his anodyne hobbies of golfing and enjoying cars. Its one feint at an amusing anecdote involves Webb conducting a pick-up orchestra in some unnamed town with a piccolo player "who was hitting sour notes because he had iron fillings in his hands." His long-time colleague at RKO, Max Steiner, left behind an unpublished memoir titled "Notes to You" now housed among the Max Steiner papers within the Film Music Archives at Brigham Young University. In nearly 900 pages comprised mostly of amusing anecdotes, not one concerns Roy Webb. Webb's letters to Christopher Palmer housed in the Special Collections Library of Syracuse University contain the most interesting biographical materials including his decision to stop composing after wildfires in November, 1961 consumed his Brentwood home. I leave the Roy Webb biography to someone more imaginative.
27. See Neil Lerner's "Preface" to *Music in the Horror Film: Listening to Fear* (New York: Routledge Press, 2010), p. ix.
28. Link describes strategies including misdirection, perverting traditional musical types, generating counterpoint between image and sound, sound effects of unseen source, and use of popular music to comment on the action. Stan Link, "Horror and Science Fiction," in *The Cambridge Companion to Film Music*, eds. Mervyn Cooke and Fiona Ford (Cambridge: Cambridge University Press, 2016), pp. 213–215.
29. K. J. Donnelly, *The Spectre of Sound: Music in Film and Television* (London: BFI, 2005), pp. 94–95.
30. Neil Lerner, "The Strange Case of Rouben Mamoulian's Sonic Stew: The Uncanny Soundtrack in *Dr. Jekyll and Mr. Hyde* (1931)," in *Music in the Horror Film*, ed. Neil Lerner (New York: Routledge, 2010), pp. 66–72.
31. Irwin Bazelon, *Knowing the Score: Notes on Film Music* (New York: Van Nostren Reinhold, 1975), p. 147.

32. Link, pp. 211–213.
33. For a discussion of Steiner's work on *King Kong*, I gravitate toward Peter Franklin's "*King Kong* and Film on Music: Out of the Fog," in *Film Music: Critical Approaches*, ed. K. J. Donnelly (Edinburgh: Edinburgh University Press, 2001), pp. 88–102. For a discussion of Waxman's contribution, I turn to William H. Rosar, "Music of the Monsters: Universal Pictures' Horror Film Scores of the Thirties," *The Quarterly Journal of the Library of Congress*, Volume 40, Number 1 (Winter, 1983), pp. 391–421.
34. Philip Hayward, "Introduction," in *Terror Tracks: Music, Sound and Horror Cinema* (London: Equinox Publishing, 2009), pp. 6–8.
35. David Neumeyer and James Buhler, "Analytical and Interpretive Approaches (I)," in *Film Music: Critical Approaches*, ed. K. J. Donnelly (New York: Continuum, 2001), p. 23.
36. Hayward, p. 7.
37. Donnelly, pp. 95–106.
38. Donnelly, p. 98.
39. Donnelly, p. 98.
40. Ellis and Lee, pp. 9–14.
41. Michael Lee, "Subverting Horror Genre Conventions in Val Lewton's *The Leopard Man*," in "The Image of Violence in Literature, Media, and Society: 1995 SASSI Conference Proceedings" (Pueblo, CO: *Society for the Academic Study of Social Imagery*, University of Southern Colorado, 1995).

1 "HAPPY MOOD OVER THIS, ROY": WEBB'S SCORE FOR *CAT PEOPLE* AS FILM ANALYSIS

Roy Webb's Victory Signature

On December 7, 1942, a year to the day from the Japanese attack on Pearl Harbor, audiences at the Rialto Theater in New York City witnessed the premiere of producer Val Lewton's first film, *Cat People*. The first image seen that night was familiar; the RKO corporate logo with its radio tower spanning the globe transmitting animated radio waves. What the audience heard at the *Cat People* premiere was new. RKO's vice president for production, Charles Koerner, instructed Roy Webb in his capacity as head of the Music Department to prepare a new "Victory Signature" to accompany the RKO logo as part of the studio's commitment to the war effort.[1] RKO, like all the Hollywood studios, was complying with the newly formed Office of War Information's request to keep things cheerful and promote happy optimism on the home front.[2]

In response to Koerner's request, Webb created a musical signature for the war effort in the form of a trope on the opening bars of Ludwig van Beethoven's Fifth Symphony with its short-short-short-long rhythm expressing the Morse code for the letter V, V for Victory and for the Roman numeral five. The BBC had previously adopted Beethoven's Fifth Symphony for its wartime signature in broadcasts to occupied Europe, so the association was not initially Webb's.[3]

Webb's "Victory Signature" (Figure 1.1) offers a variation on Beethoven's famous motif. Beethoven's rhythm remains intact, as does the first intervalic descent from G to E-flat. Webb's first modification emerges in his choice to sustain both the G and E-flat while maintaining the "V" rhythm in his upper

Figure 1.1 Roy Webb, "Victory Signature"

pedal. From there, Webb introduces more changes. Where Beethoven next presents his motif on F descending to D-flat, Webb drops immediately to D-flat and moves to A. Webb's concluding pitch collection of D-flat, E-flat, G, and A closes his "Victory Signature" with a whole-tone discordancy not present in Beethoven's symphony. This signature would grace all but one of RKO's releases scored by Webb from late 1942 through the end of the war in 1945.

Why would Roy Webb respond to a request for an optimistic, wartime corporate signature in this way? Why would Webb resist any reference to a victory topic such as fanfare figures, the major mode, ascending lines, or bright timbres all present in the pre-war and wartime corporate signatures for MGM, Warner Brothers, and Universal Pictures?

As *Cat People* was the first film where Webb deployed his "Victory Signature," perhaps in examining his work for that film we may discover a reasonable basis to speculate regarding Webb's motives. At the center of this discussion of Webb's contribution to *Cat People* lurks the claim that Roy Webb ignored many of the instructions he received on this film. From the "Victory Signature" to the choices for source music within the film's diegesis to the tone and placement of original underscore, Webb appears to have kept his own counsel.

The Origins of the Lewton Unit

History remembers Charles Koerner best as the man who fired Orson Welles. Prior to becoming RKO's chief of production in June 1942, Koerner was vice president for exhibition at RKO, which entailed running RKO's lucrative theater chain. As head of exhibition, his division was consistently the only one to turn a profit during the years 1938–1942 when George Schaefer served as president of RKO. In his new role, in which he served until 1946, Koerner purged the lot not only of Orson Welles, but of all the filmmakers who consistently lost money including William Dieterle and Pare Lorentz. He emblazoned his corporate philosophy on RKO's letterhead: "Showmanship in place of genius."

"B" pictures became RKO's mainstay under Koerner. Yet while the geniuses were sent packing, the artisans who toiled so admirably on their films as cinematographers, set decorators, sound designers, and composers remained. Their work distinguished RKO's "B" product of the 1940s.

To facilitate rapid and inexpensive production of "B" pictures, Koerner established several small production units, including its horror unit. For an associate producer in charge of horror, Koerner looked off RKO's Gower Street lot for fresh blood. This led to his hiring Val Lewton away from Selznick-International at MGM where Lewton toiled as David O. Selznick's story editor. Prior to working for Selznick, Lewton had been a largely unsuccessful journalist and minor novelist in New York, where his family had relocated from Yalta, Russia when Lewton was aged five. The Lewtons moved in with Val Lewton's aunt, the important star of silent films and Broadway dramas, Alla Nazimova. Lewton's mother also worked in film as a reader and story editor at MGM's east coast office.

In choosing Lewton for the position of assistant producer in charge of RKO's new horror unit, Koerner took something of a chance. Lewton possessed no credentials outside the story department. In his new role as producer, Lewton made the most of his exacting attention to the scripts for his films and left the making of them to an able and intimate circle. Complicating Lewton's work, Koerner hedged his bet on Lewton by choosing all of Lewton's titles through a system of market pre-testing.[4] The first title Koerner's system selected was "Cat People." This title struck Lewton, who hated horror films, as impossibly tawdry. Koerner further mandated that Lewton's films have budgets of US$150,000 and shooting schedules of three weeks.[5]

Music for "B" Horror

"B" pictures of the sort Lewton found himself tasked to make almost never enjoy original musical scores. To place the oddness of Lewton's decision to purchase an original score for *Cat People* in its economic context, we must look at the film's budget. The entire film's initial budget came in at just under US$119,000.[6] Here is a list of costs related to the film's music.

Bakaleinikov, 2 weeks @ $500/ week	$1,000
Pianist	$30
Scoring	$2,000
Arranging	$600
Copying	$300
Labor and supplies	$50
Librarian	$140
3 Balkan musicians, $16.50/day	$49.50
Sound and lab	$439
Steve Soldi, organ grinder	$300
TOTAL	$5,308.50[7]

Music and musicians occupied nearly 5 percent of the film's planned budget. By contrast, a film using library cues would spend almost nothing on its music.

Lewton had two excellent reasons for his expenditure on music. First, consider the studio's music library. RKO produced few horror films prior to Lewton's arrival at RKO. Merian C. Cooper produced most of them with *The Most Dangerous Game* (1932), *King Kong* (1933), and *She* (1935). Each film boasts an exotic locale and a score by Max Steiner ideally suited to each specific film's generous allotment of action sequences. The studio's final horror film prior to Lewton's arrival was Dieterle's magnificently expensive *The Hunchback of Notre Dame* (1939) with a sumptuous score by Alfred Newman expanding Dieterle's epic vision. *Cat People*'s action unfolds in the recognizable American present with a tiny cast engaged in everyday occupations. As an intentionally mundane anti-epic set in contemporary America, nothing of Steiner's or Newman's earlier material could be repurposed for its underscore.

Reforming Horror

The second reason why Lewton needed to invest in an original score for his films centers on the burden his approach to horror placed upon each film's soundtrack. Over the course of weeks, Lewton met with his team of hand-picked colleagues and studio-assigned personnel.

The personnel who formed the early story meetings on *Cat People* included Lewton's young secretary, Jessie Ponitz, who already knew the studio's workings very well. She also proved invaluable for her ideas on cinematic horror, which Lewton prompted her to share. She recalled, "When Val asked for your opinion, you felt that he seriously wanted to hear what you had to say. You felt so much a part of the picture he was making. It was the same with everybody else; there was a great sense of collaboration."[8]

The people who constituted "everybody else" changed over the years. Initially Lewton and Ponitz were joined by Jacques Tourneur, a second-unit director for Selznick who had done considerable work with Lewton on the revolutionary scenes in *A Tale of Two Cities* (1935); Mark Robson, an editor at RKO assigned to work with Lewton immediately after he assisted on the controversial re-edit of *The Magnificent Ambersons* (1942); and DeWitt Bodeen, a playwright Lewton met in the MGM story department.

This team discussed all manner of topics, but mostly they considered what frightened them in films. Lewton arranged screenings of several Universal horror pictures by way of providing the group an illustration of what he did not want to do. The team's most celebrated viewing was of Universal's smash hit, *The Wolf Man* (1941). That film opened on December 12, 1941 to mostly negative reviews, but thanks to a strong cast, a good script by Curt Siodmak, and a budget of US$180,000 (some wisely spent on Jack Pierce's superb werewolf make-up), the film was grossing millions of dollars for cash-strapped Universal.[9]

Set in modern times, *The Wolf Man* tells the tale of Larry Talbot (Lon Chaney, Jr.), second son to Sir John Talbot (Claude Rains), a Welsh aristocrat. The American-educated Larry returns to his father's estate on the death of his older brother. Larry meets Gwen (Evelyn Ankers), the daughter of a local antique dealer, and while the two of them visit a gypsy fortune teller (Bela Lugosi), a friend of Gwen's is murdered by a wolf, which is in turn slain by Larry with a silver-handled cane, but not before the wolf bites him. That was no wolf, but a werewolf, and now Larry bears the curse to become a werewolf himself at each full moon. Eventually Larry's wolf form threatens Gwen before Sir John is able to destroy his son, again using the silver-handled cane.

The Wolf Man is a monster movie in the fullest sense. The werewolf appears onscreen frequently during the latter half of the film. These appearances of a monster frightening primarily Gwen in thick billowing fog among leafless trees provide the film with its essence. When the wolf man strikes, the film's score by the team of Frank Skinner, Hans Salter, and Charles Previn provides obliging underscore that loudly intensifies the action on the screen.[10]

Despite its box office success and many excellent qualities, nothing about the film inspired fear in Lewton and his cohorts. *Cat People* unfolds in a world where *The Wolf Man* exists not as a supernatural horror, but as a film. In other words, *Cat People* exists in the same world as its audience. At one point in *Cat People*, the film's psychiatrist, Dr. Judd (Tom Conway), has just been warned that his patient, Irena (Simone Simon), is a supernatural shape-changer. He quips, "You want me to carry a gun perhaps with a silver bullet." Characters in Lewton's first film reveal that they know the ersatz folklore contained within rival Universal's *The Wolf Man*.

Mark Robson stated his view of the Universal style rather bluntly: "At Universal the prevailing idea of horror was a werewolf chasing a girl in a nightgown up a tree."[11] While Robson erred in his details – no werewolf ever chased anyone up a tree in *The Wolf Man* or in any of its four sequels – his jibe captures the tone of Lewton's unit. Lewton described his aims somewhat more affirmatively in an interview with *The Los Angeles Times*:

> We tossed away the horror formula right from the beginning. No grisly stuff for us. No masklike faces hardly human, with gnashing teeth and hair standing on end. No creaking physical manifestations. No horror piled on horror. You can't keep up horror that's long sustained. It becomes something to laugh at. But take a sweet love story, or a story of sexual antagonisms, about people like the rest of us, not freaks, and cut in your horror here and there by suggestion, and you've got something.[12]

The Lewton unit's visual approach to horror marries director of photography Nicholas Musuraca's chiaroscuro lighting with the relentless ordinariness of Lewton's mundane settings. All of the film's suspense scenes find the screen largely filled with shadow. In order to take full advantage of the film's shadowy look, Lewton needed an aural metaphor for his visual shadows. The Universal approach of firing up the underscore during scenes of suspense would not do.

Sound Contributes to Lewton's Reforms

Among the sonic innovations in Lewton's first production, the scenes of suggested horror – such as Alice (Jane Randolph) making her frightful walk across the Central Park transverse or the scene in the swimming pool – unfold without underscore.[13] Silence in the underscore and suggestive sound effects supply the aural metaphor for the shadowy visuals.

The film's famous "jump scare," or as the Lewton unit dubbed it, the first "bus," occurs in one of these suspenseful scenes when the frightened Alice is suddenly joined onscreen by a bus entering from the right side of the screen as the soundtrack was suddenly saturated with the sound of pneumatic brakes. DeWitt Bodeen reports that audiences at the premiere jumped out of their seats,[14] confirming Kevin Donnelly's argument that "jump scares" transcend the representational function of narrative cinema and enter in the sensational.[15] The technique would appear in all of Lewton's horror films.[16]

For the film's one scene of actual violence, the murder of Dr. Judd, composer Roy Webb supplied a suitable agitato in a ferocious harmonic language of modernist cant as whole-tone collections growl over a heavily accented descending whole-tone scalar pattern in the low strings. Here Webb traveled well-worn paths. His contribution to Lewton's reforms were reserved for other aspects of the film than its isolated moment of actual violence.

In a bold departure from the usual procedure during pre-production on studio-era films, Lewton invited Webb to attend several story meetings as the ideas for *Cat People* unfolded.[17] While Lewton wanted to discuss how musical underscore could elevate his low-budget film and intensify its suspense, Webb witnessed the unit's attention to detail and its ambition to alter the trajectory of the horror film away from the monster movie ideals practiced at Universal Pictures into a more sophisticated genre locating the monstrous within people's fears about themselves. While this is the most celebrated facet of Lewton's intervention into the horror genre, it comes with a crucial corollary. Lewton wanted to break the binary codes of horror that cast good against evil, a pleasing normalcy against an alien and monstrous threat. Webb contributed music well suited to this facet of Lewton's project.

Webb Ignores the Script

Music is mentioned in *Cat People*'s shooting script three times. In all three cases, the instructions in the script do not emerge on the film's soundtrack. The first mention appears at the very beginning of the film as Oliver (Kent Smith) first approaches Irena at the zoo. The second concerns the lullaby Irena hums in her apartment during Oliver's first visit. And the last, and least important, concerns the tune being sung by the zookeeper (Alec Craig) as he sweeps the panther's cage, and Irena returns his key.

Dispensing with this last one quickly, in the shooting script, the zookeeper sings "The Bombardment of Bristol." This obscure piece of doggerel verse selected by either Bodeen or Lewton, who always created the final draft of his scripts,[18] describes how "the refusal of the town of Bristol, Connecticut, to supply the British ships with stores on October 7, 1775, led to the bombardment of the town. Had the British aim been better, it would have been an atrocity."[19]

The choice of this text ridiculing the British aim seems unfortunate. At the time the script was written, the United States and Great Britain were allies in the fight against fascism. For the film, the zookeeper sings instead, the song "Nothing Else to Do." The tune belonged to RKO for its having been written by Bernard Herrmann for the film *The Devil and Daniel Webster* (1941). Webb provided Craig with a handwritten copy of the lyrics suggesting his involvement in the choice.[20]

While "Nothing Else to Do" offers a less ally-antagonizing option, the following substitution provides an analysis of the entire film. In the film's first scene, Irena, a Serbian sketch artist for a fashion magazine, draws a panther in its cage at the Central Park Zoo. Oliver sees her, finds her attractive, and approaches her with a clumsy series of pick-up lines. Lewton's final draft of the script for *Cat People*, reads: "Over the scene is the wheezy music of the Triumphal March from 'Aida,' as played on a hand organ."[21] In the finished film, Webb made a substitution. RKO Music Department records for October 6, 1942 show that Webb was present when Steve Soldi, the hand organ performer who appears in the film, showed up to record the soundtrack for the scene. Webb brought his own arrangement of four lines from the Act Two quintet in Friedrich Von Flotow's opera *Martha*.

Unraveling Webb's substitution reveals the composer selected a less widely recognized opera quote, but one far more apt to a canny reading of the film as a whole. The moment in the opera arises as Lady Harriet has just publicly accused Lyonel of insanity, and the chorus has obliged her by binding Lyonel with ropes. Now, fettered like a madman, Lyonel sings a rebuke to Lady Harriet, who came to him in disguise only to fall in and out of love with him. Here is a translation of the text for the passage Webb quoted in *Cat People*.

> Ah, may Heav'n above forgive you,
> That my life you could destroy!
> 'Twas your pleasure to deceive me,
> With my breaking heart to toy.[22]

How might this substitution provide an analysis of the film? Oliver approaches Irena dishonestly for being emotionally attached to his co-worker, Alice, as the film begins.[23] Irena wants nothing more than to be left alone; but when aggressively courted by Oliver she succumbs to the promises of companionship. Oliver falls quickly in and out of love with Irena while belatedly acknowledging his love for Alice. Irena's life is literally destroyed through his deception. The connection to the opera becomes even clearer when Oliver and Alice later seek to commit Irena to an asylum through a misguided accusation of insanity similar to that of Lady Harriet in *Martha*. By invoking this precise moment in *Martha*, Webb, an enthusiastic operagoer during his youth in New York

City when *Martha* enjoyed numerous English-language productions,[24] reveals a reading of the film that is far from obvious.

While many analyses of the film acknowledge the callow nature of the film's protagonists in Oliver and Alice, Webb's view, made clear in his obscure opera reference, amplifies any reading of the film as a radical departure from horror norms. For the purposes of this analysis and all subsequent ones, we look to Andrew Tudor for an articulation of horror norms.[25]

In a statistical examination of all horror films exhibited in the United Kingdom from 1931–1984, Tudor outlines the generic codes of horror films. The narrative structure of horror is tripartite, according to Tudor, with the first offering a projection of normalcy followed by a lengthy period of disorder during which a "monster" threatens "victims" and the "pursuers" gather knowledge and power to contain the monstrous threat. The culmination of this section sees the pursuers triumph over the threat. The final and usually shortest section finds order restored, albeit always provisionally as everyone must live in a world where the monster is now understood as real and sequels potentially loom. This structure gives rise to three conventional functions for characters: threat (major and minor), pursuer (expert and everyman), and victim (actual and potential).

Irena can easily be seen as the film's "major threat." But who are her "pursuers"? Tudor casts these figures as the characters responsible for the containment of the film's threat. During the 1930s, aristocrats or scientists with vague specialties served as pursuers, while the 1940s witnessed more journalists and psychiatrists in these roles. A liberal dose of "everyman" figures, as Tudor calls them, people with neither expertise nor experience other than contact with the monstrous, appear in this role during both decades. Both Dr. Judd and Oliver seem more interested in getting what they want from Irena, which is sex in both cases, rather than actually helping her or containing the threat she poses. To help her, they would first need to listen to her, and neither does. One could argue that Dr. Judd's sword cane finishes off Irena, but after being stabbed she manages to reach the panther's cage and use the key in an apparent suicide. Neither Dr. Judd nor Oliver contains the threat Irena poses.

While "monster" and "pursuer" are important to Tudor's typology of characters in horror, the third category of "victim" is equally important even though most horror films of the 1930s and 1940s neglect them as narratively disposable. Dr. Judd is the only person aside from Irena killed in the film, and as a psychiatrist provides a classic "expert" who functions to pursue the monster. Alice is clearly the film's "potential victim," the female lead who is threatened but saved, although in Alice's case she never quite needs saving. Irena is not a victim in the usual sense, the sense Tudor provides, yet we have Webb's opera quote substitution casting her as precisely that.

Irena steps outside the horror conventions and functions in multiple capacities. Under Tudor's rubric, Irena is a monster (she threatens Alice and kills

Dr. Judd) and pursuer (she contains herself first with self-imposed loneliness and later with suicide) and victim (deceived and betrayed by Oliver, she is the film's Lyonel). With one character residing in all three of Tudor's archetypes, *Cat People* lives up to Lewton's promise of throwing out the horror formula.

The third mention of music in the shooting script for *Cat People* concerns the lullaby Irena hums in her apartment during Oliver's visit. The script asks Irena to sing Stravinsky's "Berceuse du chat." A cradlesong similar in text to "Do, do l'enfant do," the French lullaby used in the film, appears as the third movement of Stravinsky's collection, but it bears no resemblance to the French tune used in the finished film. As Irena will introduce the tune into the diegesis of the film, we should be grateful that Simone Simon was not asked to sing Stravinsky's shrilly dissonant, Russian-language work cited in the script.

Stories abound in the literature concerning the important and necessary substitution of "Do, do l'enfant do" in lieu of Stravinsky's song. DeWitt Bodeen provided the earliest to find print and his version of events remains the most plausible for being the simplest. One day Simone Simon "hummed a bewitching little nursery tune at Val's request for Roy Webb of the Music Department, and that simple little rhyme became the *leitmotif* of the film's music score."[26] While the use of the term "leitmotif" is enjoying greater precision in the literature on film music today, my main quibble with Bodeen is the use of the singular article "the." To be sure the cradlesong provides Webb with the most important musical motif in the film, but there are many others, all of them pointing toward Irena.

All Motifs Signify Irena

In his score for *Cat People*, Webb follows a pattern practiced earlier by his former colleague at RKO, Max Steiner, in *King Kong*. In that score, Claudia Gorbman observes Steiner honoring the long-established association of music with the fantastic and the feminine.[27]

In *Cat People* all the music is associated exclusively with Irena, who embodies the fantastic and the feminine as well as the foreign within the film. Webb provided names for many of the motifs in his score. Here is a list of themes Webb named and their relationship to Irena: "Irena" (obvious), "Lullaby" (the tune Irena hums), "Cat Theme" (heard not simply when cats appear, but when cats respond to Irena's presence or Irena feels her curse drawing her), "Lalage" (Irena's perfume), "Escape" (a melancholy theme heard only when Irena considers her own death), and "King John" (Irena's statue of the historical figure who defeated the Cat People in her village). The tune associated with Irena's statue of King John, a restrained and modal *religioso* in the key of B minor but with not a single A# to lead the material into tonality, also serves as a musical emblem for Irena's desire for punishment, a desire she fulfills with the key to the panther's cage. The tune does not sound on each appearance of the statue, but only when Irena refers to the legends of her birthplace.

While all of Webb's motifs signify some aspect of Irena, the lullaby stands as the most important. It appears by far the most frequently. After emerging in Webb's "Main Title" cue, the lullaby next enters the film when Irena hums it. Her performance connects the tune to her. That the tune is a cradlesong renders it an ideal signifier for her curse, which found her in the cradle. She is, like the lycanthropes of earlier horror films, blameless. But the text of the lullaby, never sung in the film but useful in understanding its role as signifier, offers some menace as well for referencing the cat as a hunter.

> Do, do, baby do, the child will sleep soon.
> Today the cat put on his handsome gray suit,
> To go hunting, hunting for mice . . .
> Do, do, baby do, the child will sleep soon.
> The cat will take off his handsome suit
> If the child is not kind . . .
> Do, do, baby do, the child will sleep soon.

Considering the moments in the film when Irena dons her fur coat and heads out to stalk Alice, the lullaby could scarcely be improved upon for conveying a network of apt associations to the film.

Webb uses the tune to track Irena's mental deterioration over the course of her marriage to Oliver. As her actions become more erratic and finally violent, Webb distorts the simple tune. For example, when Irena throws the canary she killed to the panther in its cage, Webb presents the first five notes of the lullaby in D-flat major with a B natural pedal before ending the brief cue with the lullaby's opening in F-flat supported by a B-flat seventh chord. The latter of these iterations introduces a dissonant polychord and typifies the lullaby's subsequent appearances by being both fragmentary and located in a dissonant context.

When Oliver tells Irena that he will give her a divorce (earlier in the film he proposed to her and accepted on her behalf, now he magnanimously grants her a divorce she did not ask for), Webb presents the five-note fragment of the lullaby first in parallel chords of B-flat and E-flat major while a series of alternating diminished and augmented chords descend ominously. Webb then jerks the parallel presentations of the lullaby fragment to A major while the descending chords in the background arrive on G major, bringing the cue to a grindingly dissonant close.

Bizarre orchestrations of the lullaby abound. For example, orchestrator Leonid Raab allocates the five-note lullaby fragment in an icy cold marimba early in the cue concerning the dead canary. The "so-mi" descents of the melody now in C major are supported by a misspelled G# diminished chord. Equally

Figure 1.2 Roy Webb, "Needful Help," mm. 10–11

unusual, Webb utilizes the lullaby during Irena's first visit to Dr. Judd. Here Raab positions the opening bars of "Do, do" in four violins. Two play false harmonics doubling the theme a perfect fourth apart, while the other two violins double them an octave lower. A novachord supports this with a weird humming comprised of an A major chord with added F# and B.[28] Sadly inaudible on the soundtrack is a lovely feature of the printed score, a timpani playing rolled chords doubling the violin parts (Figure 1.2, "Do, do, l'enfant do" deteriorates]

Normalcy Needs a Record Player

The most unusual use of "Do, do, l'enfant do" arises at two important moments in the film and again reveal Webb operating against instructions but in service of Lewton's reforms. The first accompanies Oliver's ham-handed proposal of marriage to Irena mere minutes into the film. Here Webb presents a tonally stable version in F major complemented by Raab's quite lovely arrangement of the entire lullaby for flute, harp, and strings.

My analysis inspired by the film's music runs into trouble here. How could Webb and the Music Department present this lovely arrangement of the cradle-song as underscore for a scene in which Oliver gets what he thinks he wants, something that will ultimately destroy Irena's happiness? The truth is, Webb did not provide this lovely underscore for the scene – Irena's record collection did.

Near the film's close, when Oliver, Alice, and Dr. Judd gather in Irena's apartment to commit Irena to an asylum, they wait for her to appear. Alice plays a record from Irena's collection to kill the time. We hear the exact same musical cue from the proposal scene on the soundtrack. Then Oliver walks over to the record player and turns it off. "Let's not play that," he says to Alice.

Webb's instructions included a spotting sheet for both scenes merely asking for underscore. Webb provides neither scene with underscore, but instead he supplies diegetic music in the form of a record of the lullaby from Irena's collection. Only now, as Irena and Oliver's marriage collapses into an accusation of insanity, do we learn that Webb has not deployed the orchestral underscore to reinforce Oliver's marriage proposal nor the scene waiting to give Irena the bad news of her pending commitment. Oliver and indeed all of the film's supposedly normal characters use Irena's record collection for their underscore, Webb having provided them none.

One other crucial scene without Irena receives no underscore from Webb. At the workplace water cooler, Oliver tells Alice about his having never been unhappy before. Alice responds with a short speech superficially about the nature of love but really about Irena being an unsuited wife for Oliver. Webb specialized in subtle underscore for scenes of dialogue like this one, but without Irena onscreen, his orchestra remains silent.

Comparing the situation in *Cat People* regarding when underscore is heard and when it is not to the similar situation in *King Kong* first discussed by Claudia Gorbman and then in greater detail by Peter Franklin might clarify how we might understand Webb's approach.[29]

Steiner's first nondiegetic cue for *King Kong*, heard in the fog bank off Skull Island, attempts to illustrate for the audience the effect of fog by presenting vague harmonies drifting in soft arpeggiations. Franklin notes that imbedded in this fog music is Kong's three-note motif. From the start, Ann (Fay Wray) joins the crew in common reaction to these sounds and all are fearful yet attracted. Later in a scene on the deck of the *Venture*, Franklin points out that Steiner cuts the music whenever the film cross-cuts from Ann and Jack (Bruce Cabot) to the Captain (Frank Reicher) and Carl Denham (Robert Armstrong). Franklin argues that the music here supports only Ann, but that Jack has been allowed access to this feminized position through his discovery, almost fearful and definitely boyish, that he loves Ann. This music aligns Ann with the musical femme fatale for its having drawn Jack into its web.

Later, however, the musical underscore fires up again when Ann is offered to Kong. Franklin here describes Steiner's score as "a confused music of modernist violence, romantic passion, and sentimental tenderness." He continues: "Fay Wray is as excessively feminized and hystericized as Kong is masculinized and brutalized." And later, after observing the Kong motif imbedded into the fog scene and before Kong has appeared, "'Her' music is really his: the music of a pop-culture icon of monstrous masculinity whose progressive feminization, relative to Ann, we witness with growing sympathy."[30]

Kong begins as perpetrator of a sexualized assault on Ann as he abducts her from the sacrificial altar and ends the film a brutalized victim at the bottom of the Empire State Building, his three-note theme undergoing suitable transformation from buried ostinato as the sounds of Skull Island promise the pleasures of adventure in Steiner's fog music to the music of sexualized violence in the mid-film to sorrowful plaint after his fall. What does not receive underscore is, to quote Franklin summarizing Gorbman, anything associated with "Logic, Everyday Reality, and Control (implicitly masculine and in need of no music)" such as the Captain and Denham.[31]

In *Cat People*, Webb relentlessly associates his underscore with Irena and carefully denies it to Alice and Oliver even when the filmmakers ask him to provide it. The Ann and Jack of *Cat People*, Alice and Oliver never receive the tender underscore horror films provide their "normal" couples. The film's music supports only Irena. As Irena's lullaby begins to fragment and appear in increasingly dissonant settings and strange orchestrations, Webb charts her deteriorating mental state. Webb offers the sort of musical victimization Kong endures both musically and narratively.

Webb's score reinforces a reading of Irena as, to return to Tudor's character typology in horror, "victim" first, "monster" second, and "pursuer" upon her suicide. Her music does not threaten Alice or Oliver as Kong's threatens Ann and the *Venture*'s hapless crew. To invert Franklin's conclusion, "Her" music remains steadfastly hers and beckons the same "increasing sympathy" Kong's prompted as that film wound to its close.

More interesting and having no analogue in *King Kong*, *Cat People*'s normal characters – everyone besides Irena – recourse to Irena's record collection for their underscore. Judging by the spotting sheets, this maneuver belonged to Webb. How might we read this situation? Perhaps both Oliver and Alice at different times long to possess Irena's warmth by playing her favorite record in the proposal scene and her allure in the case of Alice playing it while killing time waiting to commit Irena to an asylum. Their respective lacks prompt them to use Irena's record to supply what is missing. But their understanding of her is artificial for fixing her in place just as records fix music in place.

Oliver never understands Irena. He claims to Alice that despite being married, he and Irena are strangers. He glibly laughs off Irena's fears about herself in one telling gesture, even giving her a mock sock to the jaw as he calls her "you crazy kid." This litany could be vastly expanded and a similar albeit shorter list of frozen projections onto Irena could be made for Dr. Judd and Alice, who also fail to understand her for never trying. In short, she is victimized as the film unfolds. Oliver's failures to understand the people he presumably cares for will be explored in greater detail in the film's unlikely sequel, *The Curse of the Cat People* (1944), confirming suspicions about him raised in this film.

Webb, who substituted *Martha* for *Aida* earlier in the film, comments analytically on the film with his refusal to provide musical accompaniment for Oliver's proposal. In doing this, Webb denies the audience any access to Oliver and Alice's interiority through music. Claudia Gorbman describes the function of orchestral music on the soundtrack of Hollywood films of the late 1930s and early 1940s as bringing "a necessary emotional, irrational, romantic, or intuitive dimension" to the objective elements of film such as "the image-track, dialogue, and sound effects." She continues: "Music is seen as augmenting the external representation, the objectivity of the image-track, with its inner truth."[32] Webb's decision to connect the function of orchestral underscore only to the character of Irena diminishes the importance of the other characters considerably. This situation does not indicate that Webb has failed to do what Gorbman observes underscore doing, as *Cat People*'s narrative demands that Webb do so. The film's "normal" characters wear their normalcy so proudly that no music could effectively augment their inner truth.

This tyranny of the normal lies at the center of *Cat People*'s narrative. Irena's husband insists that he's normal, and therefore Irena is normal for loving him. In her water cooler confession to Oliver, Alice emphasizes her normalcy by casting aspersions on Irena's self-doubt. Dr. Judd's psychiatry trades in an unreflective insistence on thinking and acting normally. He concludes his second session with Irena with this stark prescription: "Think normal thoughts, lead a normal life."

The film never treats normalcy more brutally, nor illustrates Irena's victimization more economically, than in Irena's sad speech about envying every woman she sees: "They're happy, they make their husbands happy, they lead normal, happy lives." Her victimization becomes so complete that she participates in it herself with this fantasy of universal normalcy.

My analysis of the music within the film leads me to conclude that Irena is the victim of a cruel normalcy. While I arrive at this conclusion largely through the music within the film, with considerable and obvious support from the film's dialogue, Kim Newman arrived at a similar conclusion through an entirely different means. He describes Oliver as a "heel" and Alice as "unsympathetic" while struggling to parse how a film with a monster could so thoroughly alienate the audience from the "normal" characters.[33] Newman sums up these "normal" characters with this withering assessment: "nothing could really make us like the calculating Alice or the cloddish Oliver."[34] This chapter's claims rub against the grain of horror genre conventions, but it is by no means alien to conclusions drawn from within the film studies community of which Newman is a perceptive practitioner.

"Happy Mood Over This, Roy"

After her first interview with Dr. Judd, Irena returns home to Oliver, with whom she has not consummated her marriage for fear of her curse. As she ascends the stairs to her apartment, Webb provides an orchestral cue he named "First Quarrel." The spotting sheet given to Webb – presumably by the studio's Music Department head or possibly the film's producer, director, editor, or some combination of these entities – begins with the instruction, "Happy mood over this, Roy."[35] Webb obliged initially by presenting his motif labeled "Irena," a sweet melody in D major, with the dutiful marking "Happily." At the first cadence, Webb arrives on a fully diminished seventh chord built on C#. Michael Klein, among others, identifies this sonority as a basic signifier of the uncanny in music.[36] This classic marker of the uncanny reminds the viewer that Irena's dual nature is incapable of the sort of bland happiness so eagerly sought by her husband or so matter-of-factly prescribed by her psychiatrist. Moreover, a C# fully diminished seventh chord offers an unlikely tonal destination for a phrase beginning stably in D major. Next Webb reiterates the motif in D major, choosing to resolve none of the tensions in the C# fully diminished seventh chord. This second pass through the D major phrase ends on a half-diminished E7 chord, which also lingers without resolution (Figure 1.3, "First Quarrel")

By placing unstable chords at the phrase's point of arrival, Webb provides an apt accompaniment, albeit one defiant of his "happy mood" instructions concerning the "inner truth" of the scene as stated on the spotting sheet. Webb undercuts Irena's happiness musically with basic signifiers for unresolved tensions and pointing unmistakably toward the uncanny origins of these tensions.

A Conclusion: "Victory Signature" Reprise

This chapter began with Roy Webb's "Victory Signature" and a promise to provide some explanation for Webb's discordant and downcast approach. Wars exact a cost in lives lost and sorrows for the living, and the War Department's instructions to keep everything optimistic and cheerful surely rang hollow for some Americans. Art historian Alexander Nemerov identified Val Lewton as one such American, persuasively arguing that the Lewton horror films strike a discord with the prevailing cheerfulness of wartime Hollywood.[37]

Perhaps Roy Webb reveals himself in his melancholy "Victory Signature" to be Lewton's fellow traveler in rapport not only with the auteur producer's

Figure 1.3 Roy Webb, "First Quarrel" from *Cat People*

sadness over the terrible cost of defeating global fascism, but with Lewton's aims as a reformer of the horror genre who was capable of seeing Irena not as the monster but as the victim of a shallow normalcy too quick to self-congratulation, too certain of its victory, and blithely unwilling to acknowledge its cost.

Notes

1. Charles Koerner, Memorandum to Music Department, August 1, 1942, RKO Radio Pictures Studio Records (Collection PASC 3). UCLA Library Special Collections, Charles E. Young Research Library, University of California, Los Angeles.
2. George Roeder, *The Censored War: American Visual Experience during World War II* (New Haven, CT: Yale University Press, 1993), pp. 7–25.
3. David B. Dennis, *Beethoven in German Politics, 1870–1989* (New Haven, CT: Yale University Press, 1996), p. 170.
4. Joel Siegel, *Val Lewton: The Reality of Terror* (New York: Viking Press, 1973), p. 21.
5. Ibid.
6. The finished film came in at US$134,000. To place this figure in perspective, the average American film made in 1942 cost about US$350,000. This includes everything from Poverty Row to "A" productions at prestigious studios. David Bordwell, *Reinventing Hollywood: How 1940s Filmmakers Changed Movie Storytelling* (Chicago: University of Chicago Press, 2017), p. 23.
7. Budget materials for *Cat People*, RKO Radio Pictures Studio Records (Collection PASC 3). UCLA Library Special Collections, Charles E. Young Research Library, University of California, Los Angeles.
8. Siegel, p. 25.
9. Tom Weaver, Michael Brunas, and John Brunas, *Universal Horrors: The Studio's Classic Films, 1931–1946*, second edition (Jefferson, NC: McFarland & Company, 2007), p. 261.
10. The use of three first-rank composers on a single film likely stems in this case from delays in the production that moved the start of shooting from September 8 to October 27, 1941. To make a December 12 opening, the post-production of the film had to be rushed. Three composers work faster than one.
11. Siegel, p. 71.
12. Gregory Mank, *The Hollywood Cauldron* (Jefferson, NC: McFarland & Company, 1994), pp. 214–215.
13. For a discussion of the soundtrack of Alice's walk, see Helen Hanson, "Sound Affects: Post-Production Sound, Soundscapes, and Sound Design in Hollywood's Studio Era," *Music, Sound, and Moving Image*, Volume 1, Number 1 (2007).
14. DeWitt Bodeen, "Val Lewton Proved that Even Low-Budget Films Can Have Artistic Integrity," *Films in Review* (Fall, 1963), pp. 217–218.
15. K. J. Donnelly, *The Spectre of Sound: Music in Film and Television* (London: BFI, 2005), pp. 94–95.
16. See Michael Lee, "Sound and Uncertainty in the Horror Films of the Lewton Unit," in *Music, Sound, and Filmmakers*, ed. James Wierzbicki (New York: Routledge Press, 2012), pp. 110–111.
17. Randall Larson, *Musique Fantastique: A Survey of Film Music in the Fantastic Cinema* (Metuchen, NJ: The Scarecrow Press, 1985), p. 45.
18. Siegel, p. 25.
19. Nellie Urner Wallington, *American History by American Poets, Volume One* (New York: Duffield and Company, 1911), p. 407.

20. Music Department files for *Cat People*, RKO Radio Pictures Studio Records (Collection PASC 3). UCLA Library Special Collections, Charles E. Young Research Library, University of California, Los Angeles.
21. DeWitt Bodeen, shooting script for *Cat People*, RKO Radio Pictures Studio Records (Collection PASC 3). UCLA Library Special Collections, Charles E. Young Research Library, University of California, Los Angeles.
22. Translation from librettist Wilhelm Friedrich's original journal by Stephen Smith found in the Berlin Classics compact disc release of a 1944 production of *Martha*, 0021632BC.
23. In the original screenplay, there is a short scene between Alice and Oliver at the zoo that precedes Oliver approaching Irena. We can see Alice's shoulder as she sips a soda, the only vestige of the film's opening as originally scripted.
24. "Roy Webb Biography," RKO Publicity Department, examined at the Margaret Herrick Library, Academy of Motion Pictures Arts and Sciences, Beverly Hills, California.
25. Andrew Tudor, *Monsters and Mad Scientists: A Cultural History of the Horror Movie* (Oxford: Basil Blackwell, 1989).
26. Bodeen, p. 217.
27. Claudia Gorbman, *Unheard Melodies: Narrative Film Music* (Bloomington: University of Indiana Press, 1987), pp. 79–81.
28. The novachord was the first analogue synthesizer capable of polyphonic performance. Manufactured by the Hammond company from 1939 to 1942, RKO's Music Department used it to sweeten the sound of thin string sections or double woodwind solo lines when players proved shaky over a few consecutive takes.
29. Gorbman, p. 80, and Peter Franklin, "*King Kong* and Film on Music: Out of the Fog," in *Film Music: Critical Approaches*, ed. K. J. Donnelly (Edinburgh: University of Edinburgh Press, 2001), pp. 88–102.
30. Peter Franklin, *Seeing Through Music: Gender and Modernism in Classic Hollywood Film Scores* (Oxford: Oxford University Press, 2011), p. 69.
31. Ibid., p. 65.
32. Gorbman, p. 79.
33. Kim Newman, *Cat People* (London: BFI Publishing, 1999), pp. 18–40.
34. Ibid., p. 40.
35. Spotting sheet for *Cat People*, Music Department files for *Cat People*, RKO Radio Pictures Studio Records (Collection PASC 3). UCLA Library Special Collections, Charles E. Young Research Library, University of California, Los Angeles.
36. Michael Klein, *Intertextuality in Western Art Music* (Bloomington: University of Indiana Press, 2005), p. 80.
37. Alexander Nemerov, *Icons of Grief: Val Lewton's Home Front Pictures* (Berkeley: University of California Press, 2005).

2 FRACTURED REASONS AND FRACTURED REASON IN *I WALKED WITH A ZOMBIE*

Val Lewton's Dog Puke Tie

Val Lewton's second film, *I Walked with a Zombie*, entered pre-production before *Cat People* reached theaters and proved its commercial viability. The studio's marketing department harbored doubts after a screening of *Cat People*. RKO's head of foreign marketing criticized the film's slow pace, concluding that its market potential was "either very high or none at all."[1] Ed Robat, head of domestic marketing,[2] wrote more generously of the film:

> Personally I enjoyed this picture very much. It is well written, beautifully produced and acted. I'd hate to attempt to predict its box office qualities, because the "horror" is so subtly done that it may not be sufficiently obvious to the masses, so they'll not get a kick out of the theme. But RKO can be proud of having made this picture.[3]

Under Charles Koerner, the studio did not need to feel proud of its pictures, so Lewton enjoyed no clout as yet for having "saved the studio" with his horror programmer.[4] This situation explains the hectoring Lewton received from Lew Ostrow, head of "B" production.

Ostrow hated *Cat People*. A few days into shooting, he tried to have Jacques Tourneur, Lewton's handpicked director, removed from the film.[5] Koerner ultimately overruled Ostrow. Then, after a test screening of the finished film for RKO executives, Ostrow ordered Lewton and Tourneur to take the leopard from the zoo scenes back to the ship drafting office to add footage of Irena in cat form into the final film.[6] Ostrow never liked Lewton's subtlety, and his dislike can be seen in those few shadowy shots.

The title *I Walked with a Zombie*, again dredged up by Koerner's "system of market pre-testing," drove Val Lewton close to despair.[7] Worse, Lew Ostrow assigned Curt Siodmak to write the script. Siodmak had considerable experience writing horror scripts for Universal Pictures including *The Wolf Man*, the very film Lewton had used to illustrate everything he did not want to do.

Val Lewton detested Lew Ostrow, but he also feared unemployment. Lewton used to show his insolence toward people above him at RKO by keeping a hideously ugly tie around. He called it his "dog puke tie" and told his unit that by wearing it in the presence of men like Ostrow, he was displaying his contempt for everyone to see.[8]

While the dog puke tie constituted an amusing form of insubordination, his more effective stroke came when he hired Ardel Wray, who had won a place on the RKO lot through the Young Writers Project, to rewrite all of Curt Siodmak's work.[9] Siodmak's script for *I Walked with a Zombie* resembles the film *White Zombie* (1932) far more than it resembles Lewton's finished product.[10] Siodmak's name appears on the credits, but nothing of his writing influenced the film.

Meanwhile, Lewton instructed Ardel Wray to write an original screenplay loosely based on Charlotte Brontë's novel *Jane Eyre*. In his waning days as Selznick's story editor, Lewton conducted research for the script of *Jane Eyre*, so the topic of Brontë's classic was fresh in his mind.

The film's credits, however, claim that the story is based not on a literary classic but an article called "I Walked with a Zombie" by *Cleveland Plain Dealer* film columnist Inez Wallace for *American Weekly Magazine*, a Sunday insert found in many Hearst papers. Wallace's article offers no narrative component but instead attempts to persuade the reader of the reality of zombies based on the author's recent trip to Haiti. She cites not only Haitian law, but also her own observations to conclude:

> When I first heard of the zombie, not a word would I listen to without an unbelieving smile. But I have come to look upon the weird legend of the zombie – those dead men and women taken from their graves and made to work by humans – as more than a legend.[11]

The only connection between Wallace's article and the finished film is the title and the similarity between her close and the opening shot of the film, a long shot of Betsy (Frances Dee) and Carrefour (Darby Jones), one of the film's two apparent zombies, as they walk along a beach while Betsy's voiceover ridicules the film's title:

> BETSY
> (narrating)
> I walked with a zombie.
> (laughs a little, self-consciously)
> It does seem an odd thing to say. Had anyone said that to me a year ago, I'm not at all sure I would have known what a zombie was. I might have had some notion – that they were strange and frightening, and perhaps a little funny.[12]

Citizen Kane's Legacy to I Walked With A Zombie

While the impact of the Inez Wallace article was minimal, it was the source of the title and belonged to William Randolph Hearst, a man spoiling for trouble with RKO after the release of *Citizen Kane* (1941). Koerner, who had not presided over the production of *Citizen Kane* and wanted peace with Hearst's papers, had bought the story from Hearst and needed to film it as a sort of peace offering for the unflattering biographical similarities between Welles's character and the actual newspaper magnate.

Citizen Kane had more influence on *I Walked with a Zombie* than mandating the purchase of an article from a Sunday newspaper supplement. J. P. Telotte's analysis of *I Walked with a Zombie* opens with a comparison of its structure to *Citizen Kane*, observing that

> just as Welles employed a variety of narrative voices, speaking consecutively and often contradictorily, to fashion his enigmatic portrait of Charles Foster Kane, so does *Zombie* display a succession of voices and perspectives – of I's and eyes – to construct its world. And as in *Kane*, those voices work to reveal just how 'partial' and 'distorted' a single perspective can be.[13]

The story of *I Walked with a Zombie* does not resemble Welles's film, but its structure does. Welles's narrators in *Citizen Kane* each tell Mr. Thompson (William Alland) his or her version of Charles Foster Kane's life, ultimately troubling the audience's relationship with cinematic narrative authority. Each narrator's tale receives lavish illustration through conventional flashbacks. David Bordwell, in his majestic overview of cinematic innovations from the era *Reinventing Hollywood: How 1940s Filmmakers Changed Movie Storytelling*, cites *Kane* as having "blended 1930s devices into a new and striking flashback construction."[14] Bordwell documents the spread of the flashback as subsequent filmmakers "absorbed and extended" *Kane*'s innovative approach.[15]

I Walked with a Zombie differs structurally from *Citizen Kane* in two key ways. First, the entire film is one continuous flashback initiated from the first shot in which we see Betsy walking with Carrefour along the beach, a fact viewers would be forgiven for forgetting. Within this all-encompassing flashback, various characters tell their versions of events. In a second difference, the audience does not see these narrations illustrated, only the narrator speaking to Betsy within her flashback. This quality demonstrates Lewton and his team "absorbing and extending," to use Bordwell's terms, the more radical aspect of *Citizen Kane*'s structure.

Fractured Reasons

In *I Walked with a Zombie*, Betsy wins a job as nurse to Jessica (Christine Jordan), the wife of Paul Holland (Tom Conway), a sugar planter who lives on the fictional West Indies island of St. Sebastian. Betsy meets her patient at night, in the tower at Fort Holland where Paul makes his home. Jessica advances frighteningly toward Betsy until Paul intervenes, having been awakened by Betsy's scream. Jessica has become mindless.

Two competing explanatory models emerge. One depends on Western Reason and sees Jessica's condition as the product of a severe tropical fever. But this perspective quickly fractures, as Wesley (James Ellison), half-brother to Paul, argues that Paul drove Jessica insane with his cruelty. The other perspective is local and unified in seeing Jessica as potentially the victim of "strange drugs" leading to her status as the living dead.

Betsy makes two attempts to cure Jessica. She turns first to Dr. Maxwell (James Bell) to employ insulin shock therapy. After this fails, Betsy takes Jessica to the Voodoo Houngon (Martin Wilkins) to cure Jessica's zombified state through local magic. Along the way, Betsy discovers her love for Paul and discovers that Wesley loved Jessica and the two planned to leave the island together. As the island's authorities plan an official inquiry, Wesley abandons his certainty that Paul drove Jessica mad and becomes convinced that Jessica is a zombie owing to his mother, Mrs. Rand (Edith Barrett), confessing to the crime. While no one else accepts this confession, Wesley does. He kills Jessica and himself. A final narrator, apparently local, describes what he believes happened, but why the audience would value this disembodied voice's authority in a film so packed with doubts about monological perspective is anyone's guess.

That final, never-seen narrator is preceded by many others. We hear from Alma (Theresa Harris), Jessica's maid; Paul, Jessica's husband; Dr. Maxwell, Jessica's friend and doctor; a local street singer (Sir Lancelot); Wesley, Jessica's lover; Mrs. Rand, Jessica's mother-in-law; and, finally, the unseen local narrator.

Together, these voices provide the fractured reasons for Jessica's condition promised in this chapter's title. By way of contrast, the local voices, Alma and the Street Singer, never claim that Jessica is a zombie. They are more circumspect. The believers at the Houmfort wish to conduct tests to verify Jessica's status. Here, the locals take the posture of uncertainty usually associated with Reason in horror films. Horror films have traded in the dichotomy of Reason and Superstition throughout their history. The analysis that follows argues that in *I Walked with a Zombie*, music plays a special role in clarifying the film's theme.

Expressive Doubling: Superstition Vs. Reason

Robin Wood and others have pointed out that the film illustrates the dichotomy of Reason and Superstition through a series of paired opposites.[16] The film features two forts, Fort Holland where Paul lives, itself an expression of colonial power extended from abroad onto the island, and the Voodoo Houmfort, where the ceremonies of the descendants of the formerly enslaved population unfold. Each fort is home to a zombie, Jessica (white and female) and Carrefour (black and male). Each zombie makes a memorable walk to the opposite fort. Jessica is taken to the Houmfort by Betsy while the Sabreur (Jieno Moxzer) sends Carrefour to Fort Holland to retrieve Jessica for tests clarifying whether or not she is a zombie. Each zombie frightens Betsy. Jessica approaches Betsy ominously in the tower while Carrefour approaches her at night at Fort Holland. Each approach proves a red herring as neither zombie means Betsy any harm. Each fort has a doctor. Maxwell appears only in Fort Holland and the entities described memorably by Alma as "better doctors" reside at the Houmfort. There are even two absent fathers: Paul's father, a sugar planter allied along with Paul to Western Reason, and Wesley's father, a missionary, and a man of faith. Wesley will later align himself with the cause of Superstition in another important gesture, fracturing the Western side of the film's central dichotomy.

Very little finds its way into the film without having an opposite presented to undermine its authority. Only Betsy seems to move fluidly between the film's rival perspectives, and when she does Telotte observes that her shifts are too swift, belying her inexperience, her romantic assumptions, and her inability to see beneath surface appearances.[17] We see this illustrated in her naively gazing at the beauty of the sea only to have Paul explain that its glitter is putrescent, or in the nice detail of her surprise at puncturing the brioche brought to her for her first breakfast on the island. This surprise, while confirming Betsy's lack of worldliness, also allows for one of many instances in the film when things reveal themselves as other than they appear. By the film's close, Betsy's romantic assumptions will serve as gateway to Wesley's violent acts.

Doublings that reinforce the essential clash of perspectives within the film extend into the musical realm. These musical pairings manifest on both the soundtrack and the image track. In terms of imagery, Fort Holland houses a grand piano and a gilt harp, two instruments unmistakably connected to the Western musical tradition of domestic music making among the upper and middle classes. The Houmfort houses drums and conches, instruments that quickly signify the rituals and beliefs of the descendants of people brought to the island in chains.

Both the Houmfort and Fort Holland house Aeolian instruments, instruments played by the wind. During their walk through the dry cane fields, Betsy and Jessica come upon a dried and hollowed gourd suspended from a strange scaffolding in the cane field. Holes have been bored into the gourd and wind passes through them to create an eerie, throbbing hum on the soundtrack. This autophone serves as an Aeolian flute. Like Aeolian harps, strings on frames placed in the outdoors where they may be randomly energized by the wind, Aeolian flutes were created to give voice to voiceless, disembodied spirits. The Aeolian flute appears just before Carrefour is seen at the crossroads and is associated with him. Later in the film, the gilt harp seen in Jessica's room functions as an Aeolian harp. A breeze passes through the garden, into Jessica's window, and across the harp's strings, energizing them faintly. We understand the source of the harp glissandi on the soundtrack mainly through the movement of curtains in close proximity to the harp.[18] The Western instrument-turned-Aeolian harp is associated with Jessica, the film's other zombie.

LeRoy Antoine's Contribution to the Soundtrack

The film's musical pairings extend far beyond prop instruments fleetingly heard on the soundtrack. The film has two composers affiliated with its soundtrack. Although Roy Webb received sole screen credit, he was joined in preparing the film's music by a Haitian musician named LeRoy Antoine. While uncredited and largely undiscussed in the literature on the film, Antoine made a crucial contribution. Through Webb and Antoine's contrasting work, the film's soundtrack offers its most striking stylistic doubling. Webb's orchestral score is heard during the film's opening and close, but otherwise serves only to back scenes in Fort Holland when characters whose perspective at the moment can be called "rational" are present. Antoine's music for the film, unlike Webb's, is diegetic and associated with the Houmfort.

On October 29, 1942, just three days after shooting on *I Walked with a Zombie* began, *The Hollywood Reporter* announced:

> LeRoy Antoine, who is one of the country's leading authorities on Haiti and Haitian folk music and voodoo, will be the technical advisor on

> *I Walked with a Zombie*. Antoine will also teach the negro actors Haitian rhythms for use in the voodoo ceremony.[19]

This press release further reveals that Antoine was born in Port Margot, Haiti. He left Haiti at age fourteen, returning for half a year in 1936 to conduct research for his co-authored book, *The Voice of Haiti*.[20] Antoine's career before and after his work on *I Walked with a Zombie* was rich and various. In addition to writing his book on the topic of music in voodoo ritual, he organized the LeRoy Antoine Haitian Dance Group when he moved to Los Angeles.[21] After his work on *I Walked with a Zombie*, Antoine created music for at least one more RKO film, *Belle of the Yukon* (1944).[22] He made a minor appearance in *Rhapsody in Blue* (1945) as a bootblack. He also was described occasionally in newspapers and trade periodicals as a Calypso singer. Sir Lancelot introduced Antoine to Lewton.[23]

Antoine's presence in the film and on its soundtrack serves to distance the film from some of the abuses associated with Hollywood colonialism. Rather than tasking the RKO Music Department with concocting fake Caribbean music to represent the indigenous side of the colonial/indigenous dichotomy, Lewton and his team chose authenticity in contrast to prevailing practices in Hollywood.[24]

Lewton placed tremendous importance on musical authenticity in his productions.[25] RKO struggled to exploit Lewton's unorthodox activities through marketing. The press book for the film contains an article drawing upon Antoine's expertise titled "Authority Versed in Voodooism Admits the Existence of Zombies." After parading out Antoine's bona fides as an authority on Haitian culture, the article moves toward crass exploitation with a pointless story of marital infidelity leading to a Haitian husband transforming his wife's lover into a zombie.[26] Lewton had his agenda, and corporate cinema of the 1940s had another.

The press release picked up by *The Hollywood Reporter* did not provide an exhaustive list of Antoine's contributions to *I Walked with a Zombie*. He brought a group of Haitian musicians and dancers selected from his troop onto the set to drum, dance, and sing for the ritual scenes. None received screen credit for their work.[27] Antoine himself was on the set for all the shooting at the Houmfort and appears in the film as the lead drummer. On set, he coached the cast on appropriate conduct for a ritual of its kind. Antoine supervised recording sessions on October 20 and 24, 1942, when his arrangements of the Haitian songs "O Marie Congo," "O Legba," "Wallee Nan Guinan," and "Levee Dumbala" were recorded. He also supervised the performance of his drummers whose work haunts much of the film's last half.[28] The song "O Legba" and some of the drumming patterns used in the film can be found in Antoine's book.[29]

The Haitian songs Antoine wove into the film were chosen with obvious care. The most frequently heard is "O Marie Congo," sung first on board the ship that carries Betsy and her new employer to St. Sebastian. Three singers from Antoine's troop representing crew members on Paul Holland's boat sing the song. Lewton's screenplay makes no mention of this or any of the tunes Antoine arranged for the film, so we must assume that Antoine suggested their use.

The song's lyrics refer to the practice of slavery, the title being the name of a slave ship, and suits a film that continually reminds its audience that St. Sebastian is a sad place. We hear "O Marie Congo" in the film's opening scene as Paul tells Betsy that, "there's no beauty here, only death and decay. Everything good dies here, even the stars." "O Marie Congo" haunts the soundtrack, acting much like the familiar image of the figurehead of St. Sebastian taken from the prow of the slave ship that brought, according to the film's carriage driver (Clinton Rosemond), "the long-ago mothers and the long-ago fathers of us all, chained to the bottom of the boat." The tune remains a presence to the film's close, weaving in and out of Roy Webb's orchestral underscore, until finally fishermen sing it as they use torchlight to lure fish to their spears before discovering Jessica's corpse.

LeRoy Antoine's most ubiquitous contributions to the film's soundtrack are the drums and conches heard sounding from the Houmfort and frequently audible within Fort Holland. We first hear the drums at Betsy's initial dinner at Fort Holland. Once Betsy brings Jessica to the Houmfort, the drumming Antoine led rarely ceases as the powers of the Houmfort seek to draw Jessica back.

Roy Webb and the Music of Fractured Reason

Forming a contrasting double with LeRoy Antoine's contributions to the music heard within the film's diegesis is Roy Webb's contribution of orchestral underscore. The two musicians' contributions offer another network of doublings within the film. For example, Antoine's music is diegetic, Webb's nondiegetic. More importantly, Antoine's music permeates, Webb's is permeable as Haitian songs introduced into the diegesis by Antoine find their way into Webb's underscore and diegetic drums easily overlap it. This observation brings this analysis to its crux. In *I Walked with a Zombie*, the dichotomy of Western/Reason against Caribbean/Superstition consistently reveals the monological perspective of the West as conflicted, fragmented, and permeated by its opposite.

For example, Fort Holland is described before it is seen. In what must be one of the most candid discussions on race in 1940s Hollywood cinema, the carriage driver who transports Betsy from the port to Fort Holland not only describes the horrors of slavery to Betsy but offers this comment on the nature of Fort Holland: "Time was Fort Holland was a fort but now no longer." Fort

Holland's failures as a fort later receive illustration. Carrefour, for example, enters effortlessly during his memorable visit near the film's close.

Webb's original material offers the film stylistic fractures that paint the film's subtext. Examination of the cue "Fort Holland" provides a fine example of this situation (Figure 2.1). We hear this cue, one of only seven Webb composed for the film,[30] as Betsy narrates her first impressions of Fort Holland upon her arrival and gives the audience a foretaste of her experiences yet to unfold there. Webb's cue provides the viewer with a limpid and dreamy accompaniment

Figure 2.1 Roy Webb, "Fort Holland"

befitting the space this music seeks to define. The cue opens with a pentatonic melody in the oboe over four pitches from the melodic line simultaneously sounding in the strings. This gives way to an undulating figure in eighth notes made up of A and C moving to B and D. These notes are supported for one measure by an E-flat major chord revealing Webb deploying bitonality. Through the next two measures this figure descends, but always with bitonal support. As Betsy's narration, which shares the soundtrack with Webb's cue, turns to a prophesy of her discovery of love, Webb lightly sounds his dreamy love motif in C# minor, but as happens throughout the score, his love theme enjoys no bass line to anchor it harmonically. The harmonic material closes on a weird simultaneity of F#-B-E-flat-A-D, a peculiar quartal sonority over blessed with augmented and diminished fourths to go with the perfect ones, as an inverted [014] set of A-G#-F appears three times by way of providing an ominous atonal ostinato. That ominous ostinato is one of the film's many misdirections as it arrives just as the image track shows Clement's shadow pass over Betsy's room. Clement (Richard Abrams) is the fort's unassuming and unthreatening butler.

Webb's musical procedures illustrate a cavalcade of diverse tendencies in Modernist music that fragmented the Western classical tradition into rival camps. With pentatonicism, tonal planing, bitonality, atonality, and finally quartal harmony presented in rapid succession and sometimes simultaneously, Webb highlights stylistic disunity. Webb's intentions are unknown and unknowable, but he has certainly concentrated considerable stylistic disunity into a single short cue while introducing Fort Holland. To a specialist, the disunity Webb indulges is inarguable. Yet, the music is subtle enough to serve as unassuming accompaniment for the scene while offering its reinforcement of the fractured nature of the Western perspective in the film at a deep, structural level.

Roy Webb's score for *I Walked with a Zombie* resembles Fort Holland, the space where it is almost entirely confined. The music is like the fort, in that it is conflicted and easily penetrated. The sound of drums and conches permeate the air within the fort. The songs Antoine provides creep into the score and undermine its resolve to represent its side of the dichotomy of Reason and Superstition with any persuasiveness. This is not a fault of the score, but its great strength.

Chris Fujiwara, in his monograph on the career of director Jacques Tourneur, makes an interesting observation about Webb's score for *I Walked with a Zombie*. He points out that, "Our sense of the characters as somehow not fully present is strengthened by the relative dearth of musical cues to underline their emotions: for long passages of the film, the score consists only of low drumbeats; some scenes of dramatic tension have no music at all."[31]

Apart from the "Main Titles" and "End Titles," Webb provides only seven short cues for the film. Going over them in terms of when they occur illuminates the function of Webb's music. After "Fort Holland," discussed above, comes "Zombie," an understated cue supporting Betsy's frightening introduction to Jessica in the tower; "Dr. Maxwell," a brief cue responding to Dr. Maxwell's explanation of Jessica's condition; "Sympathy," intensifying the emotional import of a conversation about love between Paul and Betsy; "Lonely Beach," music for Betsy's narration as she explains how she discovered her love for Paul; "Operation," underscoring the disappointing aftermath of the insulin shock treatment administered to Jessica; and "Return from the Houmfort," music supporting Paul and Betsy's conversation after Betsy's return to Fort Holland.

Missing from this list are, as Fujiwara observes, many key scenes. For example, nothing accompanies Mrs. Rand's important speeches in the dispensary, at the Houmfort, or when she finally confesses her complicity in Jessica's zombification. The latter of these is glaring, for if we concede that an orchestral cue would be inappropriate at the Houmfort, the confession takes place in Paul's living room at the center of Fort Holland. A pattern emerges in these absences just as one did in *Cat People* whenever Irena was not present. Mrs. Rand lacks orchestral support underlining her emotional confession because in it she admits that she was "possessed by their gods." Webb's music is not merely attached to certain characters or a certain place, but to a seemingly rational, specifically Western perspective. This situation reverses Claudia Gorbman's claim cited in the previous chapter situating orchestral music in league with the feminine, emotional, and irrational. Or more likely, it does not. Instead, the film's underscore emphasizes the falsehood in the proposition that there is some higher access to rationality uniquely belonging to the West.

Accompanying only scenes with Western characters thinking Western thoughts and acting in Western ways, Webb's music actively undermines the rationality the Western characters assume motivates their thoughts and actions. Webb's music is only tenuously grounded in harmonic and rhetorical stability. Rarely do the melodies reside in diatonic pitch space and they are often supported by unstable, non-tertian harmonies. In addition, the compositional styles used by Webb are so destabilized that the music can gain no rhetorical solidity as revealed in his cue "Fort Holland."

Criticizing the Colonial Project

Limited in what and whom it can support, permeated by LeRoy Antoine's Haitian music, and fractured in style and structure, Roy Webb's score for *I Walked with a Zombie* points toward an analytical conclusion about the film's deeper motives. In *I Walked with a Zombie*, the clash of monologics, one Western and one Caribbean, favors the Caribbean. The side of certainty, of Reason's cold and objective light, of the colonial project of Westerners, appears shabbily made.

The music does not bear this burden alone. The Western characters are themselves shaky in their commitments. Dr. Maxwell's ambitious application of Western medicine fails. Paul makes mercurial and unexplained changes of mind as he careens from tenderness toward Betsy to cool indifference. His half-brother describes Paul as "quite the Byronic character," linking Paul to the irrational project of Romanticism. For his part, Wesley is in the end convinced that Jessica is now a zombie. Prior to killing her and then himself, he needs help to enter his home, a space incapable of holding out anyone for being a "fort no longer." Wesley has lost the knack to enter Paul's sanctuary. Mrs. Rand, formerly a missionary's wife, begins by denying belief in voodoo. She ends by admitting that she turned to voodoo to thwart Jessica's efforts to run away with Wesley, a course that clearly shocks the faithful at the Houmfort.

The Western characters all fail to live up to the ideals of rational thought and action. But when they turn to the island's beliefs, they do harm. The colonial project comes off looking rather bad in the film, a film visually punctuated by the figurehead from a slave ship and aurally by a song about slavery. Lewton and his team offer their modest critique of colonialism in *I Walked with a Zombie*, a film admittedly largely about its white characters. Later Caribbean filmmakers will arise and make films telling their story of the colonial project in the West Indies with the authority that can only come from living with its consequences.[32] Among Hollywood films of the 1940s, *I Walked with a Zombie* at minimum rubbed against the grain through its handling of its theme.

To be sure, the film trades in some "B" movie assumptions, rendering the island and its inhabitants a little frightening. But in each case, these frights turn out to be another of the film's misdirections. Carrefour, played by the magnificently lank Darby Jones, appears frightening. The film trades in some conventions of "othering" commonplace in Hollywood films of the era. Yet, as Betsy's narration at the film's opening about her having walked with a zombie unfolds, there she is in long shot walking calmly with Carrefour along the beach. From the film's beginning, the "B" movie stereotypes about a non-white threat are undermined. Later, when Carrefour enters Fort Holland to retrieve Jessica for additional ritual tests, his visual handling is nearly identical to the earlier visual handling of Jessica in the tower. Both approach from medium point-of-view shots to an extreme close-up, and both shots culminate in a sudden shout on the soundtrack.

Two Performances: Sir Lancelot's "Shame and Sorrow"

One more musical pairing exists on the soundtrack of *I Walked with a Zombie*. The film features two composers whose work is performed within the film's diegesis. The Western figure is Frédéric Chopin, whose music Paul Holland performs on the grand piano inside Fort Holland. The Caribbean figure is Sir

Lancelot who played the role of the street singer and wrote the song "Shame and Sorrow," which he performs on-screen.

Sir Lancelot was born Lancelot Pinard on Trinidad. His family sent him to New York City to study medicine, but he interrupted his studies for a two-week engagement singing at the Village Vanguard. This engagement was extended to a full year, lasting until 1940, and his medical training fell to the wayside. He first came to Hollywood to appear in Columbia Pictures' *Two Yanks in Trinidad* (1941). *I Walked with a Zombie* marks his first credited performance and led to two more appearances in Lewton films and a reprise of his role as the street singer, along with Darby Jones as Carrefour, in RKO's *Zombies on Broadway* (1945). He later appeared in *To Have and Have Not* (1945) and the noir thriller *Brute Force* (1947).

His composition "Shame and Sorrow," known also by the title "The Fort Holland Song," provides a cryptic narration of action that occurs before the film begins.[33] Apparently Lewton participated in the creation of "Shame and Sorrow" insofar as he helped Sir Lancelot write the lyrics.[34]

Initially Sir Lancelot appears in a small crowd where he sings "The British Grenadiers." That scene centers on Betsy and Wesley chatting at an outdoor bar on Betsy's day off. As they talk, Sir Lancelot switches songs to "Shame and Sorrow," which narrates the troubles between Wesley, Paul, and Jessica. Hearing this performance, Wesley becomes agitated and tries to drown out the song with an irrelevant narration of his own about Clement and a donkey. He fails. Betsy wants to listen, so Wesley wordlessly instructs the bartender, T Joseph (Arthur Walker), to silence the singer. Later in the same scene, after a dissolve allows the sun to set and Wesley to drink himself into a stupor, we find Betsy alone in the dark. Sir Lancelot approaches and completes his song. He walks toward her menacingly as he sings and stares at her intently, his narrative lyrics now enfolding Betsy into his story.

J. P. Telotte observes that this scene mirrors the film's structure as a whole, in which narration overlays narration.[35] The song's lyrics end with a sudden repositioning of Betsy from outsider to insider by implicating her in the friction between the half-brothers and introducing the story's next love triangle of Paul and Wesley fighting over Betsy. Telotte points out that this crucial move costs Betsy an objective narrative voice in the film's events.[36] The audience will hear her in voiceover only one subsequent time, and then only to comment on her discovery of love for Paul.

Two Performances: Paul Holland's Chopin Étude

Sir Lancelot's musical performance marks a stark contrast to a later musical performance seen in the film, Paul Holland playing Chopin's E major Étude, Op. 10, No. 3. Sir Lancelot's song has an intended audience, Betsy, and is therefore a quasi-public performance rather than a private moment captured surreptitiously. In her scene with Paul, Betsy, again the listener, has been placed in the powerful position of gazing on Paul. In her scene with Sir Lancelot, she is the recipient of Sir Lancelot's menacing gaze as he moves toward her while singing and integrates her into his song. The power imbalance in the scene with Sir Lancelot is useful in setting up the opposed imbalance in the piano scene.

The oppositions between Sir Lancelot's song and Paul Holland's performance of Chopin beyond the Western/Caribbean dichotomies discussed at length above are so numerous as to feel intentional. They include Betsy as "object of the gaze"/ Betsy gazing,[37] narrative song/autonomous artwork, traditional/classical, public/private, threatening/alluring, to name some of the more obvious ones.

The vigor of Sir Lancelot's scene with his physical approach and insinuations about Paul's and Wesley's intentions toward Betsy contrasts starkly to the limpid scene that soon follows in which Paul plays the piano. The piano embodies the values of Reason in a complex way for the film.

In an interesting scene scripted but never shot, Jessica wanders past the piano and depresses random keys with no motivation.[38] For Lewton and Wray, playing the piano marks the player with the mastery and control enabled by Reason. Paul Holland, Reason's most insistent champion in the film, plays the piano, and his playing draws Betsy to him. It serves as the first entrée toward intimacy between them. Wray's and Lewton's screenplay differs notably from the finished film in terms of Paul's repertory.

> INT. BETSY'S BEDROOM – NIGHT
>> The room is in darkness. Betsy stands leaning against one of the jalousies, looking out through the slit between two panels. Over the scene comes the sad, masculine sorrow of the Liebestod. It is being played well and forcefully on the piano in the living room.[39]

Here the writers were ill-served by Lewton's poor background in music and Wray's youth. The *Liebestod*, the last scene of Richard Wagner's music drama *Tristan und Isolde*, would hardly suit the scene. For one thing, it was not written for piano, though Franz Liszt published a faithful piano transcription. Lewton probably meant Franz Liszt's *Liebestraum*. When RKO in-house pianist Norman Bennet joined the set to play off camera during the shooting of Paul's scene at the piano, he either selected or was instructed to play Frédéric Chopin's E major Étude. The choice constitutes a huge improvement given the intimate context – a salon piano owned by a wealthy amateur player.

With the use of Chopin's Étude yet another duality is introduced into the film, one that is both subtle and historically rich in hermeneutic potentials.

For a model of analysis examining the role of quoted music within the diegesis of horror films, Isabella van Elferen provides several in her book *Gothic Music: The Sounds of the Uncanny* (2012). She discusses, for example, how Dr. Jekyll's performances of J. S. Bach's Chorale Prelude "Ich ruf zu dir: Herr Jesu Christ" (BWV 639) and Toccata and Fugue in D Minor (BWV 565) in *Dr. Jekyll and Mr. Hyde* (1931) provide a legible hermeneutic code for the audience to assess Dr. Jekyll's character as "Bach was the composer of sacred music that is as virtuous as the chaste lover Jekyll; the musical superhuman who could play and compose things so complicated they nearly surpass human intellect, just like Jekyll's potion."[40]

Like J. S. Bach in *Dr. Jekyll and Mr. Hyde*, Chopin brings a network of signifiers to *I Walked with a Zombie*.[41] Rose Rosengard Subotnik argues, "Chopin's achievement helped mark a shift in Western thought away from metaphysical beliefs, and even away from complete confidence in the innate rationality of any structure . . . toward a fragmented, essentially aesthetic view of human reality."[42]

Chopin provides an apt choice of music for Paul, who, like his fractured fort and fractured Reason, provides a fractured self. He is at once considerate and even tender toward Betsy, and then a moment later cold and even cruel. He commands his plantation as a patriarchal heir to his father's fortune with brittle certitude. Yet, his masculinity is in crisis for he lost his lovely wife's affection to his half-brother. Chopin's presence in this scene reinforces the idea that the supposedly reasoned Western perspective, with all its attendant manners and thoughts, is in a weakened position, the object of a woman's gaze. For while Western rationality is caricatured as sturdily objective, music itself has been traditionally seen as notably subjective. Chopin provides a paragon of subjectivity and a stark double for Sir Lancelot's assertive, canny Calypso number.

Equally relevant to a discussion of a film about zombies, Jim Samson observes that, "the image of Chopin the consumptive, with 'the pallor of the grave,' was given a kind of explanatory value by some French critics."[43] Chopin functioned and functions in the popular imagination as a living dead owing to his celebrated sickliness immortalized in Hollywood cinema with the scene of Chopin (Paul Muni) bleeding on the piano keys in *A Song to Remember* (1945).

Later, Webb's score takes up the Chopin Étude first in offering an embellished version accompanied by strings and winds. This cue, titled "Lonely Beach," supports Betsy as she confesses her love for Paul, a love she cannot account for as he had just thrust her from the room where she found him playing the piano. Later, when Paul finally confesses his love, Webb's score again appropriates the Étude during the cue "Return to the Houmfort." Betsy at that point in the film has tried twice to make Paul happy by returning Jessica to health, the first by Western medicine, the second by voodoo. Now having failed, she admits her failure. Webb quotes Chopin, and Paul's reserve falters. He tells her about his tender feelings for her to the strains of the Étude he performed earlier as arranged by Webb.

The Étude is more than a borrowed love theme for the film, however. Paul's love may well have destroyed Jessica, and it threatens to do the same to Betsy. The intimacy Chopin's Étude instills is fraught with the dangers that so irrational an emotion as love might prompt. Chopin's music reveals the fractures in Western Reason's structure,[44] which attempts to build the impermeable and lasting edifice akin to the fort in which Paul resides. Paul's pat answers to all hints and whispers of an alternate explanatory mode to his own indicate his structural aspirations. As the film winds down, his explanatory model finds itself repeatedly rocked by enticing counterclaims including his mother's admission that she was "possessed by their gods" and drugged and murdered Paul's wife. Betsy speaks to the audience for the last time in voiceover as Webb's cue based on Chopin roils like the sea in the background. Her confession about love and the confusion it causes her allies Chopin's music with inexpressible feelings:

> BETSY
> (narrating)
> I don't know how their own love is
> revealed to other women – maybe in
> their sweethearts' arms – I don't
> know. To me it came that night
> after Paul Holland almost thrust me
> from the room, and certainly thrust
> me from his life. I said to myself,
> 'I love him.' And even as I said
> it, I knew he still loved his wife.
> Then because I loved him, I felt I
> had to restore her to him – to
> make her what she had been before –
> to make him happy.[45]

In *I Walked with a Zombie*, Chopin provides a complex hermeneutic field. His music balances the film's Calypso number by providing the Western alternative to on-screen performance of Caribbean music in a film where everything comes in balanced pairs. While the Calypso number is specific in its meanings, even referencing the characters in the film by name, Chopin's Étude provides inexpressible feelings and an invitation to a love that makes no sense to the lovers, a love that may well be dangerous for Betsy in light of Paul's history. As an exemplar of the Western perspective's objectivity and Reason, Chopin's music provides a subjectivity that reveals the fractures imbedded deep within that perspective.

More than an interrogation of the unreliable cinematic narrator, *I Walked with a Zombie* is a compact meditation on one of horror's classic dualities, Reason and Superstition. Through its music, the film presents the advocates of Reason as fractured against one another and themselves, and thoroughly enmeshed in the irrational. Just as the musical choices in *Cat People* serve as a form of critique of unreflective normalcy, the musical choices in *I Walked with a Zombie* offer a rare albeit modest critique of the colonial project.

Notes

1. Marketing Department screening reports on *Cat People*, RKO Radio Pictures Studio Records (Collection PASC 3). UCLA Library Special Collections, Charles E. Young Research Library, University of California, Los Angeles.
2. Ed Robat was a holdover from before Charles Koerner's ascent to head of production. His comments reflect the old ways at RKO when genius was prized over showmanship.
3. Marketing Department screening reports on *Cat People*, RKO Radio Pictures Studio Records (Collection PASC 3). UCLA Library Special Collections, Charles E. Young Research Library, University of California, Los Angeles.
4. Joel Siegel, *Val Lewton: The Reality of Terror* (New York: Viking Press, 1973), p. 40.
5. Ibid., p. 35.
6. Ibid., pp. 35–36.
7. Ibid., p. 41.
8. Ibid., p. 18.
9. Ibid., pp. 40–41.
10. Edmund Bansak, *Fearing the Dark: The Val Lewton Career* (Jefferson, NC: MacFarland & Company, 1995), p. 147.
11. Inez Wallace, "I Walked with a Zombie," *American Weekly Magazine*. This insert was undated and appeared in various issues depending on the newspaper.
12. Ardel Wray, final shooting script for *I Walked with a Zombie*, RKO Radio Pictures Studio Records (Collection PASC 3). UCLA Library Special Collections, Charles E. Young Research Library, University of California, Los Angeles.
13. J. P. Telotte, *Dreams of Darkness: Fantasy and the Films of Val Lewton* (Urbana: University of Illinois Press, 1985), p. 42.
14. David Bordwell, *Reinventing Hollywood: How 1940s Filmmakers Changed Movie Storytelling* (Chicago: University of Chicago Press, 2017), p. 101.
15. Ibid., pp. 67–101.
16. Robin Wood, *Hollywood from Vietnam to Reagan... and Beyond* (New York City: Columbia University Press, 2003), pp. 133–134.
17. Telotte, pp. 46–52.
18. This small detail clearly mattered to Lewton, who describes it in his final draft of the screenplay. One can easily imagine that Lewton's love for Samuel Taylor Coleridge, quoted at length in his later film *The Seventh Victim*, led him to introduce Aeolian

instruments into the film. Coleridge's poem *The Aeolian Harp* (1795) was a Lewton favorite.
19. *Hollywood Reporter*, October 29, 1942.
20. Laura Bowman and LeRoy Antoine, *The Voice of Haiti* (New York City: Clarence Williams Music, 1938).
21. "Russian Benefit Draws Big Crowd," *Los Angeles Times*, April 19, 1942.
22. "Filmland Briefs," *Los Angeles Times*, April 29, 1944.
23. Scott MacQueen, "The Val Lewton Thrillers." CD liner notes for *Roy Webb Music for the Val Lewton Films* (Munich: Marco Polo, 2000), p. 32.
24. For a discussion of prevailing practices concerning the creation of music "typical of certain races, nationalities, and locales" see James Buhler, *Theories of the Soundtrack* (Oxford: Oxford University Press, 2019), pp. 194–197.
25. Gestures toward musical authenticity on the part of Lewton, such as hiring LeRoy Antoine, became a mania for him. He took on a similar musical advisor, an Apache musician named Dr. Willowbird, for his final film, the Universal-International western *Apache Drums* (1951). What may have been high-minded for Lewton, the studio transformed into something low. An article in the press book for *Apache Drums*, "Authentic Music in Indian Film" reads in part: "Universal-International Studio scored a first in the musical field when Dr. Willowbird, noted authority on Indian lore, was signed to supervise authentic Apache music for the soundtrack of the Technicolor Apache Drums . . . An orchestra comprised of 20 Apache Indians was used to record the music highlighted by an Apache religious chant sung by the Redskins as part of their ceremonial preparations for going into battle. The film's background music also includes an Apache drinking song and several warpath numbers."
26. "Authority Versed in Voodooism Admits the Existence of Zombies," in Press Book for *I Walked with a Zombie* (1943), p. 5.
27. We know that the two featured dancers at the Houmfort were Jeni Le Gon and Kathleen Hartfield, members of Antoine's troop thanks to photo captions published among the film's publicity materials. These photos are in the collection of The Academy of Motion Picture Arts and Sciences, Margaret Herrick Library.
28. Production materials for *I Walked with a Zombie*, RKO Radio Pictures Studio Records (Collection PASC 3). UCLA Library Special Collections, Charles E. Young Research Library, University of California, Los Angeles.
29. Bowman and Antoine, pp. 12–13 and 39–41.
30. Compare Webb producing only seven cues for *I Walked with a Zombie* to the twenty-one cues composed for *Cat People* and you have a sense of the scope of LeRoy Antoine's contribution.
31. Chris Fujiwara, *Jacques Tourneur: The Cinema of Nightfall* (Baltimore, MD: Johns Hopkins University Press, 1998), p. 87.
32. For a strong early example, see Thomás Gutiérrez Alea's film *La última cena* (1976) in which a Spanish aristocrat in Cuba decides on Holy Thursday to use twelve of his enslaved workers to stage Leonardo da Vinci's *Last Supper*. The dinner discussion strays in fascinating directions. The next day, Good Friday, he departs to reflect on the success of the previous evening just as his enslaved workers rise in revolt.

33. Sir Lancelot recorded the song during the 1950s. It even became a hit in the United Kingdom, albeit with altered lyrics and performed by Odetta.
34. Bansak, p. 148.
35. Telotte, pp. 49–50.
36. Ibid., p. 50.
37. Here, of course, I refer to the theory first proposed by Laura Mulvey in her essay, "Visual Pleasure in Narrative Cinema," *Screen* (Autumn, 1975), pp. 6–18 and reprinted many times elsewhere.
38. The screenplay reads: "Her fingers move strangely over the keyboard, now and again striking a hesitant note, but making no music, only an occasional dissonance." The screenplay next tells us that Paul is the audience for this pathetic, mindless recital. All of the scene is observed by Betsy. Ardel Wray, shooting script for *I Walked with a Zombie*.
39. Ardel Wray, final shooting script for *I Walked with a Zombie*, RKO Radio Pictures Studio Records (Collection PASC 3). UCLA Library Special Collections, Charles E. Young Research Library, University of California, Los Angeles.
40. Isabella van Elferen, *Gothic Music: The Sounds of the Uncanny* (Cardiff: University Press of Wales, 2012), pp. 46–47.
41. From this point forward in the chapter, I owe a debt to my friend and colleague, Sarah Ellis, who co-authored with me the article "Monsters, Meaning, and the Music of Chopin in American Horror Films of the 1930s and '40s," *Journal of Musicological Research*, Volume 39, Issue 1 (Winter, 2020).
42. Rose Rosengard Subotnik, *Developing Variations: Style and Ideology in Western Music* (Minneapolis: University of Minnesota Press, 1991), p. 163.
43. Jim Samson, "Chopin Reception: Theory, History, and Analysis," in *Chopin Studies 2*, eds. John Rink and Jim Samson (Cambridge: Cambridge University Press, 1994), p. 3.
44. The terms "force" and "structure" used in this chapter's close arrive here through Jacques Derrida by way of Lawrence Kramer, *Music as Cultural Practice, 1800–1900* (Berkeley: University of California Press, 1993).
45. Ardel Wray, final shooting script for *I Walked with a Zombie*, RKO Radio Pictures Studio Records (Collection PASC 3). UCLA Library Special Collections, Charles E. Young Research Library, University of California, Los Angeles.

3 THE LEOPARD MAN AS PENITENTIAL HORROR FILM

STRANGE DUTIES

Hollywood composers during the studio era performed many tasks unusual for a modern musician. Roy Webb's strangest duty for *The Leopard Man* involved composing a seventeenth-century penitential chant for the film's climax. The RKO Music Department could have drawn such a chant from the vast repertory of the Roman Catholic Church. Webb's participation in preparing penitential music for the film, I argue in the chapter to follow, drew him into the larger, penitential project of the film as a whole.

For Lewton, the entire task of making horror films functioned as a strange duty. Lewton hated horror films. In a letter to his mother and sister, he complained that, "I'm to work on such wretched and uninteresting material." Later he frets on what "making cheap things" will ultimately cost him.[1] This lamentation runs throughout his correspondence with family, even leading him to defend the New York critics who wrote negative reviews of *I Walked with a Zombie*.[2]

While *The Leopard Man*'s climax unfolds against the backdrop of a penitential rite performed to atone for a slaughter of peaceful Puebloans by the conquistadors, the film itself can be seen as a sort of penitential rite for its makers. The film's violence is rooted in the creation of violent entertainment as a publicity stunt meant to advance an entertainer's career goes wrong. The result sees a leopard released into an unsuspecting community. A girl is killed, and a mild-mannered museum curator becomes homicidal after viewing the corpse. He then emulates the leopard's violence. By criticizing the field of entertainment and its production of unintended consequences through the manufacture of violent imagery, *The Leopard Man* functions as a form of penance for its reluctant makers. To achieve this strange end, the Lewton unit subverted horror genre conventions by creating a victim-centered horror film.

Producing a Victim-Centered Horror Film

Pre-production of *The Leopard Man* began in February 1943. By that time the box office reports on *Cat People* had begun flowing in. The news was good, maybe even astounding. Lewton's experiment in suggested horror had won favor with a massive audience.

RKO rewarded director Jacques Tourneur, who had by then already finished shooting *I Walked with a Zombie*, with a US$5,000 bonus and a contract sending him on to make "A" budget pictures upon completing a third film with Lewton. Lewton was not so fortunate. Charles Koerner felt he was too valuable now making "B" horror films. He received no salary increase, no bonus, and no change in his duties.[3] Proven commercial success also failed to excuse Lewton from producing films to titles chosen by Koerner. Wanting to capitalize on *Cat People*'s success, Koerner chose a related title next with "The Leopard Man." This close relationship of the two titles allowed Lewton to repurpose some of his work finding a story for the earlier film. Lewton had considered using as the source for *Cat People* an RKO property called *Black Alibi*, a nasty detective novel by Cornell Woolrich about an Argentinian policeman who uses the fact that a leopard has escaped in town to launch a series of grisly murders using the leopard as his "black alibi."

In concocting a story based on Woolrich's novel, Lewton changed the source material considerably. He changed location from Argentina to New Mexico. He also substituted in a new murderer. In place of the novel's psychopathic police inspector, Lewton's killer is a mild-mannered local archeologist who runs a small museum of natural history. This change in killer is not superficial. Woolrich provides no explanation for his killer's conduct. Lewton does. His killer is motivated to kill by the unintended consequences of frightening people through entertainment.

The most glaring change concerns the novel's and the film's divergent handling of the story's three victims. In the novel, these women are presented in a most unflattering light typical of Woolrich's bleak worldview. In the film, the three victims are the film's central and sympathetic focus in a reversal of the usual approach in horror films.

For the discussion of "the usual approach in horror films," I turn again to Andrew Tudor. Of victims Tudor writes:

> Inevitably, victims or potential victims are the most numerous of horror-movie characters. For much of the early genre history, however, they are the least interesting, playing out their roles as monster-fodder and serving little more purpose than that. Though we may feel vaguely sorry for the doomed burghers who fall victim to Frankenstein's monster, or the half-suspecting young women into whom Dracula sinks his fangs, we are only really involved with them in the momentary tension of their capture and demise . . . they are there to provide the human ground over which monster and expert, threat and defender, disordering and ordering impulses can battle it out. Second-class citizens of the genre, they are narratively dispensable because physically entirely disposable.[4]

Using *The Wolf Man* as a point of comparison, there are two victims in that film. The first is Jenny Williams (Fay Helm), who dies at the hands of Bela the Gypsy (Bela Lugosi) while he takes werewolf form. She's mourned later in the film, but in an unflattering way. We meet her mother (Doris Lloyd), who makes a hateful nuisance of herself as she misdirects her grief into persecution of the wholly innocent Gwen (Evelyn Ankers). The second victim, Richardson (Tom Stevenson) the gravedigger, has no lines. He appears seconds before he is killed. His death prompts only a passing mention later.

By contrast, we learn a great deal about the victims in *The Leopard Man*. The film elevates one, Clo-Clo (Margo), to second billing, and the other two, Teresa Delgado (Margaret Landry) and Consuelo Contreras (Tula Parma), occupy considerable screen time. All are mourned within the film. This treatment strays both from genre conventions and from the original source material.

On introducing Teresa Delgado, Ardel Wray's and Val Lewton's screenplay reads:

> This is Teresa Delgado, a wisp of a young girl, whose childish, smooth face might go unnoticed if it were not for her enormous and wistful dark eyes. She has on a skimpy cotton dress drawn in at the waist with a five-and-ten cent store belt.[5]

There's nothing extraordinary in this description until you compare it to Cornell Woolrich's introduction to the same character:

> She was fairly tall for her age, and particularly her racial antecedents; already full-grown in height if not girth. She was about eighteen or seventeen. Or perhaps sixteen; they didn't keep very strict count of

ages in this household. Her skin was the pale gold of wheat, but would probably darken with age.[6]

Woolrich's omniscient narrator seems barely acquainted with the girl, and its prophecies about her mounting girth and darkening skin will not come true, as she dies fourteen pages later. Woolrich describes her body for his readers with a comparable lack of sentiment:

> It was as though clots of red mud had been pelted at the outside of the door, until, adhering, they formed a sort of spattered mound up against it. There were rags mixed in with it, and snarls of hair, and even tiny crumbs of coral broken off a string.
> The mass sidled, disintegrating all over the threshold.[7]

Teresa appears more available for accurate description by Woolrich only after she has served her purpose in dying. The situation worsens with Clo-Clo. In *Black Alibi*, Woolrich describes her as a fat, greedy prostitute introduced mere pages before her death. Her literary form bears no resemblance to the lively character in the film, who is neither fat nor a prostitute, and has ample opportunity to humanize her gold-digging ways.

Lewton took a risk filling the film with sympathetic victims in violation of the basic codes of the genre. Critics showered the film with vitriol, most objecting to its grim content and confusing narrative. Bosley Crowther of *The New York Times* described the film as containing "three gruesome murders, painfully drawn out."[8] Lewton biographer Joel Siegel disliked the film, concluding that it amounts to little more than "an exercise in sadistic voyeurism."[9] Even the film's director, Jacques Tourneur, remembered it with no fondness: "Personally, I don't like *The Leopard Man*. It's episodic, a series of vignettes. It got very confusing."[10]

The film's confusion stems from its victim-centered narrative. By focusing on victims rather than "pursuers" and "monsters," the entire structure of a horror story must be recast. The resulting episodic structure emerges from the lack of a centrifugal force within the film in the form of a single main character. Each victim stars in her own segment of the film.

A Victim-Centered Plot Summary

Since *The Leopard Man* complicates generic and narrative film practices, a brief summary is necessary to support a detailed analysis of the film's penitential nature.

In the dressing rooms of the El Pueblo nightclub, two rival entertainers, Clo-Clo, a local dancer, and Kiki (Jean Brooks), a singer, prepare. Jerry

(Dennis O'Keefe), Kiki's manager, enters with a leopard on a leash. He wants his client to make a spectacular entrance during Clo-Clo's act. Kiki agrees. Initially Jerry's stunt works as all eyes turn to Kiki, then Clo-Clo frightens the leopard by clattering her castanets, Kiki loses hold of the leash, and the leopard escapes.

Sheriff Robles (Ben Bard) leads the hunt for the leopard. Charlie How-Come (Abner Biberman), who rented his leopard to Jerry, criticizes Robles's efforts.

> CHARLIE HOW-COME
> You don't get the idea, Mister.
> These cops banging those pans,
> flashing those lights – they're
> going to scare that poor cat of
> mine, Cats are funny. They don't
> want to hurt you – but if you
> scare them – they go crazy. These
> cops don't know what they're doing.[11]

Clo-Clo walks home clicking her castanets. She passes soothsayer Maria (Isabell Jewel), who urges Clo-Clo to select a card. Clo-Clo draws the ace of spades, the death card. Clo-Clo laughs off this portent. As Clo-Clo continues toward home, she passes the Delgado house, and the camera ceases stalking Clo-Clo and lingers with the Delgados.

Señora Delgado (Kate Drain Lawson) needs her daughter Teresa to go to the grocery store to buy cornmeal. Teresa refuses out of fear of the leopard. Her brother, Pedro (Bobby Spindola), illustrates her fears by forming a hand shadow of a leopard. Señora Delgado insists, locking the door behind Teresa. Teresa tries the small grocery nearby, but the proprietress declines to reopen. She walks across an arroyo to the large grocery. On her way home, Teresa and the leopard see one another. Teresa flees. Señora Delgado and Pedro hear Teresa outside the locked door begging to be let in until Teresa's blood streams under the door.

At the coroner's office, Pedro repeats his leopard shadow puppet as Robles comforts the Delgados. Robles invites Jerry to help hunt the leopard. Dr. Galbraith (James Bell), director of a natural history museum, serves as an expert witness. Clo-Clo passes by. The camera follows her to a flower stall, where Clo-Clo encounters a servant of the Contreras family named Rosita (Fely Franquelli). The camera follows Rosita back to the Contreras house.

The wealthy Consuelo Contreras receives a birthday surprise, flowers and a traditional Mexican birthday song sung by her elders. She conspires to meet her boyfriend, Raoul (Richard Martin), secretly at 4 p.m. inside the city's walled cemetery. The graveyard caretaker (Brandon Hurst) warns Consuelo that "the doors are locked at 6." She arrives later than she hoped. After placing her birthday flowers on her father's grave, she goes to find Raoul, but he is gone. Six o'clock comes and goes. Now trapped inside the cemetery, Consuelo panics. She hears someone outside the walls and asks for help. He goes to get a ladder. She sees a tree branch near the wall bend, then suddenly stiffen, as she reacts in horror to an attack by something unseen.

Galbraith points out the clear signs of a leopard attack including claw marks on the tree. Jerry disagrees, citing Charlie's expertise. With nothing to frighten it, why would the leopard attack?

Clo-Clo receives a US$100 bill from a wealthy patron at the nightclub. At home later, she discovers that she lost the money. She heads out into the dark, vacant streets to find it. She hears someone coming. Assuming her boyfriend approaches, she puts on lipstick. The lipstick falls from her hand as she is attacked.

Jerry sees the lipstick as confirmation of his theory that these recent deaths were not caused by the leopard. Jerry's theory is confirmed when Charlie finds his leopard shot in the head in a nearby arroyo. Jerry remembers the place. His feet were too sore to head up that arroyo, so Galbraith went alone. Jerry, Kiki, a young woman from the nightclub (Ariel Heath), and Raoul conspire to trap Galbraith. The El Pueblo is closed for the weekend owing to a local ceremony. Each year, the town commemorates the murder of innocent Pueblanos by conquistadores with a penitential procession.

Heading home, Galbraith passes the walled cemetery and hears a woman's voice cry out for help. As he passes the alley where Clo-Clo died, he hears castanets from the shadows. In the museum, he hears more castanets. Suddenly Kiki appears feigning that she wants to watch the procession. Her effort to provoke an attack fails when the castanets fall from her pocket. Raoul and Jerry spring out of the shadows demanding that Galbraith confess. He flees into the penitential procession. Jerry and Raoul find him there. Tormented, Galbraith confesses, claiming that the sight of Teresa's mutilated body haunted him and led him to kill. As he confesses, Raoul shoots him. Kiki and Jerry confess their love for each other and vow to end their hardboiled ways.

The Root of Violence in the Image of Violence

This victim-centered narrative clearly lacks the centrifugal force a main character provides. Jerry and Kiki serve as the film's "pursuers" and they are in the most scenes, but they drift from view for large stretches of the film. The killers are both weak and frightened. The leopard is mostly seen on a leash, more a pet than a wild animal. Galbraith provides an odd "monster." He spends the film either trying to help the film's "pursuers" or being terrorized by them.

Here we come to the crux of the matter. *The Leopard Man* situates the origins of violence within the image of violence itself. Galbraith's looking upon Teresa's body prompts his psychopathic response. Lewton's and Wray's screenplay draws attention to the irresponsibility of profiting from scaring people and as a result inviting horrific images into the world. Pedro Delgado casts shadow leopards on the wall first to frighten his sister. "They're big, and they jump on you" he laughs as Teresa cringes. Later, at the funeral parlor, Pedro again makes his leopard shadow in a fit of childish irresponsibility. This film twice violated the Production Code when it showed the bleeding wound on a waiter's hand after the leopard clawed him while escaping from the El Pueblo and when Teresa's blood flowed under the door. In both Pedro's casting of leopard shadows and the Code violations, Lewton took pains to link his film to the manufacture of irresponsible images. Given that he hated producing horror films, we can understand his criticizing the enterprise within one of them.

Webs of Collective Guilt

The penitential rite at the film's close draws attention to the deflection of responsibility away from an individual or individuals who committed the violence to an entire community in perpetuity. This theme stands equal to the victim-centered narrative in the film. A web of collective guilt spreads out to ensnare all the characters until finally the entire community shares in it.

Consider by way of example Teresa Delgado's death. She was killed by the leopard. Yet that is only the direct cause of her death. The proximate causes, those causes that meet the legal standard of "but for" in determining what caused an accident, abound in the film. Here is a list of proximate causes for Teresa's death. Jerry dreams up a publicity scheme involving a leopard. Charlie rents out his leopard to Jerry. Kiki participates in the scheme. Clo-Clo frightens the leopard, causing Kiki to lose hold of its leash. Robles botches the effort to capture the leopard and in the process frightens it into violence. Señora Delgado sends her daughter out into a darkened town with an escaped leopard in it. She does this because her husband's temper will result in shouting if there's no cornmeal for his dinner. The shouting matters because the neighbors will judge the Delgados' poverty. Señora Calderon (Belle Mitchell), proprietor of the nearby grocery store, refuses to sell the frightened girl cornmeal after she has closed. These proximate causes form a web of collective responsibility and need for communal atonement.

Similar webs of collective guilt exist for the murders of Consuelo and Clo-Clo. Galbraith is the cause of their deaths. But the film situates his psychopathy in his seeing Teresa's body, so all of the above proximate causes apply in the cases of Consuelo and Clo-Clo along with a good many more specific to each woman's death.

Roy Webb's Victim-Centered Score

Significantly, the murders in the film receive no underscore. In her analysis, Catherine Haworth notes that this provides space on the soundtrack for a heightened awareness of environmental sounds including footsteps and breathing. From the perspective of practical storytelling, this approach misleads the audience to hear the murder and misunderstand its cause as the leopard.[12] Seeing a mild-mannered museum curator approaching dressed in a leopard skin would ruin the film but hearing a comparable sonic environment with each death works extremely well.

Webb contributes to each murder scene, however, in an interesting way. Teresa's walk home receives no underscore. But when she is killed, after the audience has had ample opportunity to hear the sound effects associated with her death, Webb's five-measure cue "Teresa's Death" begins. In his autograph score, he labeled the first chord "death"[13] (Figure 3.1, Webb's "death chord"). A variation on the chord reappears in the cue "The Ace of Spades" and subsequently whenever Maria reveals the "death card" to Clo-Clo and again in the aftermath of Clo-Clo's murder.

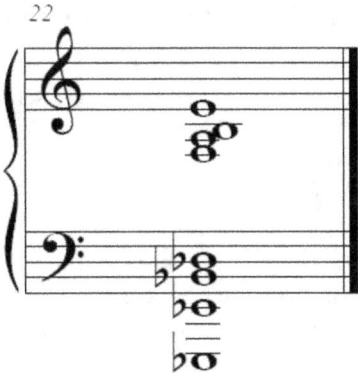

Figure 3.1 Roy Webb, "Theresa's Death" from *The Leopard Man*, m. 22

In Consuelo's scene of imprisonment within the walled cemetery, a strange and different death chord finds its way into the soundtrack. Webb's cue "Cemetery Scene" intensifies Consuelo's mounting panic in a rather standard way, urgent harmonies and snatches of melody that dart up, backtrack down, almost as though trapped themselves. Just as the image track finds Consuelo under the stern gaze of a statue of a male saint in the cemetery, the entire orchestra reaches a D diminished chord when suddenly the orchestra cuts out, leaving only the novachord now playing a D minor chord in inversion. This electronic keyboard instrument, used extensively by Leonid Raab, orchestrator for *The Leopard Man*, to sweeten the often-thin RKO string sections or double wind lines, almost never enjoys solo material. The novachord holds its D minor chord for fully thirty-one seconds before disappearing into the sounds of the wind and the shuffle of Consuelo's shoes on the soft earth. Raab's odd orchestration couples with a strange duration and seems to suspend time in a musical illustration of the cemetery gatekeeper's warning to Consuelo: "Time is strange. A moment can be as short as a breath or as long as eternity. Don't linger."

The silences during the murders themselves coupled with the unusual musical treatment before the death of Consuelo and after the deaths of Teresa and Clo-Clo serve the film's victim-centered structure. They intensify the audience's experience of the violence in what ranks among Lewton's most violent films, but without recourse to the sort of "agitato" Webb provided for Dr. Judd's death in *Cat People*. Placing an "agitato" at a moment of violence in a horror film is how victims are usually treated musically within the genre. The Lewton unit gives the audience something original and motivated by the film's highly original structural approach.

Roy Webb's Penitential Chant

Music in the film supports the victim-centered narrative, the theme of collective responsibility, and the film's implication of itself in its own violence in ways both obvious and obscure. The most obvious but crucial was Webb's "Chant" (Figure 3.2). In the final shooting script, Lewton and Ardel Wray describe the chant this way:

> Outside we can see the processionists marching. The pin points of their candles are making bright spots against the dark background of their robes and the night sky. The leader chants and the rest answer him monotonously, over and over again.[14]

Webb could have selected a pre-existing chant of a similar sort from the vast repertory of the Catholic Church. Instead, he composed an original chant lacking the sort of historical accuracy the Lewton unit prized. Reconstructing Webb's thinking leads to the possibility that the anachronism of Webb's chant invites the critical listener to look beyond the confines of the film's narrative for the chant's meaning by endangering its status as alternate reality. Doing so

Figure 3.2 Roy Webb, "Chant"

provides a useful musical key to what I see as the larger structure of the film. The film is itself structured as a penitential rite designed to atone for the sin of trading in violent imagery of the sort necessitated by the horror genre.

Music from a "Fantastical Gap": Roy Webb As Penitent

Webb's music migrates between the nondiegetic underscore and the film's diegesis with considerable fluidity. Indeed, these migrations come so frequently that, by the film's close, it is unclear as to whether the characters or even just one character can hear them or not. For example, we know Galbraith hears castanets in the museum when Kiki drops them. But who is playing castanets mere moments before by the alley where Galbraith murdered Clo-Clo? Kiki and her one female accomplice cannot be in three places at one time to plead for help behind the cemetery wall, play castanets in the alley, and at the museum. Is Galbraith alone hearing Clo-Clo's castanets in the alley where he murdered her?

Robynn Stilwell theorizes the effects of music of unclear source in film. She writes,

> The movies have taught us how to construct our phenomenological geography, and when we are set adrift, we are not only uneasy, we are open to being guided in any number of directions. It is the multiplicity of possibilities that make the gap both observable and fantastical – fantastical because it changes the state, not only of the filmic moment, but also of the observer's relationship to it.[15]

Stilwell offers an excellent explanatory model for the situation in *The Leopard Man*'s soundtrack.

One of the most telling migrations of music from nondiegetic to diegetic presence on the soundtrack concerns the castanets first heard in Webb's "Main Titles." After the "Victory Signature," Webb presents a seven-measure-long flourish in the manner of an agitato befitting a climactic scene. From there Webb elides into a bolero with a very prominent castanet part throughout. As the "Main Titles" fade out, the castanets continue to play until they overlap with Clo-Clo's obviously diegetic castanets when we catch our first glimpse of her in the film's opening shot. The result is a sophisticated aural elision from the obviously nondiegetic "Main Titles" to the equally obvious diegesis of Clo-Clo rehearsing.

Clo-Clo's castanets serve to signify her presence as she clatters them in the initial rehearsal, uses them skillfully in her performance, and clicks them cheerfully as she walks through the town with a pleasing variety of meanings to each clack. When they are heard in Webb's score, she and the score become one. And finally, in order to capture Galbraith, Catherine Haworth points out that Kiki must take them up and become Clo-Clo.

In her thorough and persuasive reading of Clo-Clo, Haworth points out that in the initial shot of the film, Kiki and Clo-Clo perform a duet, pounding out the same rhythm. When Clo-Clo frightens the leopard, her music becomes dangerous, linking her with the status of femme fatale often associated with the sort of exotic beauty that threatens Kiki's status and drives Jerry to hire the leopard. Later, Kiki must become Clo-Clo, adopting her sounds just as Galbraith adopted the sounds of the leopard when he killed his two victims.[16]

Clo-Clo's richness as a character allows her to play many roles: rival to Kiki; entree into the film's ubiquitous examination of the pressures of poverty; likable member of the community who seems to know everyone; and, finally, victim. Her multi-faceted position within the film far exceeds the description of victim in Tudor's typology. She is not a character aptly described as "the least interesting" and "narratively dispensable."

In addition to Clo-Clo's castanets fluidly floating between diegesis and nondiegesis and even occupying Stilwell's "fantastical gap" as Galbraith walks through the alley, other music heard on the streets or in the nightclub exists within a "fantastical gap." Street music exemplifies this ambiguity. For example, when Clo-Clo passes by Teresa, we hear a faint sound of an accordion. The source of this music is never seen. Similarly, when Clo-Clo receives a flower from Consuelo's maid, Rosita, a small ensemble plays a popular tune softly on the soundtrack. We never see them. Guitars also come and go on the soundtrack during Clo-Clo's walks through the streets.

Of these faint, offscreen performances, the accordion proves the most interesting. We hear it first as Clo-Clo approaches the soothsayer's shop while on her way home from work. The haunting tune, composed by Webb for the film, plays softly throughout this encounter. It then seemingly follows Clo-Clo for several more blocks, suggesting that it is a nondiegetic cue. With the film's atmosphere already charged with fortune telling and portents of death, Stilwell's quote above seems all the more useful to this analysis. Eventually Webb orchestrates the tune and places it into the film's underscore. This again occurs at the soothsayer's shop in a cue called "The Ace of Spades." This appearance is important as the ace of spades, or death card, appears whenever Maria tells Clo-Clo's fortune. This accordion music even finds its way into the "End Titles."

Roy Webb's music moves between diegesis and nondiegesis freely, which is not so unique in and of itself. Tunes written for films and performed within them move to the underscore in many films of the era, especially when characters are popular entertainers. To illustrate what matters about it here, consider that this film features possibly the only appearance by Roy Webb in any film he scored. When Clo-Clo chats with the wealthy man in the bar, Webb sits at the piano improvising on his cue written for the accordion.

The film features a villain who, as Haworth points out, aurally impersonates the leopard as he kills. It also features a group of "pursuers" who embody the film's victims through sound to trap their killer. All of this unfolds in a film foregrounding collective responsibility for violence.

The filmmakers implicate the act of filmmaking into their theme of collective responsibility by illustrating how gruesome images, such as the sight of Teresa's body, become a proximate cause for a psychopath's crimes. That motivation does not exist in the Woolrich source material. To clarify the filmmakers' consciousness of their own responsibility, they put Pedro's irresponsible shadow casting into the film. They concocted dialogue to specifically draw the audience's attention to the mercenary side of entertaining. And the film shows a penitential rite including its anachronistic music as a way of alerting the audience to the collective nature of responsibility for violent wrongs. As the chanting of the processionists indicates, responsibility can span generations.

Webb's music and Webb himself move into the world of the film and out again, implicating the film's music into the mercenary project of horror film production and sharing in the penitential nature of the film as a whole. By criticizing all phases of making horror films, *The Leopard Man* appears a penitential rite for all of its makers, not only its auteur producer.

Notes

1. Val Lewton, Letter to Nina and Lucy Lewton, undated [1942]. Val Lewton Papers, 1924–1982. Library of Congress, Washington, DC.
2. Joel Siegel, *Val Lewton: The Reality of Terror* (New York: Viking Press, 1973), p. 48.
3. Ibid., p. 39.
4. Andrew Tudor, *Monsters and Mad Scientists: A Cultural History of the Horror Movie* (Oxford: Basil Blackwell, 1989), p. 89.
5. Ardel Wray, shooting script for *The Leopard Man*, RKO Radio Pictures Studio Records (Collection PASC 3). UCLA Library Special Collections, Charles E. Young Research Library, University of California, Los Angeles.
6. Cornell Woolrich, *Black Alibi* (New York: Ballentine, 1982), pp. 21–22.
7. Ibid., p. 37.
8. Bosley Crowther, "Boo to You," *The New York Times* (May 20, 1943).
9. Siegel, *Val Lewton*, p. 119.
10. Joel Siegel, "Tourneur Remembers," *Cinefantastique* (April 1973), p. 25.
11. Wray, "The Leopard Man," p. 13.
12. Catherine Haworth, "Dames, Darlings, and Detectives: Women, Agency and the Soundtrack in RKO Radio Pictures Crime Films," PhD dissertation, University of Leeds, 2010, pp. 199–208.
13. Roy Webb, autograph short score for *The Leopard Man*, RKO Radio Pictures Studio Records (Collection PASC 3). UCLA Library Special Collections, Charles E. Young Research Library, University of California, Los Angeles.
14. Ardel Wray, "The Leopard Man," p. 104.
15. Robynn Stilwell, "The Fantastical Gap between Diegetic and Nondiegetic," in *Beyond the Soundtrack: Representing Music in Cinema*, eds. Daniel Goldmark, Lawrence Kramer, and Richard Leppert (Berkeley: University of California Press, 2007), p. 200.
16. Haworth, pp. 199–208.

4 SEARCHING FOR MEANING IN *THE SEVENTH VICTIM*

Production History from A to B

After producing two box office hits in *Cat People* and *I Walked with a Zombie*, RKO granted Val Lewton his fondest wish, an "A" budget for his next picture. He finally found surcease to his penitential production of "B" horror films. Lewton and writers Charles O'Neal and DeWitt Bodeen set to work on a script to Koerner's latest title, *The Seventh Victim*. Lewton liked this title as it differed from the previous three for containing no reference to a monster.[1]

With a completed script of ninety-pages' length appropriate for an "A" budget film, Charles Koerner delivered Lewton a setback by assigning director Edward Dmytryk to the project. Lewton wanted to promote his editor, Mark Robson, to the director's chair out of both loyalty and friendship.[2] Dmytryk was another veteran of Universal Picture's horror cycle, having just completed *Captive Wild Woman* (1943). He was also enjoying "savior of the studio" status at RKO for his *Hitler's Children* (1943) having matched *Cat People* at the box office. Had Lewton given him a chance, they may have worked well together given their similar leftist politics. Dmytryk became one of the Hollywood Ten accused by Senator Joseph McCarthy of communist affiliations. Lewton helped form The Committee for the First Amendment, a support group for the Hollywood Ten. By 1945, the FBI concluded that Lewton was "a known communist" and began recording the license plates of cars owned by people with whom Lewton associated.[3]

Despite their shared political sensibilities, Lewton protested RKO's choice of Dmytryk long and loud (likely while wearing his "dog puke tie"), but to no avail. RKO held firm and would not assign a first-time director to an "A" budget project. Lewton had to choose between loyalty to Robson or his long-hoped-for "A" budget.[4] Lewton chose Robson, and the film's budget shrank to a punitive US$114,000. An obstinate Lewton had Robson shoot the entire script. A ninety-one-minute version of the film was screened only to have RKO executives insist on cutting it to seventy-one minutes, a more orthodox running time for a "B" picture.[5]

Editor John Lockert performed a magical job cutting the film down to a "B" running time.[6] The ellipses that stem from his cuts provide a narrative rich with dead ends and lost threads. For example, a very minor character named Natalie Cortez (Evelyn Brent), the one-armed member of a society of urbane Satanists, received lavish treatment in the screenplay. In the script, she was a concert pianist who lost her arm in an accident. During her arduous recovery, she plunged into depression and had a long-standing affair with her psychiatrist, Dr. Judd (Tom Conway).[7] In a scene where she attempts to recruit Judd to her group, known as the Palladists, she lays out the rationale for the society's embrace of evil. In supplying her missing backstory and turning her into a font of exposition, the "A" budget script burdens the story with unhelpful detail while denying the audience the pleasure of unanswered questions. Lockert cut down Natalie Cortez's role to a much more minor and more mysterious figure. Her connection to the Palladists and the physical evidence of her injury receive no burdensome explanations, rather they add to the film's melancholy sensibility.[8]

The fall from an "A" to a "B" budget led to Lewton making economies throughout the production. In terms of music, this resulted in Webb's first recycling of older cues in one of Lewton's films. The scale of this recycling was small, limited to one scene. The rest of the score for *The Seventh Victim* is original. Important to the premise of this book, nothing of the recycled material came from previous Lewton horror films. The normal approach, undertaken on the studio's series of detective films featuring the Falcon, for example, would see cues recycled from the first film in the second to save money.[9] This illustrates how Webb's approach on Lewton's films painted the text too closely for recycling. Instead, Webb recycled two cues from *Stranger on the Third Floor* (1940), a very early example of film noir.[10] Webb used the borrowed material during an early scene where two characters break into a cosmetics firm at night. That Webb borrowed from an earlier crime film rather than from the previous three scores for Lewton illustrates the singularity of the material Webb produced for Lewton.[11] Almost nothing of it would be recycled, not even on the sequel to *Cat People*.[12]

Madrigalisms in Webb's Material for *The Seventh Victim*

For *The Seventh Victim*, Webb's approach lurches toward the madrigalistic insofar as conventions of text-tone relations often found in vocal music prevail.

Webb paints three ideas in his score, all deeply connected to the central theme of the film.

Lewton rendered the film's theme instantly legible in the first shot, for having emblazoned it on stained glass at the grim boarding school where the film begins.

> I RUNNE TO DEATH AND DEATH MEETS ME AS FAST,
> AND ALL MY PLEASURES ARE LIKE YESTERDAY.
> John Donne, *Holy Sonnets VII*[13]

The first theme Webb paints concerns fruitless striving for meaning. The second concerns repetitious behaviors of the sort Sigmund Freud would describe as "repetition compulsion" in *Beyond the Pleasure Principle*.[14] Freud came to see repetitious behavior as closely associated with the death impulse. The idea simplified is that the patient repeats behaviors again and again to deny death while actually associating strongly with it. And third among Webb's madrigalisms is a repetition of a chord or tone in iambic rhythm, which he labeled in his autograph short score as "death."[15] In all three cases, Webb's madrigalisms link to John Donne's couplet.

An Overview of the Film

The Seventh Victim begins at a boarding school with a young woman named Mary (Kim Hunter), learning that her sister and only relative, Jacqueline (Jean Brooks), has failed to pay her tuition. Mary travels to New York to find Jacqueline. As she searches, she begins to replicate her sister's choices, even falling in love with her sister's estranged husband, Gregory Ward (Hugh Beaumont). Mary discovers that Jacqueline's life had become one vast and fruitless search for happiness. Mary meets two women who strongly intimate that they have had same-sex liaisons with Jacqueline.[16] She meets Jacqueline's psychiatrist and lover, Dr. Judd (Tom Conway). She finds that Jacqueline rented a room above an Italian restaurant,[17] a room she seldom visits. Inside that room, the only furnishing is a chair beneath a rope noose. Finally, Mary learns that her sister's search for meaning led Jacqueline to the Palladists, a cult of urbane Manhattanites who worship Satan. Two seemingly exclusive rules govern the Palladists. The first mandates that anyone who "speaks of their being or their deeds in the marketplace" must die. The second is a pledge to non-violence, "for violence once undertaken becomes its own master, and may serve either good or evil." Having broken the first mandate by discussing her involvement with the Palladists with her psychiatrist, Jacqueline now faces the second, a sinister effort by the Palladists to convince her that life is not worth living.

As Mary searches, she quickly assimilates into a new life. She takes on a job teaching at a kindergarten in Greenwich Village and begins a romantic attachment with her sister's husband. Eventually Mary loses interest in finding her sister, her own life having taken on so many of the trappings of her sister's life. The role of searcher falls to a failed poet named Jason Hoag (Erford Gage), one of the many people in Jacqueline's orbit who befriends Mary. Jason's failure to win Mary's heart coupled with his failed career add to the film's melancholy atmosphere.

Lewton and his team packed the film with melancholy insights into the human condition. One elaborate tracking shot early in the film captures the film's essence. Mary visits the Missing Person's Bureau to report Jacqueline's disappearance. To establish this scene, the camera tracks slowly down four stations where business-like officers take reports of somber people who cannot find a loved one. The first petitioner reveals that the woman he seeks is only sixteen. The second officer asks what the missing person was wearing when last seen. An older woman pensively replies, "He went out without his hat and coat. It's very cold for such an old man." In the next exchange, the missing person had no unusual or identifying marks. And last we come to Mary, searching for her sister.

In presenting these three isolated moments from what appear to be tragedies, this one shot captures the film's fixation on the ubiquity of sorrow and loss. None of the first three petitioners appears again. Their loved ones may be anywhere and nowhere. Their stories erupt into the film for an instant then blend in with the dozens of other tiny, similar tragedies and disappointments that make up the film.

The Seventh Victim offers its viewers a fabric of missing persons and fruitless searches. Some gaps in the story are intentional, like the petitioner's stories. Some are unintentional, the product of John Lockert's studio-mandated sudden and drastic cuts to the film. Taken together, the film offers a surprising structure organized more around a theme than a story. The theme of the film is the quote from Donne's *Holy Sonnet I* absent the rest of the sonnet and the other eighteen Donne wrote for the collection. While Donne's work meditates on the problems of faith in a world of sin and sorrow, *The Seventh Victim* secularizes the theme and denies it any reassurance rooted in faith. The film's theme boils down to an assertion that life is full of suffering, meaningless pleasures, and then it ends.

While Jacqueline's long and fruitless search for meaning unfolds prior to the film, Lewton peppered the film with other instances of fruitless striving for happiness. The melancholy poet, Jason Hoag, finds a fresh muse on meeting Mary. He falls in love with her, resumes writing, then on failing to win her favor "plays Cyrano" in wooing her for Jacqueline's boring husband, Gregory. He tries to publish again after a long silence. The screenplay reveals that the publisher rejects his work, but this detail was cut from the film. Instead, the audience only hears Dr. Judd's skepticism about Jason's style being out of tune with the times.

More dire are the Palladists, each of whom has been motivated by loss and futility to turn toward the secret worship of evil. Selecting as an object of worship a figure singular within its cosmology for being both despised and defeated suggests an embrace of futility itself. For their part, the Palladists justify their love of evil through the rhetorical sleight of hand demanding from their opponents proof in the context of faith: "I prefer to worship Satanic majesty and power, who can deny me? Give me one proof that good is superior to evil." Their heterodox posture is purely willful.

Webb's Madrigalism for the Futile Search for Happiness

Webb illustrates fruitless striving through misshapen melodic phrases that almost exclusively ascend. While arch shapes dominate the construction of melodies in Common Practice music, Webb's score for *The Seventh Victim* assiduously eschews them. Webb's ascending antecedent phrases are never balanced with descending consequents.

Webb introduces this particular madrigalism in his "Main Title" cue. After establishing the key of D-flat minor, Webb's first phrase begins with all ascending intervals moving up the tonic scale (Figure 4.1). Next the winds enter ascending up by step from F-flat to A-flat. The next two measures provide a slightly embellished restatement of these first two measures until the winds ascend to the unexpected chromatic tone of A natural, an important move for being a musical misstep as the melody overshoots the dominant effectively linking the nondiegetic music to an important motif of missteps in the film.[18] Webb extends the motif of relentless ascent over the next eight measures of

Figure 4.1 Roy Webb, "Main Title" from *The Seventh Victim*, melody m. 3–8

the "Main Title." Webb associates this connotative detail only when the film's characters demonstrate fruitless striving for happiness.

Webb establishes the connection between striving and ascending musical material in his cue "Principal's Office." The imposing headmistress of the boarding school, Mrs. Lowood (Ottola Nesmith), provides Mary the option to return to the school in the event she fails to find her sister. Throughout, her assistant, Gilchrist (Eve March) looks on avidly. As Mary leaves, Gilchrist shows her out. On reaching the hallway, Gilchrist warns Mary never to come back. The short, vaguely ominous scene ends abruptly with a sharp shout from the headmistress summoning Gilchrist, who wordlessly complies with this command.

Webb's brief cue paints the text in minute detail. As Mrs. Lowood explains that she will pay for Mary to go to New York to find her sister, the violins slowly ascend from their lowest string to the B a tenth above. When Gilchrist escorts Mary to the door, the violins ascend quickly from c" to the D-flat a minor ninth above. This lavish ascending figure accompanies the beginning of Mary's journey toward a new life. Coinciding with Gilchrist's first line, "don't come back," the violins plunge down an octave and commence a downward chromatic sequence. Gilchrist is one of the film's many tragic minor figures like the petitioners at the Bureau of Missing Persons. Yet, unlike them, her striving has ended.

The madrigalistic ascents appear throughout the film, but one last illustration of narratively motivated ascents must suffice. Webb's cue "Love Scene" serves as an elision between the scene where Dr. Judd and Jason Hoag confront the Palladists and Mary and Gregory's discussion of their mutual feelings. Webb enfolds this important moment into the theme of fruitless striving through a madrigalistic ascent of both melodic and accompanimental material in his underscore as Dr. Judd "proves" these Satanists wrong with an awkward recitation of the Lord's Prayer, awkward for coming from an amoral seducer. Webb provides a lavish portion of heavenly clichés in the major mode, including ascending arpeggios in the harp and a prim plagal cadence from D major to A major. The remainder of the cue underscores a cut to Mary and Ward quietly admitting their love for one another. Mary is in danger of sharing her sister's fate of marrying a dullard. This grim potentiality was foreshadowed in a telling moment when the freshly discovered Jacqueline recoils at the sight of her bland husband. Insofar as Jacqueline's marriage to Ward appears as one of her many failed attempts to discover happiness, Webb's cue ends on a series of ascending chords with harp arpeggiation reinforcing the ascending madrigalism just as it had during the Lord's Prayer and with comparable irony.

By placing his madrigalism of futility behind scenes of half-embarrassed religiosity and tame expressions of erotic sentiment from an inexperienced youth and a dangerously dull husband, Webb reveals the sophistication of

Figure 4.2 Roy Webb, "Love Theme" from *The Seventh Victim*

his madrigalistic approach. Rather than ascending on each prompt in the dialogue, Webb calibrates the tone of his ascents to serve as the sort of commentary prized by the performer-consumers of sixteenth-century madrigals. Here Webb undermines the value of the cynical Dr. Judd's prayer and Ward's bland verbalization of love through the ironic tone of his heavenly music and by having firmly established melodic ascents as signifiers of fruitless striving. Indeed, Gregory's acknowledgment of his love for Mary finds a deceptive cadence from F major to d minor in Webb's underscore at measure 10 of his cue "Love Theme" (Figure 4.2).

Fruitless Striving in the Diegetic Music

While Roy Webb's score presents musical ascents to paint striving for happiness in the film's underscore, the RKO Music Department chose source music to reinforce this connection. Whether Webb selected the pieces in question or someone else (and here pianist Norm Bennett offers a solid candidacy for being the pianist who played them on the set), there is no mistaking the intent of connecting source music in the film to Webb's madrigalism for striving.

As Jason Hoag tries to help Mary find Jacqueline, he takes her to find Dr. Judd, certain that Judd knows where Jacqueline is hiding. Hoag finds Judd at a party in the home of Natalie Cortez. From her piano, we hear Johannes Brahms's Waltz in A-flat Major, Op. 39, No. 15, followed by the first movement of Beethoven's Piano Sonata No. 14 in C# minor, "Moonlight."[19] These two chestnuts have in common a strong primacy of ascending material. In the Brahms, both the melody and accompaniment emphasize upward motion. In his Sonata, Beethoven deploys exclusively ascending arpeggiated accompaniment. One would be sore pressed to find two more ascent-centric excerpts from the piano's standard literature. The scene unfolds at a party where several of the Palladists and a good many people from Jacqueline's circle of pleasure seekers enjoy cocktails as Dr. Judd performs a card trick. Source music rich with the film's madrigalism for fruitless striving serves a scene of empty pleasure well.

Later in the film, another pianistic ascent clarifies the film's thematic use of source music. As Jacqueline makes her way from the clutches of the Palladists to her noose waiting in room no. 7 above the Italian restaurant, a member of the Palladists (Wally Brown) pursues her. No longer able to hear his gumshoes in an alley, Jacqueline backs to a wall and feels her way through the alley, much too frightened to look. Her fingers reach the fabric of a man's coat. The Palladist grabs Jacqueline's arm and pulls out a knife. Just as his switchblade clicks open, a gesture meant to frighten Jacqueline rather than kill her as the Palladists are pledged to non-violence, the soundtrack fills with sudden laughter. The dancers from the Ivy Lane Theater pour out of the theater's backstage and into the alley. The Palladist hides his face and retreats. Jacqueline runs into the arms of a large man in Roman attire who the screenplay tells us is a dancer dressed as Gambrinus (Adia Kuznetzoff), the Roman god of mirth and fecundity. "There's a man following me," she explains. "I shouldn't wonder, babe, I shouldn't wonder" he replies without missing a beat. Part of the swirling show of distractions, the world of fruitless striving for happiness, the dancer's concerns are instinctive. "Please help me," Jacqueline persists. "I'll help you to a beer and a sandwich. Come along, babe," he concludes.

The dancer leads Jacqueline to Cleary's, a low and raucous pub. Inside we hear frantic piano music hammering out a bumptious ragtime devoid of the striding dignity usually associated with that genre. As the first chorus ends, we hear a transition in which the pianist plays an ascending scale that runs almost the entire length of the keyboard. This wildly unusual flourish fits the moment brilliantly. If ascending material signifies the futile struggle for meaning, then Cleary's pub and the arms of Gambrinus represent an oasis where a manic and desperate quest for distraction from suffering prevails.

Musical Repetition and the Death Impulse

A closely related madrigalism appears throughout Webb's score to represent repetition compulsion. J. P. Telotte's psychoanalytic reading of the film sees repetition as one of two options the world of the film provides its characters.[20]

He sees this theme even in the film's title, for where we find a seventh, six more came before.[21] Rote lessons fill the sound world of Mary's childhood home at the boarding school and persist to the film's final encounter between Mimi (Elizabeth Russell), the consumptive woman who rents the room at The Dante adjacent to Jacqueline's, and Jacqueline. Mimi insists that she is tired of waiting for her illness to claim her life. She wants to "go out and laugh and dance and do all the things I used to do." As Mimi heads out to repeat her past, the film's final shot, Webb presents a repetitious travesty of a waltz in which the melody is exclusively comprised of six repetitions of a three-note descending figure outlining a tritone – A-G-E-flat (a 0-4-6 whole-tone collection) and accompanied exclusively by repeated chords on beats two and three using the same three pitches heard in the melody.

Cellular musical repetitions fill the score during passages of the film illustrative of the thematic weight of repetitious behavior within it. The cue Webb composed supporting Jacqueline's story about her captivity at La Sagesse, simply called "Jacqueline," features nothing but four tiny repetitious cells. Orchestrator Maurice De Packh felt sufficiently confused by this cue as to spare the studio's copyist confusion by writing, "That is all!" at the end of his score.[22] Clearly De Packh felt that a piece of music should do more than whir away with tiny repetitions. But these little repetitious cells appear frequently in Webb's score always in conjunction with scenes of repetitious behavior.

This madrigalism also finds its way into the film's source music. During the meeting of the Palladists at which the cultists try to convince Jacqueline that her life really has no meaning and she should commit suicide, Natalie Cortez sits at her piano and lazily plays parallel augmented triads over and over while waiting for Jacqueline to sip poisoned wine. Natalie's performance lends the proceedings an aura of the uncanny for using this classic harmonic signifier, but also reinforces the film's concern with unconscious repetitive behavior as key to understanding the film's application of Freud's Death Impulse.

Madrigalistic Musique Concrète

After its opening shot of stained glass, the film cuts to a marvelous tracking shot of Mary ascending her boarding school's massive staircase as a collage of sounds emerge around her. Here the work of the film's sound designer, John C. Grubb, takes center stage. The collage begins with the sound of a classroom of girls conjugating the Latin verb "amare" (to love). This is overlapped by a voice lesson in which the student sings scales while moving up by a half-step after each one, and another student reciting the nine times table.

After her meeting with the headmistress and the doleful Gilchrist, Mary's journey down the stairs marks the start of her search for Jacqueline and receives a similar sound collage featuring a class conjugating the French verb "recherche" (to search), a different student singing the vocal exercise heard earlier, a teacher's voice correcting an inaccurate recitation of the American presidents in chronological order, Mary's own voice reciting the final verse of Oliver Wendall Holmes's poem "The Chambered Nautilus" with its exhortation to "leave thy low-vaulted past,"[23] and finally two strokes from a grandfather clock seen at the bottom of the stairs.

Each of these elements within the collage serves the film's subtexts. The sung scales each a half-step higher than the last links the collage to the madrigalism of fruitless striving in Webb's score and simultaneously to the theme of repetition. Mary's journey striving toward her place within the world of adults is underway. The verb "to search" underscores the rationale for her journey, while the verb "to love" provides a foretoken of her major discovery on that journey. The times table offers an endless sequence with no logical conclusion, much like the singer's journey up the chromatic scale. The botched recitation of presidents foretoken Mary's many missteps to come including her unwise attachment to Jacqueline's husband. "The Chambered Nautilus," indeed the entire pair of sound collages, contribute to Telotte's conclusion, "leaving this sheltered world, a world of comforting repetitions, Mary must search for both her sister and herself."[24]

The soundtrack in this sequence cannot possibly be providing the audience with Mary's actual aural experiences as Mary hears her own voice reciting "The Chambered Nautilus." This sound collage points toward another "fantastical gap," to cite Robynn Stilwell again.[25] These sounds of unseen source serve to foreshadow future events. But as they unfold, the audience has no awareness of that function. In the moment, these unsourced sounds open up the film as a catalyst for individual audience reactions in the manner Stilwell theorized by opening gates backward to the pleasures and petty humiliations inherent to gaining an education, and forward to the inevitable end. The greatness of *The Seventh Victim* may well be revealed in this moment of uncertainty for an audience treated to a horror film that quietly asks if there is a rational basis for human happiness.

A Musical Figure Marked "Death"

Webb conveniently labeled his third madrigalism in the score "death" on most appearances,[26] but here the connection of text to tones is more abstract than ascending musical material conveying striving or ostinati indicating repetition. For "death," Webb repeats a chord in iambic rhythm. Before appearing in Webb's score, we can hear these death chords foreshadowed again in Grubb's collage on the staircase, for the two strokes of the grandfather clock inevitably form an iambic rhythm for the second stroke of the chime lingering far longer than the interrupted first stroke.

Webb presents his death chords first at the opening of the cue "Room No. 7" when Mr. Romari (Chef Milani) assists Mary's search by opening the door to the room Jacqueline rented but never occupied. Neither of the pair of repeated chords heard as this cue begins are tertian. The first iamb features A-flat-C-D (another 0-4-6 whole-tone collection connecting this chord to Mimi's waltz discussed above) while the second moves up to C-D-F. Mr. Romari has not yet opened the door, merely reached its exterior. The subsequent dialogue, some in Italian, concerns Mr. Romari's curiosity to see inside the door and by doing so learn something about Jacqueline. Webb underscores this dialogue with urgent chromatic ascent in both the melody and interior contrapuntal lines. When the door opens, the camera pans up from a chair to a noose. The pan is accompanied by a rapidly ascending scalar figure doubled at the second and the fourth (all 0-4-6 whole-tone sets), just like the opening iambic chords. When the camera reaches Jacqueline's noose, Webb restates his iambic chords now made up only of D and G supporting a dissonant simultaneity in the high strings.

Webb's cue "Symbol of the Palladists" commences just as Jason Hoag shows Mary a parallelogram with a split triangle within it; a symbol Jason has learned represents the secret cult. Webb repeats the opening of his cue "Room No. 7" with its iambic presentation of identical dissonances precisely as the screen fills with the symbol of the Palladists, and again when Jason utters the name, "Palladists" during the subsequent dialogue. Here Webb connects the cult with death, fitting as they are striving to convince Jacqueline, their seventh victim, to end her own life.

In the next scene, we find the Palladists discussing their options. Jacqueline must die, but they are powerless to kill her for being pledged to non-violence. Webb places iambic chords under every mention of their deadly intentions in his cue "The Palladists." The same happens in the cue "Jacqueline Is Found" which opens with Webb's death motif as Jason informs Dr. Judd that Jacqueline is a murderer. This cue also finds the iambic chords on every reference to death.

The last and most ominous articulation of Webb's death motif comes at the very beginning of Webb's "End Title" cue. As Mimi, the woman with consumption, heads down the stairs to "have fun" in the repetitious way she always used to, the soundtrack reveals Jacqueline's suicide with the sound of the chair falling from beneath the noose in room no. 7.[27] Webb presents a simultaneity of C-D-E-flat-A in iambic rhythm immediately afterward.[28]

The ending of the film is daring in the extreme. The Production Code forbade suicide as a mechanism for bringing closure to a film's plot. Moreover, the suicide itself could not be shown for fear of the Code requiring rewrites, but also because Hollywood films of the 1940s would never trade in such graphic imagery.[29]

The ending of *The Seventh Victim* could easily have been used by Michel Chion as an exemplar of one of the six rhetorical effects of sound that he hears in film as "emotively effective."[30] The type in this case is "the acousmatization of the unshowable" wherein the filmmakers cut away from a character who is about "to be killed or commit suicide."[31] The film's "emotively effective" solution to portraying Jacqueline's suicide allows the audience to hear the chair clatter as Mimi walks past Jacqueline's closed door. The examples cited by Chion concern the readily comprehensible sound of a gunshot to indicate a character's offscreen death. The clatter of a chair proves riskier as critics and audiences have found the ending of the film confusing, a situation anathema to classical Hollywood cinematic style, which strives to "narrate causal information as clearly as possible."[32]

Critics at the time confirm the confusion caused by the film's ending. *The Film Daily* review concludes, "The plot has been developed in a confusing manner. The end in particular will leave audiences in a bit of a quandary."[33] Bosley Crowther at *The New York Times* wondered if the film had been screened "upside down and backwards."[34] All of the exhibitors who opined in *The Motion Picture Herald*'s "What the Picture Did for Me" section described negative audience reactions, with one offering that "This is the worst one of this series. It didn't quite make sense . . . It has a terrible ending. Pass it up."[35]

Webb's score intervenes to clarify the scene with its rehearsal of the "death" chords sounded so frequently to paint the text throughout the film. Here Roy Webb's methods prove more cinematically conservative than the rest of the Lewton unit for striving to clarify the narrative. This situation should not be surprising. Val Lewton prided himself on risky behavior in his work, and Mark Robson, the film's director, found himself in that complex role for the first time. Roy Webb was the veteran for having worked on sound films for RKO through his entire professional life. He even worked to clarify the intended meaning of his music in this case by labeling the chords heard after the chair falls "death" for the benefit of his orchestrator and likely no one else. Here we get a glimpse, perhaps, of Webb himself fiercely striving to contribute clarification for "the unshowable" moment in a film he feared had strayed from the ideals of classical Hollywood filmmaking.

Not all madrigalisms in scores receive clarifying labels from their composers, but the film's death motif reveals itself clearly and insistently throughout Webb's score. Less clear than the death chord is the ascending signifier for fruitless striving, but even it can be heard so consistently that, once pointed out, it cannot escape notice. Similarly, Webb fusing his "death" chord into Mimi's waltz by using the same whole-tone pitch set suggests method to the score's painting of the text.

While the film's conclusion with its juxtaposition of Mimi departing to repeat the activities of happier times against Jacqueline's suicide does not constitute a sound collage of comparable density to the one heard earlier on the staircase, it does offer an appropriate bookend for existing at least in part outside the diegesis of the film. To be sure, Webb's clarifying score is nondiegetic. The chair is diegetic although potentially difficult to parse in the moment. Then come the film's last words. They are spoken by the now deceased Jacqueline, who speaks to the audience from a "fantastical gap," that uncanny space first theorized by Robynn Stilwell. Lending a character who just died offscreen a voiceover adds to the potential confusion of her "unshowable" death. Her words are the film's first – "I runne to death and death meets me as fast, and all my pleasures are like yesterday."

Notes

1. Joel Siegel, *Val Lewton: The Reality of Terror* (New York: Viking Press, 1973), p. 52.
2. Ibid., pp. 48–49.
3. "Val Lewton File" from "Michael Ravnitzky Papers," National Security Archive at George Washington University.
4. Siegel, pp. 50–51.
5. Production materials mention a version running ninety-one minutes, sixteen seconds being both printed and screened. RKO Radio Pictures Studio Records (Collection PASC 3). UCLA Library Special Collections, Charles E. Young Research Library, University of California, Los Angeles. Edmund Bansak confirms the existence of a longer version at one time citing both DeWitt Bodeen and Val Lewton, Jr. See Edmund Bansak, *Fearing the Dark: The Val Lewton Career* (Jefferson, NC: MacFarland & Company, 1995) p. 185.
6. John Lockert's work as editor never enjoys praise in the literature on Lewton. It should. He edited three of Lewton's films including this one, *Youth Runs Wild*, and *The Ghost Ship*, which would be his last editing job. Lockert died in 1944 at the age of forty-six.
7. Dr. Judd died at the end of *Cat People*. His appearance here either means that this is a prequel, or the Lewton unit was parodying the absurdity of Universal horror films in which dead characters return willy-nilly.
8. Charles O'Neal and DeWitt Bodeen, shooting script for *The Seventh Victim*, RKO Radio Pictures Studio Records (Collection PASC 3). UCLA Library Special Collections, Charles E. Young Research Library, University of California, Los Angeles.
9. Koerner reined in costs on the studio's "B" series. *The Falcon's Brother* (1942), the first Falcon film made under Koerner, credits Roy Webb as composer although the film recycles materials composed for the series' earlier installments by Paul Sawtell. The second film under Koerner, *The Falcon and the Co-eds* (1943), does not credit a composer, despite all of the underscore having been recycled from both Sawtell's and Webb's earlier cues for the series. I owe a debt to Catherine Haworth who pointed this out in her 2018 presentation at Music and the Moving Image.
10. *Stranger on the Third Floor* figures into many discussions of film noir. In many ways the film is too early to participate fully in the style. For one thing, it presents an unequivocally happy ending. But the atmosphere of paranoia and persecution within both the film's narrative and style leads to its inclusion as an important forbearer if not an actual example.

11. One other cost-cutting measure in the film's music is the reuse of the hand organ quote of *Martha*, now heard without its explanatory power.
12. Webb did recycle most of the "Main Title" cue from *Cat People* in *The Curse of the Cat People*. The ending of the cue had to be changed, however, due to the differences in each film's opening. The result is a slightly modified version of the earlier cue.
13. The quote is actually the third and fourth line from John Donne's *Holy Sonnet I*. This error must have chagrined the poetry-loving Lewton.
14. Sigmund Freud, *Beyond the Pleasure Principle (The Standard Edition)*, James Strachey, translator (New York: Liveright Publishing Corporation, 1961), p. 40.
15. Roy Webb, autograph short score for *The Seventh Victim*, RKO Radio Pictures Studio Records (Collection PASC 3). UCLA Library Special Collections, Charles E. Young Research Library, University of California, Los Angeles.
16. The lesbian subtext in the film shines through rather clearly. The most exhaustive discussion of it can be found in Harry Benshoff, *Monsters in the Closet: Homosexuality and the Horror Film* (Manchester: University of Manchester Press, 1997), pp. 102–104.
17. The restaurant is named "The Dante," a fitting choice for the poet being associated in the popular imagination almost entirely with the consequences of death.
18. We see Mary first traveling in the opposite direction of her classmates. She has to be redirected first by Mrs. Lowood, then by the hairdresser, and again and again throughout the film.
19. According to RKO Recording Logs, Norman Bennet is the pianist. He was the long-time house pianist at RKO. He recorded this standard repertory in a single take. RKO Radio Pictures Studio Records (Collection PASC 3). UCLA Library Special Collections, Charles E. Young Research Library, University of California, Los Angeles.
20. J. P. Telotte, *Dreams of Darkness: Fantasy and the Films of Val Lewton* (Urbana: University of Illinois Press, 1985), p. 82.
21. Ibid., p. 78.
22. Maurice De Packh, orchestral score for "Jacqueline" from *The Seventh Victim*, RKO Radio Pictures Studio Records (Collection PASC 3). UCLA Library Special Collections, Charles E. Young Research Library, University of California, Los Angeles.
23. Here is the full text recited in the film: "Build thee more stately mansions, O my soul, / As the swift seasons roll! / Leave they low-vaulted past! / Let each new temple, nobler than the last / Shut thee from heaven with a dome more vast, / Till thou at length are free, / Leaving thine outgrown shell by life›s unresting sea."
24. Telotte, p. 82.
25. Robynn Stilwell, "The Fantastical Gap between Diegetic and Nondiegetic," in *Beyond the Soundtrack: Representing Music in Cinema*, eds. Daniel Goldmark, Lawrence Kramer, and Richard Leppert (Berkeley: University of California Press, 2007), pp. 184–202.
26. Roy Webb, autograph short score for *The Seventh Victim*, RKO Radio Pictures Studio Records (Collection PASC 3). UCLA Library Special Collections, Charles E. Young Research Library, University of California, Los Angeles.

27. The moment is as clear-cut a violation of the Production Code as can be found, for suicide could never be a tool of plot resolution. By playing it entirely on the soundtrack, the filmmakers sneaked their violation past Joseph Breen's office undetected.
28. Leonid Raab orchestrated this scene. He labeled this chord "death" in his score. Clearly the Music Department staff found this detail important.
29. Interestingly *The Seventh Victim* is the third Lewton horror film to violate the injunction against suicide as a mechanism for plot resolution. Irena commits suicide "by panther" in *Cat People* and Wesley Rand intentionally walks into the ocean to drown in *I Walked with a Zombie*.
30. Michel Chion, *Film, A Sound Art*, Claudia Gorbman, translator (New York: Columbia University Press, 2009) pp. 208–212.
31. Ibid., p. 209.
32. David Bordwell, Janet Staiger, and Kristin Thompson, *The Classical Hollywood Cinema: Film Style and Mode of Production to 1960* (New York: Columbia University Press, 1985), p. 265.
33. "The Seventh Victim," *The Film Daily* (January 15, 1943).
34. Bosley Crowther, "Who's Looney Again?" *The New York Times* (September 18, 1943).
35. "What the Picture Did for Me," *The Motion Picture Herald* (September 21, 1943).

5 A WARTIME FABLE IN THE SOUNDS OF *THE GHOST SHIP*

A Wartime Fable

As *The Ghost Ship* entered production in August 1943, Americans – including the Lewton unit – were fixated on the world war unfolding around them. The daily headlines drew attention to the Allies' hard-won, incremental progress in Sicily, the Solomon Islands, and along the Russian front. The all-engrossing war effort of the summer of 1943 led to the production of the Lewton unit's film most clearly informed by the war.

The action of *The Ghost Ship* takes place aboard the merchant ship *Altair* as it delivers sheep to San Sebastian, the fictional Caribbean island where *I Walked with a Zombie* took place.[1] Although the film never mentions the war, oblique wartime references can be found within it. For example, when the Bosun (Dewey Robinson) calls the roll before the *Altair* leaves port, the First Officer (Ben Bard) comments on one sailor, "He's a Finn, keep an eye on that man, I don't want any trouble aboard ship." The lone sailor so singled out is a mute known to the crew only as "The Finn" (Skelton Knaggs). The line tumbles past without receiving any notice in the literature on the film, but it refers directly to the war. Finland was allied with Germany during the war, hence the First Officer's concern over potential trouble. While at port in San Sebastian, another minor war reference finds its way into the film when German sailors in the apparently neutral port physically accost the *Altair*'s Trinidadian crew member, Billy Radd (Sir Lancelot).

These references to the war establish *The Ghost Ship*'s wartime context. The film's narrative also speaks to another wartime preoccupation. The film's central plot deals with authoritarianism and most importantly to the moral indifference of the masses to authoritarianism's abuse of the individual. Insofar as America's enemies were fascist dictatorships in Europe and Japan, a film dealing with an authoritarian ship captain's descent into madness and violence inevitably resonated with the times.

Stories of power-mad sea captains abound prior to *The Ghost Ship*, so Lewton may not have needed a global war against fascism for inspiration. J. P. Telotte sees the film's inspiration in Jack London's *The Sea Wolf* and Joseph Conrad's *The Secret Sharer*, the former for providing a similar dynamic between a young man on his first voyage and a disciplinarian captain.[2] Edmund Bansak points out similarities with *Journey into Fear* (1943), the film Mark Robson edited immediately prior to directing *The Seventh Victim*.[3] Harry Benshoff cites Conrad's *Secret Sharer* for its homoerotic content as a forerunner along with Herman Melville's *Billy Budd*.[4]

Whatever the sources, much in *The Ghost Ship* feels conventional, even borrowed.[5] Like *The Seventh Victim*, the film offers an initiation story. But where the earlier film provides a complex narrative almost defying coherent summary, *The Ghost Ship* tells its tale with linear precision.

The film begins with Tom Merriam (Russell Wade), a young Third Officer heading toward his first voyage, giving a blind street musician (Alec Craig) a coin for luck. The blind man warns Tom that the *Altair* is a bad ship. Tom passes The Finn, who reveals in voiceover that he is mute and will be watchful on this deadly voyage.

On board the *Altair*, we meet the crew during a roll call that culminates in the discovery that one crew member is dead on the deck. Soon after, Tom meets Captain Stone (Richard Dix), who specially selected Merriam for his Third Officer for both men having comparable backgrounds as orphans. At sea, Stone reveals a fondness for Tom as he shares his philosophy that authority provides great satisfaction to its wielder. Stone goes so far as to suggest that a captain's authority grants him the power of life and death over his crew. Tom finds the captain's remarks valuable, but mostly he enjoys the attention of a father figure.

As the seas swell, Tom wants to secure a huge hook that Captain Stone recently ordered repainted. "A line will mar the paint," the captain explains by way of denying Tom's request for permission to stopper it. During the night, the hook begins to swing dangerously, so sailors must risk their lives securing it.

Then, a Greek sailor named Peter (Eddie Borden) falls ill with appendicitis requiring an emergency surgery aboard the ship. The captain is poised to perform the procedure with a doctor radioing instructions from Panama. Captain Stone balks, so Tom performs the surgery.

Now short two crew members, a sailor named Louie (Lawrence Tierney) confronts the captain, pointing out that according to regulations, the ship should put in to port to replenish its crew. Later, Captain Stone traps Louie in the ship's chain locker, crushing him to death. Tom finds the body and realizes that Captain Stone murdered Louie.

In port at San Sebastian, Tom denounces Captain Stone to the shipping line. At an informal hearing, none of the crew supports Tom's accusation. A misinformed Peter believes that Captain Stone saved his life. Sparks (Edmond Glover), the ship's radio operator, knows the truth but says nothing. The incident with the swinging hook comes up, but no one knows that Captain Stone gave Tom the order not to secure it.

Defeated, Tom quits his job. He receives a ride from a woman named Ellen Roberts (Edith Barrett), who has a romantic attachment to Captain Stone. She points out to Tom how like the captain he is, lonely and austere. She arranges for Tom to meet her sister back in San Pedro.

Ellen reveals to Stone that she is now divorced, and the two of them are free to marry. Stone declines, indicating that he no longer trusts his mental stability.

While still in port, German sailors assault Billy Radd when he refuses to sing for them. Tom intervenes on his behalf and is knocked unconscious. Billy, unaware of Tom's resignation, brings Tom aboard the *Altair*.

Tom awakens to find himself on the *Altair* as it sails for San Pedro. Captain Stone allows Tom to try and turn the crew against Stone's authority. Stone articulates a bald case for the efficiency of authoritarianism, as the film reaches its thematic climax. Stone's rant concludes with his assessment of the crew: "You'll find them too lazy, too cowardly, too disinterested, Merriam. That's what I want you to learn. Men are worthless cattle, and a few men are given authority to drive them." Tom counters, "I know people aren't that way. They're usually good and kind, willing to help each other. It's only hard to get them to understand."

Tom has no success convincing the crew. Next, he searches for a simple means of personal protection by trying to steal a knife, a sharp seaman's tool, and finally a gun, but in each case Stone thwarts him. The Finn observes the unfolding drama from the shadowy margins, providing voiceover commentary for the audience.

Finally, Tom wins an ally in Sparks, who receives a cable from Ellen asking if Tom is aboard the *Altair*. Captain Stone has Sparks send the reply that Tom is not aboard. Sparks consults with Tom, promising to take the incriminating evidence to the other officers. Leaving Tom's cabin, Captain Stone murders Sparks, then asks Tom to send the wireless communication that Sparks has fallen overboard. Tom and the captain struggle, but the crew overwhelms Tom. They bind Tom and leave him on his bunk. Captain Stone administers a sedative to the terrified former officer.

The Finn finds the captain's misleading message about Tom and brings it to the officers. After hearing the other officers seriously considering Tom's accusations, Captain Stone enters Tom's cabin with a large knife and murderous intentions. The Finn intervenes and fights Stone, killing him. The film ends with Tom piloting the *Altair*. The Finn stands at his side, promising in voiceover that Tom is safe "and his belief in men, and men's essential goodness is secure."[6] Back at port, Tom gives a coin to the same street singer before meeting Ellen's sister (Shirley O'Hara), portrayed only in silhouette.

Several tropes common in initiation tales define the contours of *The Ghost Ship*'s story. Lewton and his team did not invent the narrative of a clash between a flawed older mentor and a younger disciple who risks becoming like that mentor unless some inner reserve can be tapped. The details distinguish this wartime retelling by emphasizing the crew. The philosophical clash of Stone and Merriam boils down to two visions of the crew, one pessimistic to the point of radical cynicism, the other optimistic. The film seems to end happily enough. Yet a parsing out of The Finn's final voiceover reveals that Tom's optimistic view of the crew is not neatly endorsed. The Finn provides an almost mystical personage with prescient knowledge and is certainly not a figure easily universalized. Sparks had to have the evidentiary equivalent of a smoking gun before trying to do anything. The rest of the crew can be summed up in their final line. While holding Stone's incriminating message in his hands, the Chief Engineer (Herbert Vigran) says, "Well, now, I don't know."

As a World War Two artifact, the film's concern with the clash of fascistic pessimism and democratic optimism does not reinforce a "happy mood" of the sort the War Department wanted from Hollywood. Alexander Nemerov explains the film's many bad reviews this way: "It satisfied neither as patriotic lore nor as engrossing distraction."[7]

THE SOUNDTRACK'S DIVIDED LOYALTIES

To organize the discussion of the soundtrack to follow, I would like to draw attention to the four types of characters within the film and suggest that their position in the narrative is closely linked to one aspect of the film's soundtrack. Captain Stone constitutes one type entirely on his own. He is the film's authoritarian villain. He holds his fellow men in contempt and articulates the philosophical basis for dictatorship. His perspective finds support in the soundtrack's sound effects.

As the protagonist, Tom Merriam singularly occupies the polar type from Stone. While equally isolated, he holds an optimistic view of his fellow men. Tom calls out injustice with courage and suffers for his silences. The film's dialogue favors his perspective.

The crew collectively represents the body of men about whom Captain Stone and Tom argue. The diegetic music speaks to the crew's position within the film. With the exception of the street singer who bookends the narrative and some accordion music heard in San Sebastian, the film's diegetic music is both made by and illustrative of the crew's posture within the fable.

The Finn, while part of the crew, exists apart from them. His opening voiceover speaks to his isolation. "This is another man I can never know," he begins on meeting Tom. In his first appearance, he reads as an ominous character with the stark lighting of his pockmarked face and billowing steam behind him. Over the course of the film, he serves as something of a Greek chorus, orienting the audience through a mixture of observation and prophecy. But at the film's close, he emerges as the film's unlikely "pursuer," to use Andrew Tudor's terminology.[8] He embodies Tom's optimism about humanity and rewards Tom's hopeful outlook by engaging Captain Stone in the film's ferocious climactic knife fight. Oddly, Roy Webb's underscore favors this minor character to a surprising degree.

With the mise-en-bande divided in its degree of support for each character or group of characters, the film's soundtrack reveals itself as one of the more innovative of an already innovative era in film.

Captain Stone's Symphony of Sound Effects

Because Lewton's approach to horror emphasizes suggestion over depiction, sound performs a crucial role in his films. Francis Sarver provided the sound design for *The Ghost Ship*.[9] While his responsibilities were many and diverse, his production of sound effects proved crucial. They center on the shipboard sonic world of the *Altair* where wind and waves unite with the mechanisms of the ship to transport the audience to the largely unfamiliar world of a merchant ship at sea. The ship's various bells and horns can be seen performed by the crew throughout the film, always energized through Stone's orders. If the crew members are the ship's orchestral performers, Captain Stone is its exacting conductor.

The film's most spectacular sequences all depend on sound effects to achieve their impact. One in particular, Stone's murder of Louie in the chain locker, finds Stone benefitting from the ship's symphony of sounds. Noise conceals his crime, as members of the crew beat on the huge chain links with hammers creating a music of rhythmic, high-pitched clangs. Once Louie enters the locker, the clanking changes tone with a darker timbre as the huge links come to rest first upon the locker's metal floor and then upon one another. The pace quickens as the momentum of the chain increases. Unbeknownst to Louie, Stone casually shuts and locks the hatch to the locker, trapping Louie within. Realizing his peril, Louie cries out for help, but by that point Sarver saturates the soundtrack with the noise of the huge chain. Louie's cries are rendered inaudible.

Similar scenes of Stone's crimes privilege sound effects. The huge hook Captain Stone insisted not be secured swings and clangs against the railings, walls, and lifeboats, awakening Tom to a terrifying symphony caused by Stone's pathological willingness to place his crew in deadly danger and later to deflect blame from himself to his subordinate.

The failure of Captain Stone in the operation scene includes radioed instructions from the doctor in Panama. We see the scalpel held in Stone's quivering hand poised to make the first incision as the matter-of-fact voice mechanically articulates the frightening instruction to make an incision of a prescribed depth and length. No cut is made, and yet the voiceover moves on with its next instruction. The sound of the patient's muffled breathing features prominently in the soundtrack. The defamiliarized and somatic sound of heavy breathing couples with the disembodied voice on the wireless describing things the audience does not wish to see. Together, these sound effects provide a melancholy "music" for a tense scene.

When Tom finds himself a prisoner on Stone's ship, we hear the clatter of his porthole covering and the rattle of his door after the locking mechanisms have been removed undoubtedly due to Captain Stone's orders. These rattles and clatters form an unnerving accompaniment for Tom's mounting panic and merge with one of Roy Webb's sparse nondiegetic cues.

Even the ubiquitous sound of wind and waves serves Captain Stone's mania. By covering over the sound of his murdering Sparks, the sound effects associated with the sea become part of Stone's symphony. Stone's dialogue clarifies that his authority only manifests at sea. "In San Pedro, I was just another captain. At sea, I am *the* captain."

These scenes of horror in *The Ghost Ship*'s soundtrack resemble a moment in *Dr. Jekyll and Mr. Hyde* (1931) analyzed by Neil Lerner. Lerner hears the first transformation scene in that film with musical ears, noting that director Rouben Mamoulian produced a "sound stew" with ingredients including a recording of Mamoulian's own heartbeat, the decay of a gong stroke (the attack having been edited out) played back in reverse, and the sound of a flickering candle.[10] Citing Irwin Bazelon, Lerner refers to this sound collage as an example of "pre-*musique concrète*."[11]

The key difference between the "sonic stews" in *Dr. Jekyll and Mr. Hyde* and *The Ghost Ship* concerns the invisible sound source in the earlier film. While not nearly so advanced or uncanny as the earlier sound collages in *Cat People* during Irena's dream, or Mary's journey up and down the staircase at Highcliff Academy in *The Seventh Victim*, the sound collages onboard the *Altair* merit notice for their thematic potentials. All the prominent sound effects embody Captain Stone's conception of authority and the dangers that authority poses to all those around him.

The sound effects in the film associated with the *Altair* serve Captain Stone well. They confirm that the crew executes his orders while burying his crimes in sound. As Captain Stone is a wartime villain, his authoritarian self-conception as arbiter of life and death over his crew not only resembles the wartime situation for more than a million Americans in uniform, but it also gestures toward the dictatorships those men and women were fighting against. The mundane aspect of Stone's reign of terror is essential to its symbolic potential. He is not some singular, supernatural threat, but the recognizably human impulse to abuse power. His sonic world, therefore, is the dehumanized network of shipboard noises he commands.

Hollywood Dialogue and Liberal Democracy

In contrast with Captain Stone, Tom Merriam depends on dialogue to make his case. His first encounter with Sparks is illustrative. Tom takes exception to Sparks's sprinkling a little Latin into his banter. Tom prefers clear communication of easily understood ideas and values. He tells Sparks, "It's a relief to find someone on board I can talk to. All I've been doing this morning is saying 'yes, sir.'" He refers to Captain Stone's lecture on the importance of authority. Yet when Sparks casts doubt on the value of Stone's words, Tom defends the captain. "I like the way he talks – the things he has to say." Tom's credulity manifests in his assumption that words matter, and that the speaker always means well.

When Tom realizes that Captain Stone is a killer, he depends on words to save himself and the crew. He uses them to denounce the captain's incompetence to the First Officer. He takes his case next to Sparks who advises him not to speak out against the captain. Then he tries to convince the crew to help him when his life is clearly imperiled. Sparks speaks for the group when he tells Tom, "I'm dead serious when I tell you I don't want to hear a word you have to say."

Tom makes himself vulnerable to attack when he does not speak. He never mentions that leaving the hook unsecured was Captain Stone's order. He also remains silent about his having performed the operation on the Greek sailor. Both of these silences work against Tom in the informal hearing in San Sebastian, as Captain Stone appears a hero and Tom a villain when the opposite is true.

Later, as Stone points a revolver at Tom's abdomen, Tom calls the captain "crazy," prompting this speech delivered with relish by Richard Dix as Captain Stone: "I never felt more sane in my life than I feel at this moment. Who is crazy – you who defied me and are helpless and discredited, or I who control my destiny and the destiny of the *Altair* and all the lives on board?"[12] Tom replies that he only wishes the crew could hear the way the captain talks. Captain Stone indicts himself in his dialogue, while Tom speaks the language of liberal democracy, which also happens to be the mother tongue of the Classic Hollywood Style.

The first two decades of sound film production in Hollywood witnessed the rise of dialogue as the crucial material conveyed in the soundtrack. As a technology, studio-era Hollywood dialogue defaults toward the network of ideological values generally associated with liberal democracy and its attendant system of government which allows for elections between competing political parties, some guaranteed freedoms protecting the person from the people, a market economy often coupled with some safeguards for the least advantaged, and equal protection under the law for all citizens.

Three populations regretted the rise of dialogue in sound film: Marxists who saw in dialogue a deadly threat to the ideals and revolutionary potentials inherent in montage; aristocratic esthetes who longed for the perpetuation of the visual poetry of silent cinema into an indefinite future; and the coterie of cinephiles attached to avant-garde experiments on film who detested art rooted in reality. Michel Chion describes these entities as "the disappointed fairies gathered around the cradle" containing sound film in its infancy.[13] Chion's disappointed fairies were not advocates of liberal democracy nor the corporate art that amused its citizens, least of all its dialogue.

The world's liberal democracies (along with their communist allies in the Soviet Union) were fighting for their lives against fascism when *The Ghost Ship* reached theaters. These theaters illustrate the alliance of corporate cinema and the general public.

When Hollywood productions of the 1930s and 1940s advanced overt political messages, they advanced a politics closely aligned to that of its audience, the optimistic and humane ideological perspective undergirding liberal democracy. The clearest space for this messaging was the dialogue.

A default politics finds its way into the dialogue track of many films, including *The Ghost Ship*. That politics is fundamentally optimistic about the common man. Consider how two famously political novels published during the studio era reached the screen with completely different results. Both novels became films clearly informed by the Classic Hollywood Style as outlined by David Bordwell and his associates. One, *The Grapes of Wrath* (published in 1939), was far left and the other, *The Fountainhead* (published in 1943), was far right.

The film version of *The Grapes of Wrath* (1940) features a good deal of dialogue taken directly from John Steinbeck's novel. The hero, Tom Joad (Henry Fonda), delivers his moving final speech about his willingness to be everywhere that common people are getting a raw deal with a quiet conviction that allows each word to sear the air of the theater. The film was both a commercial success and a critical smash hit with Frank Nugent of *The New York Times* declaring the film an instant classic.[14] The film's message confirms the ideals of an audience that struggled together through a Great Depression and soon a world war.

By contrast, Ayn Rand's novel *The Fountainhead* presents a pessimistic vision of the common man as befits a far-right fantasy of individual genius untrammeled by concern for the less fortunate. Rand wrote the screenplay adaptation of her novel, preserving much of its dialogue verbatim. Despite an "A" list cast including Gary Cooper, Patricia Neal, and *Cat People*'s Kent Smith, a three-million-dollar budget, and the directorial labors of distinguished veteran King Vidor, the film failed miserably. Audiences shunned it as it lost nearly a million dollars on its release. Critics savaged it in no small part for the confusion its dialogue caused. You cannot have your protagonist speechify on his indifference to the plight of the common man in a film made under the ideals of the Classic Hollywood Style without causing confusion. *The Hollywood Reporter* remarked that, "the characters are downright weird" reflecting the confusion that anti-democratic and illiberal dialogue causes within the era's cinematic style.[15] John McCarten summarized the film's reception in *The New Yorker* when describing the film as "the most asinine and inept movie that has come out of Hollywood in years."[16]

The film's dialogue, largely lifted from the novel, echoes Captain Stone's misanthropy and clarifies how the dialogue of a film made using the Classical Hollywood Style cannot place the words of villains in the mouths of heroes without becoming absurd. Audiences are conditioned by the medium of film dialogue to expect heroes to speak the optimistic language of Tom Merriam and the far more expansive and poetic Tom Joad, while villains talk like Captain Stone and Howard Roarke. This reality supersedes the impact of casting likable Gary Cooper in the distribution of the audience's affections. *The Fountainhead* became an instant laughing stock, failing at the box office for having been rejected by the "common man" it so thoroughly hates.

Yet if we examine Tom's role in the film using Andrew Tudor's typology of characters, he could be seen as a "pursuer," a character who strives to contain the film's threat. The film's dialogue makes Tom seem a hero for his voicing the ideals of liberal democracy, and no one struggles harder than he to save the crew. But he is also what Tudor calls a "potential victim."[17] His feminized name – Captain Stone calls him "Merriam" exclusively throughout the film's second half – and his weakened role (drugged and bound during the film's climax) reinforce his primary role as potential victim rather than pursuer. He raises his voice against tyranny, aligning it with the ideals of liberalism,[18] then, he chillingly fails to alter his fate. This is, after all, a horror movie.

The Crew

The crew of the *Altair*, including all of its officers save Stone and Merriam, are the contested characters of the film. While Captain Stone and Tom have their views about the crew, what about the crew itself? Unfortunately, they largely confirm Stone's pessimism about them rather than Tom's optimism. They evince no agency over events as Stone kills three of their own with minimal protest. They manage to remain ignorant of the injustice Tom sees so clearly.

Music proves one or their most powerful tools for not seeing or hearing the reality that threatens them. The crew of the *Altair* is strangely musical. Their talents include bagpiping, harmonica playing, singing, whistling, stomping, and clapping.

Starting with the bagpipes, we hear them first as Peter is introduced along with the rest of the crew at the initial roll call. Mr. Bounds calls Peter "Scotty" but Peter points out that he is not Scottish, but Greek. As Tom performs the appendectomy, we hear the bagpipes being played despite Peter being the patient. Louie gives them a try until another crew member asks him if he's sure he won't contract appendicitis from playing Peter's bagpipes. Louie promptly ceases his playing. The scene is mildly funny but makes a broader point about the alienation of the crew from one another.

The bagpipes are joined later in the film by a harmonica played by one of the sailors passing time as the crew works. As Tom moves from man to man trying to incite rebellion against the homicidal captain, the men use the pretext of this performance to ignore him. Their impromptu attention to music overwhelms Tom's call for action.

When Tom goes to his only friend on the ship, Sparks, to plead his case that Captain Stone murdered Louie, we find Sparks dancing with an imaginary partner as he uses the wireless to listen to music on his headset. Tom interrupts Sparks's reverie to tell him that the captain is insane. Sparks casually agrees but clarifies that he intends to remain willfully ignorant. Sparks resumes listening to the music until Tom physically restrains him. This dialogue passes between them before Sparks can resume listening to music instead of Tom.

> TOM
> Let me tell you from the beginning.
>
> SPARKS
> Not me. Don't tell me. I like my job and I want to keep it.
>
> TOM
> When we get to port, I'm going to tell the company agent.

Sparks shakes his head.

> SPARKS
> You'll lose a good job. Even if I believed you, I'd advise you not to do it.[19]

By showing Sparks dancing to music only he can hear and striving to curtail Tom's dialogue in order to resume his solipsistic listening, the film argues that the crew's isolation is a willful act. Sparks offers a pragmatic alternative to Tom's idealism, but given the default stance of dialogue supporting the ideals of liberal democracy he cannot help coming off sounding weak. Unlike the other crew members, Sparks will eventually wise up, but only when presented with clear evidence of evil intentions handed to him by Captain Stone himself. Sparks's tardy shift from isolation to showing communal concern for his fellows offers no profile in courage.

Sir Lancelot, who played the role of Billy Radd, composed two original Calypso songs for *The Ghost Ship*.[20] He had composed the memorable song "Shame and Sorrow" for *I Walked with a Zombie* and now only a few months after its successful release found himself working with Lewton for the second time. His song, "I'm Billy Radd," offers the sort of improvised lyrics that typify workplace Calypso singing. Sir Lancelot's lyrics introduce the singer to the listener by identifying himself first, then offering a litany of his likes and dislikes. Fitting given the role of the crew within the film, the first verse acknowledges that the singer is neither so good nor so bad. That admission of moral ambivalence reveals Sir Lancelot as keenly in touch with the film's theme and his character's role within it.

In the film's climactic scene as Captain Stone first tries to kill Tom, then fights The Finn to the death, the crew performs "I'm Billy Radd" on deck. This informal jamboree involves the harmonica, whistling, clapping, stomping, and the character Billy Radd singing his signature tune. The counterpoint between the visual track with its bloody struggle and the cheerful music made by the crew leads to the stark interpretation that Captain Stone's misanthropic pessimism may be accurate in this case. The crew is "Billy Radd" insofar as they are all one in refusing to see what is happening around them. Ironic, as it was Billy Radd who Tom tried to protect from the German sailors.

This rare moment of "counterpoint" between the image track and soundtrack in Lewton's horror cycle arrives at a moment of important tension in the film's commentary on society's indifference in the face of authoritarian violence. James Buhler presents an important overview and extension of historical theories of the soundtrack. His discussion of moments of "counterpoint" between a violent image track and cheerful music offers this summation:

> At one extreme, anempathetic music or sound can nevertheless remain expressive: a death occurs, say, and the sound of the motor keeps going, happy children resound in the background, joyful music plays on the radio, and so forth. Composer Max Steiner (1937) recognized the dramatic power of this device: imagine, he says, a nightclub with a jazz orchestra playing and a daughter notified of her father's death: 'it would

be absolutely wrong to change from the hot tune in progress to music appropriate to her mood ... No greater counterpoint has ever been found than gay music underlying a tragic scene' (224–25). The juxtaposition registers the indifference of the world (Chion 1994).[21]

Here the expressive potential of the performance of "I'm Billy Rad" while Captain Stone tries to kill Tom points clearly toward my analysis of the film's wartime theme. Buhler's and Chion's phrase "the indifference of the world" resonates even more strongly in this example because it is the crew, the men making the merry music, who are both threatened by the Captain's homicidal streak and responsible to do something about it.

While not as dramatically linked to the action as "Shame and Sorrow" was in *I Walked with a Zombie*, the tune and rhythm of "I'm Billy Rad" seems much catchier than its more celebrated predecessor. The text for "I'm Billy Rad," with its self-absorption, apparently typifies improvised Calypso texts for being about the singer. Here that tradition seems apt. Billy, like all the crew members except The Finn, is lost in a self-absorption that shields him from aiding Tom in the pressing life-and-death drama unfolding mere yards away.

Sir Lancelot's other song composed for *The Ghost Ship* – "Here We Come to San Sebastian" – is heard in its entirety as the *Altair* arrives in San Sebastian. Sir Lancelot's voice once again receives the accompaniment of a harmonica. Sir Lancelot's lyrics reveal Billy Radd as steadfast in his concern for pleasure. In many ways Billy is The Finn's opposite. He has no idea what is happening around him. Billy's glowing testimonials for all the officers given to Mr. Roberts (Boyd Davis) at the informal hearing indicate how hard he tries not to know what is going on. He repeatedly says on behalf of the crew, "We just can't understand it." Later, after Tom aids him when the Germans attack him, Billy clearly has no idea that Tom has quit.

The diegetic music within the film's soundtrack belongs to the crew. They use it to pass the time doing menial chores, or to express their various enthusiasms. More alarmingly, they use it to isolate themselves from their responsibilities to one another in a context in which they are all under direct threat.

A Digression about "Blow the Man Down"

One other performance of diegetic music occurs in the film, albeit on shore. At the film's opening and close, Tom passes a blind street musician who sings passages of "Blow the Man Down" as he accompanies himself on a zither. Typical of the Lewton unit, the choice of song was not arbitrary. While "Blow the Man Down" is surely the most recognizable sea shanty ever sung, Lewton researched the song's provenance and variants before submitting fifty-six lines of text to the Production Code Office for approval for use in the film. The correspondence on *The Ghost Ship* between Lewton and the Breen Office was easily Lewton's most complicated.[22] For example, we find the censors quite concerned about homosexual potentials in the script, even warning Lewton against any "pansy gags associated with this sailor business." As Harry Benshoff points out, many such gags did enter into the film; for example, the exchange between two crew members about the sovereignty of a captain at sea includes this exchange: "Why a captain can even marry you." The other sailor responds, "Not me, I have a wife."[23] Why Lewton saw fit to send fifty-six lines of a sea shanty for approval suggests that Lewton may have been bored that day and wanted to complicate someone's life at the Production Code Office for their having made his life more complicated with their hectoring about his script.

Lewton took great care in selecting which of the many versions of "Blow the Man Down" he would use. The version Lewton chose is neither the oldest nor the most famous version of the song.[24] The oldest concerns the Blackball line, a Dutch-owned line of packet ships that ran the first commercial passenger lines between New York and Liverpool. The Blackball line was notorious for its terrible treatment of its crews. The text of the song in this earliest instantiation seems inappropriate for Lewton's film insofar as it deals primarily with the fact that no able seaman would ship with the Blackball line, hence the line's famous use of incompetent beginners. One couplet captures its tone:

> There's tinkers an' tailors an' sogers an' all,
> All ship as prime sailors aboard the Blackball.

Lewton's dramatic situation differs from that on the Blackball line. The *Altair* is surely a ship where the captain mistreats the crew; but the crew, unlike those on Blackball packets, is able. The version Lewton chose is a variant called "The Fishes." In this version, a captain finds "his ship lay becalmed in a tropical sea." He summons a seal by whistling, and before long all manner of sea creatures have jumped on deck to help get the ship moving again. The captain repays his able crew of volunteers with murderous conduct.

> The mackerel the skipper did scoff for his tea,
> The herring he salted, the seal harpooned he.
>
> He baited a hook, an' he thought it a lark,
> To catch as he did that hoary ol' shark.
>
> The eel it wuz tasty, the hake it wuz strong,
> The flounder he speared with a lance o' three prongs.

The skate he speared next, but the porpose wuz fast,
The conger it grinned an' it grinned to the last.

He caught the ol' whale, which was no simple task,
An' soon with whale oil he had filled up each cask.

With the head o' the codfish he made a fine pipe,
The sprat then he salted, but twas only a bite.

The breeze it blew merrily, an' merrily sailed he,
But what an ol bastard that skipper must be![25]

Lewton chose a version of the song in which we find the crew able, even superhumanly so, but the captain murderous. No other version evinces this combination. The film only allows the audience to hear the first few lines of the song, but for a perfectionist such as Lewton it mattered that "The Fishes" variant of "Blow the Man Down" was sung and not a version with a different distribution of praise and blame.

The Finn

Roy Webb's nondiegetic underscore favors an unlikely figure in The Finn. The character has a name, Pollo Lindstrom, shouted during the initial roll call. His role in the film takes several peculiar turns before he winds up assuming the role of the film's "pursuer" for being the man who kills Captain Stone.

The Finn functions initially as a red herring. When Tom first boards the *Altair* he asks The Finn where he can find Captain Stone. The Finn's somber demeanor and the menacing way he wordlessly gestures with his knife join Webb's orchestral underscore to render him a seeming threat. That first cue Webb produced elides the blind musician's rendition of "Blow the Man Down" (sung in B major) to a vamp featuring a B-flat major seventh chord superimposed on a G major chord supporting a strange five-note scalar pattern comprised of half-steps, whole steps, and an augmented second (Figure 5.1) The orchestration of this ostinato presents all the harsh dissonances of this passage very gently. For example, the G major chord appears only in three solo violins. The effect of a quiet rendition of such discordant material renders it subtly menacing. Then, as Tom moves on, The Finn offers his first of many voiceover narrations in which he reveals that he is a mute, and therefore cut off from other men. But he promises that he can "hear things other men can never hear, know things other men can never know."

In subsequent appearances, The Finn emphasizes his willingness to watch the events unfolding around him including both Captain Stone's murderous

Figure 5.1 Roy Webb, "Finn" from *The Ghost Ship*

conduct and Tom's ambition to resist. The ostinato described here appears in virtually all of the cues associated with The Finn. In its first appearance, Webb extends the polychord B-flat7/G to the end, while placing a baleful bassoon solo in A-flat minor above it. With its complex harmony and unusual melodic material, Webb imparts on The Finn layers of musical complexity befitting his multifarious role in the film.

Scanning the whole of Webb's contribution to the soundtrack finds him paying uncommon attention to The Finn. Here is an overview of all Webb's cues for the film.

0'–1'	Main Title	
3'–4'	Finn	The Finn is introduced
9'–10'	Finn	The same music is reprised as The Finn reflects on Jensen's death
26'	Finn's Theme	The Finn is seen on watch as a transition
41'–43'	Too Late	Ellen and Captain Stone on the *Altair*'s deck
45'–46'	Tom Merriam	Tom wakes up on board the *Altair* after quitting
48'–54'	Fear	Tom discovers troubling signs that the captain plans to kill him
57'–58'	I Will Watch	The Finn identifies with Tom and plans to watch out for him
63'–64'	If the Boy Is Right	Stone overhears the officers, The Finn watches
65'–66'	The Boy Is Right	Stone plans to kill Tom, The Finn watches
67'	Death of Stone	The Finn has killed Stone and reacts to his death
68'	The Boy Is Safe	The Finn narrates as Tom commands the ship
69'	End Title	

On examining the cues for the film and the dramatic circumstances they support, it becomes clear that the orchestral music overwhelmingly accompanies The Finn. Not one cue appears on the soundtrack until the forty-first minute of the sixty-nine-minute film without The Finn dominating the screen. The forty-first minute of the film marks the point when the *Altair* reaches San Sebastian. During that phase of the film, Webb's music supports the film's only female character, Ellen, reflecting the normative practice of associating orchestral underscore with the feminine.[26] On the *Altair*'s return to sea, Webb's music returns to supporting The Finn.

Roy Webb's score for *The Ghost Ship* is slim, sparser even than that produced for *I Walked with a Zombie* wherein Webb supported only half the story. The choice of connecting the film's orchestral underscore largely to support The Finn offers a surprising violation of normative practices. Webb's score for the film almost never intensifies the impact of scenes of action nor clarifies the hidden truth within the film's characters apart from The Finn.

Insofar as this chapter is concerned with how *The Ghost Ship* can be seen as a wartime fable about the urgency of questioning authority, especially authority hostile to the ideals of liberal democracy, privileging The Finn with the luxury of orchestral underscore makes sense. He becomes the film's unlikely hero, or to use Tudor's terminology, its only effective "pursuer." He alone lives up to the ideals about the essential goodness of the common man haltingly articulated by Tom throughout the film. The Finn has privileged access to the soundtrack by speaking on it in voiceover and by enjoying the vast majority of its orchestral underscore, thus bonding the audience more readily to him.

A Conclusion: "Blow the Man Down" Reprised

Some commentators on *The Ghost Ship* conclude that the film features an optimistic ending.[27] Parsing through the soundtrack of the ending allows the music to render its more complicated verdict.

Webb's cue "The Boy Is Safe" draws its title from The Finn's final voiceover narration: "The boy is safe, and his belief in men and Man's essential goodness is secure. He stands beside me in command. All's well."[28] Webb's orchestral support covers a series of parallel dissonant trichords (0-2-7 sets) over an F# pedal before ending on a deceptive cadence of G major (with major seventh as the F# pedal remains) resolving to B major. That Webb offered a deceptive cadence to support The Finn's optimism may be telling as the film repeatedly undercuts Tom's idealistic notions about the common man.

This brief cue supporting The Finn's final, optimistic voiceover narration elides directly into the blind street musician singing "Blow the Man Down" in B major. Tom and the street singer begin to reproduce their exact dialogue from the film's opening. Alexander Nemerov sees this as evidence that Tom has gone nowhere and little has changed.[29]

Roy Webb has his orchestra join the performance of "Blow the Man Down" as his End Titles begin. After wrapping up the song, Webb has the orchestra race toward an unusually prim cadential formula. The last three chords, like the ending of "The Boy Is Safe," feature an F# pedal: B major: I vi IV vi64 ii7 #iv7 IV9 V7 I64. The ending of *The Ghost Ship* offers one of Webb's most tonally stable sequences composed for the entire series. Maybe Webb saw some hope in Tom meeting Ellen's sister's shadow as promised, the film's final image.

Here we find Webb's music performing a "standard" task of film music as outlined by Claudia Gorbman, "It *interprets* the image, pinpoints and channels the 'correct' meaning of the narrative events depicted" in order "to ward off the displeasure of uncertain signification."[30] Yet in this case, Webb's music sends mixed messages. His deceptive cadence undercuts the authority of The Finn's voiceover, but the cheerful transition from "Blow the Man Down" to the End Title's final, optimistic cadential formula signifies the very ideals heard in The Finn's optimistic final voiceover.

My own view tends toward Nemerov's. The film fails to clarify what if anything Tom learned about humanity in the laboratory Captain Stone provided aboard the *Altair*. The film's close provides little comfort. The wartime fable pitted the pessimism and misanthropy of fascist dictatorship against the optimism and humanity of liberal democracy. For the most part, the laboratory of the *Altair* saw the crew and officers, the common man, confirm Captain Stone's conclusions. The Finn rushes to aid Tom because his disability cuts him off from the society of other men, allowing him a unique perspective. If liberal democracy hangs by the thread of an alienated, prescient sailor to save the day, then its cause appears to be in dire shape.

Here I part ways with Roy Webb, who I believe allowed a conventional reading of the film's content to shape his End Title rather than painting the text with the sort of insight he demonstrated in the earlier films. We might close by defending his choice with a reference to the film's wartime context. Perhaps Webb fully comprehended the film's mixed message as evidenced in his deceptive cadence but wanted to see things Tom's way and provided his cadential formula to satisfy a hopeful personal agenda.

Notes

1. The script for *I Walked with a Zombie* consistently refers to the island as "St. Sebastian" while the script for *The Ghost Ship* refers to it as "San Sebastian." This explains the two spellings in this book for the same fictional island.
2. J. P. Telotte, *Dreams of Darkness: Fantasy and the Films of Val Lewton* (Urbana: University of Illinois Press, 1985), pp. 95–96.
3. Edmund Bansak, *Fearing the Dark: The Val Lewton Career* (Jefferson, NC: MacFarland & Company, 1995), pp. 218–220.
4. Harry Benshoff, *Monsters in the Closet: Homosexuality and the Horror Film* (Manchester: University of Manchester Press, 1997), p. 105.

5. In addition to its plot similarities to familiar literary classics, much more is borrowed in the film. The set is a leftover from RKO's production of *Pacific Liner* (1939). Its presence on the RKO lot inspired Charles Koerner to ask Lewton for a horror film set on a ship. Also recycled is the presence of Richard Dix in the film. By this point, Dix's career as a leading man was over, but the actor owed RKO one last film on his contract. Koerner felt this asset needed to be used and assigned Dix to Lewton. Finally, RKO lost a plagiarism case launched by two writers, Samuel Golding and Norbert Faulkner, who felt *The Ghost Ship* owed something to an unsolicited manuscript they had left with Lewton's secretary, who returned it unread. Two judges found the case believable, and the film was pulled from release in February 1944.
6. Interestingly, this speech does not appear in the final shooting script. It had to have been added during the production. Donald Henderson Clarke, *The Ghost Ship* shooting script, RKO Radio Pictures Studio Records (Collection PASC 3). UCLA Library Special Collections, Charles E. Young Research Library, University of California, Los Angeles.
7. Alexander Nemerov, *Icons of Grief: Val Lewton's Home Front Pictures* (Berkeley: University of California Press, 2005), p. 65.
8. Andrew Tudor, *Monsters and Mad Scientists: A Cultural History of the Horror Movie* (Oxford: Basil Blackwell, 1989), pp. 22–23.
9. *The Ghost Ship* was Francis M. Sarver's first job recording sound for film. He was thirty-five years old and had been an assistant in the sound department prior to this assignment. He would record two more films for Lewton, *The Curse of the Cat People* (1944) and *Mademoiselle Fifi* (1945). He worked at RKO until finally being laid off in 1954 as the studio wound down production. The credits for his last film for RKO, *Cattle Queen of Montana* (1954), find his name inaccurately presented as Francis N. Sarver, a fitting farewell gesture from a studio by then badly mismanaged by hands-on owner Howard Hughes.
10. Neil Lerner, "The Strange Case of Rouben Mamoulian's Sonic Stew: The Uncanny Soundtrack in *Dr. Jekyll and Mr. Hyde* (1931)," in *Music in the Horror Film*, ed. Neil Lerner (New York: Routledge, 2010), pp. 66–72.
11. Irwin Bazelon, *Knowing the Score: Notes on Film Music* (New York: Van Nostren Reinhold, 1975), p. 147.
12. This moment is particularly interesting in light of Sarah Kozloff's work on film dialogue. This speech functions simultaneously to achieve two aesthetic effects described in Kozloff's work: "Thematic messages/authorial commentary" by clarifying the film's ideological potentials and "Opportunities for 'star turns'" by providing Dix a moment of distilled madness. Sarah Kozloff, *Overhearing Film Dialogue* (Berkeley: University of California Press, 2000), pp. 56–61.
13. Michel Chion, *Film, A Sound Art*, Claudia Gorbman, translator (New York: Columbia University Press, 2009), pp. 201–208.
14. Frank Nugent, "The Grapes of Wrath," *The New York Times* (January 25, 1940).
15. "The Fountainhead" Review, *The Hollywood Reporter* (June 12, 1949).
16. John McCarten, "The Current Cinema," *The New Yorker* (July 16, 1949), p. 47.
17. Tudor, pp. 119–121.

18. In discussing two speeches at the ends of *Love Actually* (2003) and *The King's Speech* (2010), Dan Wang connects dialogue in these films with "theories of liberal subjectivity that emphasize the way in which speaking itself produces an efflorescence of personhood." Dan Wang, "The Voice of Feeling: Liberal Subjects, Music, and Cinematic Speech," *The Oxford Handbook of Voice Studies*, eds. Nina Sun Eidsheim and Katherine Meizel (Oxford: Oxford University Press, 2019), p. 127.
19. Donald Henderson Clarke, "The Ghost Ship."
20. Sir Lancelot's songs were used in *The Ghost Ship* by special permission of their author. Clearly, he intended to introduce them into his repertoire after leaving Hollywood. Only the song from *I Walked with a Zombie* seems to have earned that honor.
21. James Buhler, *Theories of the Soundtrack* (Oxford: Oxford University Press, 2019), pp. 13–14.
22. MPAA Files, "*The Ghost Ship*," Margaret Herrick Library, Academy of Motion Pictures Arts and Sciences, Beverly Hills, California.
23. Benshoff, p. 108.
24. The discussion here of "Blow the Man Down" is entirely informed by Stan Hugill, *Shanties from the Seven Seas* (Mystic, CT: Mystic Seaport Press, 1994), pp. 154–167.
25. Ibid., p. 165.
26. Claudia Gorbman, *Unheard Melodies: Narrative Film Music* (Bloomington: University of Indiana Press, 1987), pp. 79–81.
27. J. P. Telotte concludes that "*The Ghost Ship* leaves us with a sense of promise fulfilled and some hope for the future"; Telotte, p. 110. Edmund Bansak offers that "*The Ghost Ship*'s conclusion is decidedly upbeat"; Bansak, p. 214.
28. This dialogue, like much of The Finn's voiceover dialogue, does not appear in the shooting script. Lewton may have added it on the day actor Skelton Knaggs recorded his voiceover material.
29. Nemerov, p. 77.
30. Gorbman, p. 58.

6 MUSIC FOR AMY AND HER FRIEND: WEBB'S SCORE FOR *THE CURSE OF THE CAT PEOPLE*

The Curse of the Cat People ranks among the strangest films made in Hollywood during the 1940s.[1] Upon its release in early March of 1944, reviewers struggled with its weird hybridity. Bosley Crowther concluded his unusually positive review with, "The whole conception and construction of this picture indicates an imaginative approach. Its chief fault is that it is cursed with the flavor and some of the claptrap from that 'Cat People' film."[2]

Ostensibly a sequel to the lucrative *Cat People*, *The Curse of the Cat People* delivers neither a curse nor a cat person, rendering it the rare sequel that rehashes nothing from its predecessor. Instead, the film offers the story of a sensitive child seeking a friend. Yet, three characters return from the earlier film . . . or do they? Jane Randolph and Kent Smith reprise their roles of Alice and Oliver, who are now married with a young daughter named Amy (Ann Carter). Simone Simon's Irena, dead at the end of *Cat People*, enters as Amy's friend. But Irena's nature is uncertain. Some scholars, like David Bordwell, see Simone Simon playing the ghost of Irena returned to aid Oliver's lonely child.[3] Others, most notably Joel Siegel, see her as purely an imaginary friend whose face Amy selected from a photograph.[4] The film's music weighs in importantly.

In addition to its role in clarifying the film's central mystery, the music in the film situates its audience in the position of a young girl, a demographic Hollywood films rarely privileged during the studio era. By reinforcing only Amy's interiority, the film's soundtrack situates the audience in rapport with Amy.

The film's music reinforces the film's presentation of childish fantasy with great realism while presenting adult reality as thoroughly infiltrated by the fantastic. Claudia Gorbman explains that music in horror and other fantasy genres normally serves to break down an audience's defenses against irrational forces. Here music aids in revealing the irrational deeply ingrained in the adult world of "logic, everyday reality, and control,"[5] while also painting the fantastical inner world of childhood.

"Universalizing" Horror at RKO

Before turning to music for some guidance in understanding this unusual film, we visit how it came to be. RKO formed the Lewton unit to compete with Universal Pictures' horror cycle. To this point the studio's efforts included selecting market-tested titles, marketing the films with lurid and misleading imagery, hiring a writer (Curt Siodmak) and a director (Edward Dmytryk) with Universal horror credits, and insisting on more shots of a leopard in *Cat People*. Lewton managed to finesse his way through these efforts, preserving his distinct approach.

Charles Koerner's next attempt to "Universalize" Lewton's productions took the form of tasking Lewton with making a sequel to *Cat People*. This mandate proved difficult to dodge, although Lewton surely tried. He objected to Koerner to no avail, even proposing an alternative non-horror film called "The Amorous Ghost."[6] RKO humored Lewton in developing this non-horror project long enough for a lengthy treatment and a draft of a script to materialize.[7] The story depicts the ghost of Casanova coming to modern America for twelve hours during which time he falls in love with a modern American woman. His love for her becomes so perfect that when his time expires she returns with him to what Lewton hoped would be an eighteenth-century conception of heaven. RKO never produced Lewton's romantic comedy/ghost story,[8] but Lewton bought time away from his duty to produce a sequel to *Cat People* through it.

"The Amorous Ghost" was only one of Lewton's efforts to dodge making *The Curse of the Cat People*. He proposed an adaptation of F. Marion Crawford's horror short story "The Screaming Skull." This project also never came to be, although RKO did purchase the rights to film the story. He proposed a non-horror film dealing with the plight of children during the war whose parents are either overseas fighting or working long hours in a munitions plant. The lack of parental supervision leads to delinquency. Initially Lewton titled this film "Are These Our Children?" but it eventually morphed into the film *Youth Runs Wild* (1944). Lewton even cheerfully took up making *The Ghost Ship* to slow down work on *The Curse of the Cat People*, managing to delay shooting long enough that the three principals – Simone Simon, Kent Smith, and Jane Randolph – had other projects, forcing still further delays on the sequel.[9]

Through his various delaying tactics, Lewton bought himself seven months of reprieve until he ran out of excuses. His final effort to thwart the sequel came in the form of an appeal to Koerner to change the project's title to "Amy and Her Friend" as that title better suited the material Lewton was developing for the film.[10] Koerner held firm.

Horror sequels were the order of the day at Universal Pictures. During the year leading up to Koerner assigning Lewton this sequel, Universal had released four horror sequels: *The Ghost of Frankenstein* (1942), *The Mummy's Tomb* (1942), *Frankenstein Meets the Wolf Man* (1943), and *Son of Dracula* (1943). All of them proved profitable and all of them repeat tropes from earlier in their series with varying degrees of relentlessness.[11] Oddly, though, Universal's horror producers had their eyes on Lewton's commercial success and launched their own series of psychological horror films based on Simon and Schuster's successful "Inner Sanctum" radio series. Each film in the series would be set in modern America with understated horror elements in emulation of Lewton's apparent horror formula. The first film in the series, *Calling Dr. Death* (1943), reached theaters mere months ahead of *The Curse of the Cat People*. This back-and-forth rivalry of borrowed "schema and revisions" in film production typifies the era's "cooperative competition," as David Bordwell describes it.[12]

The most outlandish effort at RKO to "Universalize" Lewton came during this period of stalling preproduction on *The Curse of the Cat People*. Charles Koerner saw how horror was handled at Universal Pictures and the trend was toward "monster rallies" in which more than one iconic monster appears in a single film. The first such film was *Frankenstein Meets the Wolf Man*. *The Hollywood Reporter* announced that RKO was producing a horror rally titled "They Creep By Night."[13] The publicity department produced a pre-production ad with copy promising:

> Not one, not two, not three . . . but ALL of the famous creeper characters you ever heard of, plus some new ones, in the wildest nightmare of terror thrills that mind can imagine! . . . Cat People, Zombies, Leopard Men; beast-women and bat-men; blood-curdlers by the dozen . . . all in a merger of monsters that will make anything else in this line look like a Sunday School picnic!

Perhaps the mere threat of this ludicrous project prompted Lewton toward compliance. Soon after the announcement of "They Creep By Night" in trade papers, Lewton sat down to write the original story for *The Curse of the Cat People*, a project he undertook entirely alone according to the film's credited screenwriter, DeWitt Bodeen.[14]

Amy and Her Friend Meets Curse of the Cat People

The story Lewton wrote for the film would be ably served by the title he proposed, "Amy and Her Friend." He made a few compromises in his conception of "Amy and Her Friend" in order to place a fig leaf on his naked insubordination, such as having Amy's parents be Oliver and Alice from *Cat People*. Now married, they live in Tarrytown, New York, the small city where Val Lewton spent much of his youth after he moved to America with his mother and sister. Alice and Oliver's daughter, Amy, resembles the young Lewton according to Joel Siegel by being a quiet, withdrawn child with a vivid imagination and no friends.[15] Mrs. Farren (Julia Dean), the aging actress Amy visits, resembles Lewton's aunt, Alla Nazimova, with whom the Lewtons lived in Tarrytown. Some of the particular instances from the film derive from Lewton's childhood experiences. The sequence wherein Amy reveals that she placed the invitations to her birthday party in a knothole of a tree, believing it to be a "magic mailbox," for example, is one Lewton claimed from his own youth.[16]

Out of loneliness, Amy turns to an imaginary friend. Lewton inserted Irena, dead at the close of *Cat People*, into the role of the imaginary friend. In an early draft, Lewton unmistakably cast Simone Simon as Irena's ghost, providing her with dialogue like, "Death's like life. Death's a part of life. It isn't frightening. It isn't the end of everything. It is quiet and nothingness. It's a part of all eternity."[17] In revisions, such didactic dialogue vanished until, after final editing of the finished film, a more delicate balance is struck between Irena as friend conjured from imagination and ghost.

The film's conflict arises when Oliver finds Amy's recourse to his deceased first wife as an imaginary friend troubling. Oliver lashes out at his daughter's flights of imagination, even accusing her of lying about how she came to possess a ring when she was telling the truth. Alice observes the conflict between her increasingly irascible husband and embattled daughter for the most part without intervention. When she does intervene, such as when she demands that Oliver allow Amy to tell her side of the story about the ring, Oliver's temper leads to shouting.

Oliver's demand for Amy to abandon her friendship with Irena leads to defiance from the child. Out of patience, Oliver resolves to punish Amy physically. The first spanking is mercifully played off-stage, but most viewers conclude that Oliver is an atrocious father.

Oliver's stubborn insistence on everything being normal in *Cat People* remains in the sequel. During the film's first scene, Amy goes on a school field trip to Sleepy Hollow. There, Amy becomes enamored with a butterfly, calling it "my friend." She chases the butterfly as it flies, and a boy named Donald (Joel Davis) captures it for her so violently that he kills it. Amy slaps Donald's face. Next, we find Alice and Oliver consulting with Amy's teacher, Miss Callahan

(Eve March). Miss Callahan describes Amy's attachment to the butterfly as a "harmless fancy." Oliver's reply feels familiar: "Amy has too many fancies – too few friends. It worries me. It doesn't seem normal."[18] Here Oliver confirms the music-based analysis of him in *Cat People* by revealing himself as too stolid, too stubborn, and far too attached to his conception of normalcy to offer any comfort to his daughter.

Lewton left little space for a sequel to *Cat People* to peek out through "Amy and Her Friend." But there are connections to the earlier film beyond Alice and Oliver being cast as Amy's parents. Oliver's past haunts him. Oliver appears quietly traumatized by his experiences with Irena and justifies his aversion to Amy's imaginative flights with his memories of how Irena destroyed herself with an overly active inner life.

Scrambled Genres

The film resulting from the studio and the producer/writer's conflicting interests hybridizes elements of a child's initiation story with a horror sequel. Many critics at the time objected to this hybridization, offering essentialist arguments insisting that the film's scrambling of generic codes constituted a grave flaw.

Variety, usually sympathetic to Lewton's films, complained:

> Made as a sequel to the profitable *Cat People*, this is highly disappointing because it fails to measure up as a horrific opus. Even though having the same principals as in the original chiller, this is an impossible lightweight. Chief trouble seems to be the oversupply of palaver and concern over a cute, but annoying child.

The review gets worse from there, and primarily blames the film having two directors for its woes.[19]

While *Variety*'s reviewer hoped for a horror film, Lewton admirer James Agee joined Bosley Crowther in complaining about the film's horror elements, describing the film's hints at "curses and were-cats" as unhelpful.[20] Despite his strongly worded reservations about the film's few horror elements, Agee went on to name the film, along with Lewton's *Youth Runs Wild*, as the best fiction film of 1944.[21]

Universalizing Amy

From Lewton's story to DeWitt Bodeen's screenplay to Lewton's last-minute rewrite,[22] the film explores the inner life of Amy and her flights of imagination far more than any horrific elements. This emphasis in the writing informs the entire production with both the image track and the soundtrack urging the audience to enter Amy's world, often positioning the audience to see as only she can and hear what only she hears.

The image track opens with the RKO Art Department's title cards featuring whimsical drawings seemingly pulled from the pages of a child's storybook. The film's lighting and photography under the supervision of Nicholas Musuraca offer viewers moments of exquisite visual poetry as only a child can experience, such as the sparkling light on icy boughs as Irena bestows her Christmas gift, as well as scenes of childish fright including the heavily shadowed bedroom as Amy wakes from her nightmare.

Costume designer Edward Stevenson adds to the film's imagery inspired by childish fancy through Irena's improbable storybook gown. While a sharp dresser who worked for a fashion magazine in *Cat People*, Irena becomes the radiant princess of a child's dream in the sequel.

Often the film's image track reveals to the audience things only Amy can see. We see Amy's hand with the ring on it in the fishpond from Amy's point of view. Similarly, as Mrs. Farren performs her melodrama of "The Legend of Sleepy Hollow," the camera takes Amy's seated position and allows the audience to witness the performance from her perspective. Actress Julia Dean in the role of Mrs. Farren looks directly at the camera as though looking into Amy's eyes.

Much of this visual manipulation concerns the person of Irena. We see her, just as Amy does, standing in the Reeds' garden. Yet her father claims that there's no one in the garden. At the film's climax, as Mrs. Farren's mentally unstable daughter Barbara (Elizabeth Russell) threatens Amy, we see, from Amy's point of view, Irena's image superimposed on Barbara's, indicating that Amy has seen the potential friend hidden within this threatening stranger. David Bordwell praised the film's subjective approach to Irena's presence or lack thereof: "As a fantasy *The Curse of the Cat People* has a unique subtlety. For once, nobody redundantly explains who can and who can't see the ghost."[23]

David Bordwell cites a host of innovations configured to grant audiences "greater intimacy with the characters, an effort to understand them from the inside,"[24] including flashbacks, voiceover narrations, point-of-view shots, dream sequences, hallucinations, and montages. In the case of *The Curse of the Cat People*, only some of these techniques find their way into the film, but always to lend the audience greater intimacy with Amy's interiority.

Amy's dream, for example, provides the audience access to Amy's mind as her recollections of Mrs. Farren's performance unfold in nightmarish distortions. Echoes of Mrs. Farren's voice concluding "forever you must ride with the Headless Horseman" fragment, jumble, and repeat, as a musical ostinato in what Irwin Bazelon would surely call "pre-*musique concrète*."[25] The sound effect of a horse's hoofbeats combines with whirring strings in Webb's cue "Nightmare" to complete the presentation of Amy's mental activity for the audience. Interestingly, the image track only shows the reality of Amy sleeping. The soundtrack does the heavy lifting of situating the audience in Amy's fantastical inner life.

Later, when Amy searches for Irena in the snowstorm, we hear those same hoofbeats now combined with Webb's score to illustrate what Amy is thinking about as she cowers in fear on the little bridge in Sleepy Hollow. The image track will later reveal that a loose chain on a truck tire provides the reality of the fantasy as it clatters in the same hoofbeat rhythm on the truck's fender.

Later in that same sequence, the audience hears the sound of hunting horns that join the sound effect of baying dogs as they hunt Amy. The music on the soundtrack comes from cut material for Webb's cue supporting the telling of "Herne, the Hunter," one of two planned melodramas intended to take place within the film. Those hunting horns provide concrete aural illustration of Amy's thoughts. This cut scene and its music will be discussed in greater detail below.

Further demonstrating the privileging of Amy's perspective is the film's Christmas scene. When the carolers join the Reeds in singing "Shepherds Shake Off Your Drowsy Sleep" at Alice's request, the audience also hears Irena singing the French carol "Il est né, le divin Enfant." The two carols form a lovely quodlibet, yet only Amy can hear it. The carolers, Edward, and the Reeds give no sign of having any idea what is happening on the film's soundtrack. The soundtrack privileges the audience to hear what only Amy can hear. This moment crystallizes the centrality of Amy to the film.

Fantasy in Reality and the Reality of Fantasy

J. P. Telotte argues that *The Curse of the Cat People* functions as a meditation on fantasy more than a film born of the nebulous genre of fantasy.[26] His psychoanalytic approach to the film begins by observing that contemporary psychologists admired it. On September 7, 1944 the Los Angeles Council of Social Agencies screened the film for an audience of teachers and child psychologists at a seminar on the depiction of childhood in film where both Lewton and director Robert Wise were invited to attend and receive praise for their work.[27] The head of child psychology at UCLA's Child Psychology Clinic, Dr. Franklin Fearing, also held a seminar to watch and praise the film for the accuracy of its depiction of childhood.[28] And finally sociologist David Riesman singled out the film for its thoughtful evocation of "the poetry and danger of childhood" in the most widely read nonfiction book of 1950, *The Lonely Crowd*.[29]

Telotte describes the film's mixture of reality and fantasy this way:

> Through the complex image of the child and his [or her] fondness for fantasizing – a fondness which can become lost in the course of growing up – *Curse of the Cat People* locates a valuable touchstone for the

larger human vesperal experience, one which marks the path by which we come to 'experience the fantasy in all realities and the basic reality of fantasy.'[30]

The quote within the quote belongs to psychologist James Hillman and captures the essential point Telotte makes about the film.[31] As a meditation on fantasy, the film draws the audience's attention time and again to the role make-believe plays in the reality Oliver strives toward and the reality within the fantasy world Amy conjures.

In the film we find adults continually engaging the fantastical. Oliver proudly builds toy boats, plays tiddlywinks, and muddles the boundary between fantasy and reality for his young daughter. The best example of this last case is his story of the old tree in the garden functioning as a magic mailbox. More importantly, he clearly cannot escape his experiences in the earlier film and begins to indulge in the fearful and fantastical belief that Amy could somehow be Irena's child.

Oliver is joined in his preoccupation with make-believe by Alice, who fondly recollects bygone mummers' plays and joins in a family colloquy on the nature of wishing as a self-appointed expert. The family's servant, Edward (Sir Lancelot), also a participant in the wishing colloquy, uses the vacuum cleaner to energize the sails on Oliver's model ships, and shares a tale of Jamaican wishing rings with Amy. Mrs. Farren trades in make-believe for having spent her life on the stage. She tells Amy an unsettlingly vivid version of "The Legend of Sleepy Hollow" and, worse, harbors a grim delusion that her daughter Barbara died in a fire even as Barbara stands beside her.

The film's soundtrack honors these adult flights of fancy and departures from reality by providing many of them with musical accompaniment. Edward, for example, sings the sea shanty "Reuben Ranzo" while aiming the vacuum cleaner at the toy boats to animate their tiny sails.

Mrs. Farren's improvised telling of "The Legend of Sleepy Hollow" receives an evocative cue from Webb titled "The Headless Horseman." Thanks to Webb's muted horn calls and whirring string tremolos up and down partial chromatic scales, the scene conjures the ghost of melodrama, a genre popular into the twentieth century, but in drastic decline after the advent of cinema. Melodramas require musical accompaniment supporting spoken dialogue or read poetry, firmly connecting it to the art of film music.

Webb composed two such works for the film; the other serves Mrs. Farren's recitation of Mistress Page's Act IV, Scene IV soliloquy from William Shakespeare's *The Merry Wives of Windsor* about the frightening ghost, Herne the Hunter, during Amy's Christmas visit to her. As Mrs. Farren realizes that her audience, Amy and Edward, do not know the play, she begins to paraphrase rather than recite the tale. The end of this second melodrama-like cue can be heard in the film as Edward and Amy take their leave, and Barbara challenges her mother to show her some measure of the kindness she shows Amy. Mrs. Farren's second story for Amy was cut from the final film, but RKO logs prove that it was shot, edited, scored, mixed, and included in the print shown to RKO executives. Cutting the scene makes sense as a second story slows down the action, but later, when Webb quotes the cue to illustrate Amy's memory as she wanders through the snowstorm – a clear reference to music in the film serving to illustrate Amy's memory of a fantastical experience – is sadly lost. My conclusion to this chapter will strive to privilege the genre of melodrama enfolded into the film. Horror films are heirs to the fantastical symbiosis of music and make-believe.

Roy Webb supplied no musical underscore for Oliver and Alice in *Cat People*, even defying spotting sheets instructing him to do so. In this film, one particular conversation between them receives orchestral underscore as they discuss Amy's worrisome imagination. As Oliver reflects on similarities between Irena and Amy, Webb's cue "Concerned" emerges on the soundtrack. Here we find Oliver at his least "normal" and most at the mercy of the fantastical side of his nature, thus Webb supplies Oliver with his first and only musical underscore illustrative of his interiority.

Amy's fantasy life is rooted in her lonely reality as her peers judge and shun her in ways that feel poignantly realistic. For example, her classmates complain that her constant dreaming spoils the fun in the film's first scene. Miss Callahan defends Amy as "just a little different," a defense certainly satisfying to adult viewers of the film, but ineffective for the classmates. The same child who voiced the complaint at the school outing (Gloria Donovan) later conspires with friends to simultaneously mock Amy's imaginative nature and ostracize her. When Amy asks to join a game of jacks, her antagonist points offscreen and shouts, "look at the giraffe." As Amy looks, the girls dash away. These painful vignettes of isolation from her peers lend Amy's dreamy childhood a dose of reality while rooting her dream life in the reality of loneliness that inspires it. This was the realism that invited the admiration of psychologists and educators at the film's release.

Enter Irena

The film's most important fantasy concerns Amy's friendship with Irena. As mentioned above, Irena's nature in the film as ghost or imaginary friend has led to disputes about what precisely the audience is seeing when we see Irena. Music may help here. In *Cat People*, I claimed that all musical motifs in the film pointed to Irena. The motifs in the sequel are more varied in their signification and merit an overview.

When Amy wishes upon the ring, the wish she believes came true when Irena came to her, Roy Webb provides the cue "Amy's Wish." The cue begins with a musical motif recycled from *Cat People*, one Webb marked as "Irena" in his autograph score and the same melody heard at the opening of Webb's cue "First Quarrel" when the spotting sheet instructed him to provide a "happy mood over this." In *The Curse of the Cat People*, the motif marked "Irena" appears often; however, it rarely appears when Irena is in the scene. After it appears in the "Main Title," it sounds next in the film's opening scene when Amy calls the butterfly "my friend." The "Irena" motif next appears in the cue under discussion, "Amy's Wish." We hear it both when Amy lazily plays with her marionette bird, and when she wishes for a friend. Webb then deploys the tune when Amy plays with Irena in the garden in a cue Webb titled "My Friend." Webb uses it next at the film's climax just as Amy calls out for her friend and sees Irena superimposed over Barbara. And finally, Webb reiterates the "Irena" motif sweetly on the soundtrack as Oliver claims to see Irena in the garden even though he is only gazing upon Amy. In each case, Webb presents the "Irena" motif from *Cat People* when Amy finds or even believes she has found a friend. Here Webb shrewdly connects the sequel to the original through an interesting repurposing of one of the earlier film's important musical motifs. The meaning of "Irena" has fanned out and expanded to embrace all objects of Amy's friendly feelings, whether real or imaginary.

Returning to the cue "Amy's Wish," after the wish is stated, Webb reintroduces the lullaby "Do, do l'enfant do" used in *Cat People* as the signifier for both Irena's cursed origins and later as a marker of her deteriorating mental state. Here the lullaby is presented through a gentle orchestration of strings and flute and a stable harmonic treatment entirely in the major mode. The audience does not yet see Irena, but her presence on the soundtrack is unmistakable.

In the next scene, as Alice takes Amy to bed, Amy tries to sing the lullaby, claiming that her friend taught it to her. The scene where Amy finds the photograph of Irena (a moment where again Webb deploys the lullaby as a signifier of the real Irena) remains more than a reel away. This is no simple imaginary friend with a face discovered in a photograph. She has taught Amy her favorite lullaby long before Amy discovers her photograph.

Webb's most interesting presentation of the lullaby finds him again distorting it to reflect shifting psychological potentials. His distortion comes in the film's climax when Amy sees Irena in Barbara. At that point, Webb expands the major mode tune to a whole-tone tune as though Irena's role has expanded to clarify the potentiality of friendship even with the tragic Barbara. This subtle gesture, easily overlooked, typifies Webb's "special care" when working with Lewton.

Webb's score for *The Curse of the Cat People* lacks the singularity of focus he employed in *Cat People* where every cue and every motif concerned Irena. In the sequel, Webb provides music for other characters.

Amy has a new motif, one that ably captures her gentle nature. "In Good Night Amy," orchestrator Leonid Raab scores a melody Webb exclusively associates with Amy in solo violin. This "Amy" theme inevitably appears in solo instruments within Raab's orchestration, underscoring her fragility and bringing the audience into intimate rapport with her interiority as only solo instruments can.

Webb composed one other new motif for the film, one associated only with the melancholy daughter Barbara. The Barbara motif, always deployed in somber registers of the double reeds or violas, first enters Webb's score at Barbara's first appearance in the garden. Webb provides a lengthy presentation of it later in the cue "Imposter," as the delusional Mrs. Farren describes Barbara's death to Barbara. At the close of the scene in which Amy visits Mrs. Farren, we hear the Barbara theme in the cue "Herne, the Hunter" as Barbara pleads for recognition of her Christmas gift after Amy and Edward depart. The last and most melancholy appearance of the theme occurs near the film's close as Barbara, her mother now dead, descends the stairs of the house to the basement where she apparently sleeps.

A Melodramatic Close

Beyond motifs signifying characters, music importantly serves the fantastical in the film, whether highlighting moments of fantasy the audience shares with Amy or underscoring the flights of fancy undertaken by the film's adults. In the film's first cue, "Introducing Amy," we hear Webb's score reinforcing the skipping of the children through a mimetic rhythm, comically conjuring the alarming "Cat Theme" from *Cat People* as boys pretend to machine-gun a black cat in a tree, accompanying the diegetic singing of "Cobbler, Cobbler Mend My Shoe," illustrating Amy's daydream that spoils the game, connecting the "Irena" theme to the butterfly, and cutting out sharply when Donald kills the butterfly. All of these moments find Webb's music lavishing mimetic effort in illustrating these childish fancies and suddenly falling silent with the termination of one of them.

Examining Webb's tropes on musical topics of the unreal inevitably leads to Webb's cue "Magic Mailbox," which features ethereal major chords in first inversion deployed in high strings and unanchored to any harmonic syntax due to the lack of a bass line. In the cue "Haunted House," whole-tone scales in trills and tremolos present augmented chords using planing in an impressionistic whirl of musical fantasy. Rolled chords on the celesta appear in moments of childish wonder as in the cue "Farren House," as Amy explores the weird bric-a-brac shrouded in darkness within the house's parlor.

What all these fantasy topics referenced in Webb's score suggest is that the film's music strives to situate the audience in Amy's role. From a bland, adult perspective, there's no wonder to a knothole in a tree or the bric-a-brac accumulated in an elderly actress's home. The music here strives to suture the audience into rapport with Amy's wonder at these mundane things.

By way of wrapping up this examination of music in *The Curse of the Cat People*, I want to return to the melodrama embedded within it where Mrs. Farren tells a version of "The Legend of Sleepy Hollow." Webb's underscore offers a conventionally spooky musical accompaniment apparently geared to intensify one of the film's skimpy feints at horror. Like the image track's camera angle providing Amy's point of view, the music here is rather more importantly inviting the audience to share Amy's emotive response. Different music lacking in fantastical topics or no music would allow the audience to evaluate Mrs. Farren as storyteller from a detached, adult perspective. Webb's fantastical music invites the audience to hear the story as Amy.

Music throughout the film could be seen as a similar melodrama. The filmmakers tell us the story, and the RKO Music Department situates the audience in Amy's experience. Remember Amy's dream. The image track shows the bland truth of a child sleeping. The soundtrack vividly paints her unconscious thoughts. The inclusion of a melodrama, and the near inclusion of one more in "Herne the Hunter," renders the entire production in rapport with the aging art of melodrama. Amy and the audience become one in experiencing the film's imbedded melodrama, just as only we and Amy can see Irena in the garden.

None of Lewton's films is more musical than *The Curse of the Cat People*. Roy Webb produced more music for it than any other film in the series, and that is supplemented by singing children, a singing butler, and three carols. Randall Larson estimates that Webb's score occupies fifty-three minutes of the film's seventy-minute running time.[32] By contrast, Webb graced *Cat People* with barely twenty-five minutes of original underscore. In this way, *The Curse of the Cat People* comes closest to the art of melodrama among Lewton's films.

A film cannot allow its audience to become Amy even for the mere seventy minutes it takes for *The Curse of the Cat People* to unfold. But a film can invite sympathy and even empathy for others by providing a simulation of their experiences. By placing Amy at the center of both the film's image track and, I argue, more importantly its soundtrack, the Lewton unit invites its audience to enter into what critic James Agee called "the poetry and danger of childhood."[33] While not the stuff of generic horror, the danger of childhood marks *The Curse of the Cat People* as a special exemplar of the innovative approaches to cinematic storytelling emerging in Hollywood during the 1940s. Few films from that period did more to universalize a young girl's concerns by inviting its audience to share them.

Notes

1. Brian Eggert begins his essay on the film writing, "*The Curse of the Cat People* remains among the strangest Hollywood sequels ever made." Brian Eggert, "The

Definitives: Appreciations and Critical Essays about Great Films: *The Curse of the Cat People*," in *Deep Focus Review* (October 22, 2017).
2. Bosley Crowther, "The Screen," *The New York Times*, March 4, 1944.
3. David Bordwell draws this conclusion in *Reinventing Hollywood: How 1940s Filmmakers Changed Movie Storytelling* (Chicago: University of Chicago Press, 2017), pp. 366–368.
4. Joel Siegel, *Val Lewton: The Reality of Terror* (New York: Viking Press, 1973), p. 55.
5. Claudia Gorbman, *Unheard Melodies: Narrative Film Music* (Bloomington: University of Indiana Press, 1987), pp. 79–80.
6. For a chronological perspective, *The Curse of the Cat People* was first mentioned in trade papers on February 17, 1943 in *The Hollywood Reporter*. The earliest mention of "The Amorous Ghost" and "The Screaming Skull" was also in *The Hollywood Reporter*, on March 10, 1943. Less than a month after receiving his assignment, Lewton had the trades announcing two other projects.
7. Val Lewton, "The Amorous Ghost," treatment and unproduced screenplay, RKO Radio Pictures Studio Records (Collection PASC 3). UCLA Library Special Collections, Charles E. Young Research Library, University of California, Los Angeles.
8. In this author's opinion, "The Amorous Ghost" materials that exist are singularly unfunny, even bordering on terrible despite an interesting premise. RKO was wise to resist Lewton's efforts to move forward with this project.
9. Edmund Bansak, *Fearing the Dark: The Val Lewton Career* (Jefferson, NC: MacFarland & Company, 1995), pp. 203–204.
10. Siegel, p. 57.
11. A sixty-one-minute running time, fully ten of which are devoted to a retelling of the action from *The Mummy's Hand* (1940), makes *The Mummy's Tomb* the most relentlessly devoted to the ideal of repetition in sequels.
12. Bordwell, pp. 29–55.
13. Bansak, p. 205.
14. John Brosnan, *The Horror People* (London: St. Martin's Press, 1976), p. 81.
15. Siegel, p. 55.
16. Ibid., p. 136.
17. Val Lewton, "The Curse of the Cat People" script. Lewton Papers, Library of Congress, pp. 98–99.
18. DeWitt Bodeen, *The Curse of the Cat People* shooting script. RKO Radio Pictures Studio Records (Collection PASC 3). UCLA Library Special Collections, Charles E. Young Research Library, University of California, Los Angeles.
19. The film's initial director was a short-subject documentary specialist named Gunther von Fritsch. Lewton promoted him to direct his first feature on *The Curse of the Cat People*. When he fell far behind schedule for being afraid of making mistakes, Lewton tapped Robert Wise, who was editing the film, to direct. See Bruce Austin, "An Interview with Robert Wise," *Literature/Film Quarterly*, Volume 6, Number 4 (Fall, 1978), pp. 296–297.
20. James Agee, "*Curse of the Cat People*," *The Nation* (April 1, 1944).
21. James Agee, "Year in Review," *The Nation* (January 20, 1945).

22. After the film was shot, Lewton decided the ending was poor. He rewrote the ending to its current form. The original featured Irena intervening in the climax by opening and shutting doors to protect Amy from the bloodthirsty Barbara. Clearly Lewton toned down the horrific content.
23. David Bordwell, p. 367.
24. Ibid., p. 275.
25. Irwin Bazelon, *Knowing the Score: Notes on Film Music* (New York: Van Nostren Reinhold, 1975), p. 147.
26. Fantasy doesn't really function as a genre in anything like the way westerns, musicals, horror films, and war pictures do. They lack a centrifugal force and can readily embrace everything from *A Midsummer Night's Dream* (1935) to *The Wizard of Oz* (1939) to *Lady and the Tramp* (1955) to *The Seventh Voyage of Sinbad* (1958), films with no common internal or external elements other than the apparent presence of the impossible.
27. Correspondence from LACSA director to Val Lewton, RKO Radio Pictures Studio Records (Collection PASC 3). UCLA Library Special Collections, Charles E. Young Research Library, University of California, Los Angeles.
28. Siegel, pp. 58–59.
29. David Reisman, *The Lonely Crowd* (New Haven, CT: Yale University Press, 1950).
30. J. P. Telotte, *Dreams of Darkness: Fantasy and the Films of Val Lewton* (Urbana: University of Illinois Press, 1985), p. 113.
31. James Hillman, *Re-Visioning Psychology* (New York: Harper & Row, 1975), p. 23.
32. Randall Larson, "The Quiet Horror Music of Roy Webb: Scoring Val Lewton (The Robert Wise Films)," *Midnight Marquee*, Issue 44 (Summer, 1992), p. 31.
33. James Agee, *Agee on Film* (New York: Grosset & Dunlap, 1969), p. 137.

7 BORIS KARLOFF AND THE SOUNDTRACK OF *THE BODY SNATCHER*

Boris Karloff, Movie Star

Val Lewton's final three horror films would all star Boris Karloff. With the advent of a bona fide movie star associated closely with the Universal approach to horror into Lewton's hermetically sealed production unit, the understated approach to horror Lewton had so carefully crafted and the Sound and Music Departments at RKO had so ably adapted to serve was effectively finished. Karloff's presence in an understated depiction of modern America of the sort Lewton cultivated would be absurd. This chapter focuses on how Boris Karloff's presence transformed the style of the Lewton unit's films. His impact on all facets of the soundtrack receives the lion's share of our concern. Let's begin by examining how Lewton and Karloff came together before digging into the impact on Lewton's sonic style.

Genre film production benefits from cultivating bankable stars associated with the genre. While every genre has its stars, horror's most luminous figure during the 1930s and 1940s was Boris Karloff. From the moment he appeared in James Whale's *Frankenstein* (1931) wearing Jack Pierce's sensational make-up, staring at the camera with his doleful eyes as it approached him in a series of jarring jump cuts, Karloff became Hollywood's most bankable monster. The following year he appeared in featured roles in three more horror vehicles, two for Universal (*The Old Dark House* and *The Mummy*) and one for MGM (*The Mask of Fu Manchu*). By the end of the decade, Karloff had fifteen starring credits in horror films.

In January 1944, as Val Lewton embarked on producing his seventh horror film, Boris Karloff was back in Hollywood following more than a year on Broadway as Jonathan Brewster, the villain in Joseph Kesselring's play *Arsenic and Old Lace*, followed by sixty-six weeks touring with the play across the country. With no contract pending, Karloff was a free agent.

Universal Pictures wanted Karloff back badly. They signed him to a two-picture deal for US$5,000 per week for twelve weeks of work. The first film was an expensive Technicolor tale about a Svengali-like Karloff who aids, then courts, and finally menaces his operetta-star patient played by the bankable singer, Susanna Foster. The strange hybrid of musical and horror called *The Climax* (1944) featured too much singing for horror fans, too much menacing for musical fans, and failed to attract either in sufficient numbers.

His next film for Universal, *House of Frankenstein* (1944), marked Karloff's return to the Frankenstein franchise. He had starred as the sad-eyed Monster in the first three films, then missed out quite intentionally on the subsequent two, *The Ghost of Frankenstein* (1942) and *Frankenstein Meets the Wolf Man* (1943). Karloff did not don Pierce's monster make-up for *House of Frankenstein*, instead playing Dr. Niemann, a brilliant but evil scientist. *House of Frankenstein* was the third of Universal's "monster rallies" and featured not only the Frankenstein Monster (Glenn Strange) and Karloff's mad scientist, but also Count Dracula (John Carradine), the hapless Wolf Man (Lon Chaney, Jr.), and a homicidal hunchbacked assistant (J. Carroll Naish). Like its monsters, the music was almost entirely recycled from other horror films. The project depressed Karloff, who was in terrible back pain during the shoot and who had to perform his own climactic stunt by sinking into quicksand with the Frankenstein monster.[1] In an interview with the *Los Angeles Times*, Karloff dismissed *House of Frankenstein* as "a monster clambake . . . it was all too much."[2]

Enter Jack Gross

1943 had been RKO's most profitable year.[3] Uncharacteristically, the Lewton unit ended the year 1944 on a commercial losing streak. *The Curse of the Cat People* underwhelmed at the box office. Film studios often applied more creativity in their accounting than in their productions, so figures must be taken with a grain of salt, but the studio reported only a US$35,000 profit for *The Curse of the Cat People*.[4] For the first time, Lewton lost the luster of unbridled box office success.

Production of *The Curse of the Cat People* had cost Lewton dearly in political capital at the studio. Charles Koerner, the man who hired Lewton, had been promoted to chief of production, leaving the executive producer position for "B" units to Sid Rogell. Rogell and Lewton butted heads frequently during the protracted pre-production of *The Curse of the Cat People*. As Lewton dragged his feet, he won a series of concessions from Koerner while giving in to Rogell's general insistence that the sequel be made. Two of these concessions resulted in two non-horror films, *Mademoiselle Fifi* and *Youth Runs Wild*. Rogell especially detested Lewton producing the costume drama *Mademoiselle Fifi*. He worked to cut Lewton's budget at every turn.[5]

Both of Lewton's non-horror productions at RKO apparently lost money, at least that is what RKO's books claimed.[6] Place them on the heels of *The Curse of the Cat People*'s disappointing performance, and Lewton found himself in real trouble for the first time.

Having backed Lewton time and again in his confrontations with Sid Rogell, Charles Koerner knew he needed to make a change. He hired Jack Gross, associate producer of three magnificently profitable horror projects at Universal,[7] to executive produce "B" pictures and directly supervise Lewton. The "universalizing" of horror at RKO was on again with a vengeance.

Lewton was miserable. In a letter to his mother and sister dated August 20, 1944, after the release of *Mademoiselle Fifi* but eleven days before the release of *Youth Runs Wild*, Lewton complained about Jack Gross, whom Lewton referred to as "an abysmally ignorant and stupid gentleman." Lewton concluded his tirade about his new boss with a tribal flair: "Jack Gross is the man who has been making those Universal horror films and so had a particular grudge against me, as our pictures had shown up his films not only from an artistic viewpoint, but also from a standpoint of profits."[8]

Lewton surely believed that Jack Gross had a grudge against him, although the cited reasons smack of self-congratulation. What Jack Gross wanted more than anything was to produce hits for his new employer, RKO. He believed that, based on his strong track record with profitable horror productions at Universal, the RKO horror product needed to look and feel like Universal's hits. To achieve this end, and to stick it to his former employer, Gross signed Boris Karloff, now lurking in Hollywood with no contract, to a two-picture deal. Lewton was consulted as a courtesy, and his expression of profound objection to this move was courteously ignored.[9] Karloff would receive US$6,000 a week with a guarantee of five weeks' work per film. His presence in *The Body Snatcher* saw the budget of the picture rise to US$194,608 with US$30,000 going to the star.[10] Suddenly Lewton was producing "B+" pictures for RKO and the stakes rose enormously that he produce a hit.

Shooting on *House of Frankenstein* ended on May 8, 1944, with Boris Karloff surely wondering if there were any better showcases for his talents out there. Ten days later, he paid a visit to Val Lewton at RKO Studios to discuss the projects that might stem from a two-picture deal. Unbeknownst to Karloff, Val Lewton never wanted this meeting.[11] The meeting was a formality. Karloff had already been signed to star in Lewton's next two films over the producer's objections. Fortunately for all concerned, the meeting went beautifully. According to Robert Wise, Karloff charmed everyone with his genial ways.[12] Lewton quickly forgot his objections to working with Universal's former horror star.

Rewriting Robert Louis Stevenson

Lewton began the work of sorting out vehicles suitable to Boris Karloff's formidable talents as a character actor in mid-May 1944. Lewton's first idea concerned an expansive meditation on Arnold Böcklin's 1880 painting *Isle of the Dead*. That film went into production prior to *The Body Snatcher*, but the shoot had to shut down owing to Karloff's back pain flaring up.[13] *The Body Snatcher* wrapped first and reached theaters first, so the film *Isle of the Dead* must wait until the next chapter.

For the story of *The Body Snatcher*, Lewton turned to Robert Louis Stevenson's short story of the same name published in 1884.[14] Lewton rewrote Stevenson considerably, inventing several characters and radically altering the temperament and function of others. In Stevenson's story, both Fettes and MacFarlane were students under the infamous historical figure Dr. Knox, who purchased the bodies of murder victims from the murderers to serve the needs of his medical students in 1828 Edinburgh. Gray is a minor character in the story. Gray appears to know something about MacFarlane's crimes and threatens the man with blackmail until MacFarlane murders Gray. Fettes and MacFarlane then dissect Gray's body for Knox's use. But later, when out robbing a remote grave to supply their teacher with a subject, MacFarlane and Fettes unearth Gray. Stevenson's tale serves as a fine little ghost story. While the ending remains recognizable, the film departs radically from Stevenson's original.

First Lewton cleverly changed the timing of events. Stevenson's story features the historical figure of Dr. Knox not as a character per se, but as the current employer and teacher of both Fettes and MacFarlane. The film takes place after Dr. Knox's scandal led to his departure from Edinburgh. MacFarlane (Henry Daniell) is not a medical student, but a doctor who is both teacher and employer to Fettes (Russell Wade). MacFarlane takes on Dr. Knox's position. This allows the film to use the historical experiences of both Dr. Knox, now "living in London like a gentleman," and the figures of William Burke and William Hare, the grave robbers for Knox who cut corners by murdering their victims. Hare gave testimony against Burke and received immunity. Burke eventually confessed to sixteen murders before he was hanged in 1829. Hare was escorted out of Scotland by authorities after mobs assembled to kill him first in Edinburgh and later in Dumfries. The disparate fates of the doctor who requested the crimes and the criminals who executed them afford Lewton a chance to comment on class disparities in the film.

Cabman Gray enters Stevenson's story only briefly, but Lewton expanded his role, clarifying his threat to MacFarlane and bestowing upon him a wealth of menacing and often amusing dialogue. Gray (Boris Karloff) also serves as Lewton's mouthpiece for the class critique within the film. He relishes tormenting Dr. MacFarlane by continually drawing attention to their ironic class disparity given that Gray could ruin MacFarlane by speaking to the authorities. Gray does not stop at holding the upper-class MacFarlane in contempt; he also justifies his own crimes as the product of an unfair economic order.[15]

Fettes differs even more notably in the film. In the story he is fully culpable in the criminality associated with grave robbing and murder. He is also a drunken lout, and not the kindly and promising medical student of the film who falls in love with the widow Marsh (Rita Corday), whose injured daughter Georgina (Sharyn Moffett) he strives to aid. The original story includes neither Mrs. Marsh nor any Georgina. Just as Hollywood had to invent the female characters in Stevenson's *Dr. Jekyll and Mr. Hyde*, Lewton had to do the same with *The Body Snatcher*.

The character of the janitor, Joseph, was concocted for the film to suit the presence of actor Bela Lugosi. Strangely, Lugosi's involvement appears to have been Lewton's idea. The actor was on the RKO lot shooting a spoof of *I Walked with a Zombie* titled *Zombies on Broadway* when Lewton wrote a memo to Jack Gross about choosing Stevenson's "The Body-Snatcher" for Karloff. The memo ends with the rationale that, "there is an excellent part for Lugosi as a resurrection man."[16] Lewton fought against hiring Karloff, but having lost, he now wanted Lugosi too. The challenge RKO intended to Universal's horror supremacy was on.

Lewton's rewrites also multiplied the minimal horrors of Stevenson's tale. To be sure, the thrilling conclusion, albeit now a hallucination rather than a supernatural manifestation, remains. Lewton's script adds numerous grisly scenes. Some made it into the final film; like the murder of the street singer (Donna Lee) and the murder and subsequent discovery of Joseph in a pool of brine. Cut from the film was Lewton's opening horror of elderly Mrs. McBride (Mary Gordon) pitifully searching through dissected bodies to find the remains of her son. Joseph Breen objected to Lewton's screenplay so strenuously that he declared it "unacceptable."[17]

Lewton had always shied away from horrors of the sort liberally deployed in his rewrite of Stevenson. Clearly the presence of Boris Karloff mattered to him. He wanted to outdo Universal's horror cycle in the thing that most differentiated his films from theirs, at least in his own mind. His labors at compounding horrors drove his screenwriter, Philip MacDonald, who feared the film would add to Lewton's box office losing streak, to ask the producer who had done such extensive rewrites to take screen credit and share the blame.[18] Lewton obliged, although he used his favorite pseudonym, Carlos Keith.

Karloff's Impact on Lewton's Reforms

None of the distinguished authors and documentarians who have provided overviews of Lewton's career highlights the hiring of Boris Karloff as an important disjunction in Lewton's output. Auteurist in sensibility, the literature on Lewton emphasizes the absence of explicit monsters in his horror films, the stylish use of shadow in the films, and the privileged place uncertainty gains through those shadows. In those areas, continuity in style exists to some extent from the first six films to the last three.

James Agee, Lewton's devoted champion, noticed the stylistic disjunction at the time, although he did not identify the source as Karloff. In his review of the third and final Lewton-Karloff collaboration, *Bedlam*, Agee offered this concern over Lewton's shift to period pieces: "I regret and somewhat fear Lewton's recent interest in costume movies, which seem to draw on his romantic-literary weaknesses more than on his best abilities, which are poetic and cinematic."[19]

Examining films from a new perspective, in this case primarily through their music, ideally yields a changed understanding. In this case, the music points toward a substantially different understanding of the stylistic continuity of the Lewton horror films. The last three, all starring Boris Karloff, find the star's presence necessitating widespread stylistic upheaval touching far more than the music. As the studios' promotion of stars figures prominently in genre histories, and indeed in the history of Hollywood under the studio system, Boris Karloff's arrival at RKO touched all phases of the productions. Consider these stylistic upheavals between Lewton's early output and the three Karloff vehicles.

The presence of considerable overt violence in *The Body Snatcher* cited above marks the first stylistic transformation. The film features three violent onscreen deaths (Joseph, Gray, and MacFarlane) and a very disturbing death only heard and not seen (the street singer).

Lewton prided himself on situating his approach to horror in realistic contemporary settings in order to bring the horror into the lives of the modern American audience. In addition to the early films' modern timeframe, with the exception of *I Walked with a Zombie*, they are all set within the United States. The shift from the realistic and domestic present to the foreign past changes many aspects of the image track. Costumes, sets, and props all change the look of the films.

Another consequence of Boris Karloff's star power joining Lewton's productions is a notable shift away from female-centered films to male-centered narratives. With the exception of *The Ghost Ship*, the earlier Lewton productions revolve around women. *Cat People*'s Irena, *I Walked with a Zombie*'s Betsy, the female victims in *The Leopard Man*'s victim-centered narrative, Mary and Jacqueline in *The Seventh Victim*, and Amy in *The Curse of the Cat People* provide a string of female leads the likes of which one Hollywood producer rarely provided in a single series, especially a horror series. While Lewton added the roles of Mrs. Marsh, Georgina, and MacFarlane's secret wife, Meg (Edith Atwater), to the story, the film is a showcase for its men. MacFarlane enjoys the most screen time, Gray has the best dialogue and plenty of it, and Fettes is the film's mild-mannered protagonist. With music so closely associated with the feminine in film, this change would yield important differences in how Roy Webb approached scoring this film, differences to be dissected below.

In terms of Lewton's reforming of the horror genre through stylistic intervention, much of that was abandoned for *The Body Snatcher*. The horror is explicit. A Grand Guignol sensibility emerges in the film that suits the presence of Boris Karloff to a tee but distances the film from its predecessors in the series. This is not a source of regret to this author, only an observation relevant to a discussion of music within the film, music which must perform distinct functions, distancing it from the task of interpreting the film as happens in *Cat People* or painting its subtexts as in *The Seventh Victim*.

Scoring a Boris Karloff Horror Vehicle

Roy Webb's orchestral underscore for *The Body Snatcher* differs in function and to some extent in style from the previous six films for Val Lewton. To demonstrate this point, Claudia Gorbman's seminal discussion of her seven principles governing "Classical Film Music" offers a useful framework for comparison. Sufficiently famous, I will quote only her fourth principle.

> IV. *Narrative Cueing*:
> – *referential/narrative*: music gives referential and narrative cues, e.g. indicating point of view, supplying formal demarcations, and establishing setting and character.
> – *connotative*: music 'interprets' and 'illustrates' narrative events.[20]

In examining Roy Webb's underscore for the first six horror films produced by the Lewton unit, the bulk of my attention has gone toward the principle of Narrative Cueing and specifically to its connotative function. In the earlier films, the connotative principle governed Webb's overall compositional approach. His music ushered the audience into the melancholy interiority of Irena in *Cat People*, fractured the monologic of Western/Colonial Reason in *I Walked with a Zombie*, offered penance for profiting on horror in *The Leopard Man*, painted the indignities of mortality in *The Seventh Victim*, distracted from the moral courage authoritarianism demands from its opponents in *The Ghost Ship*, and vivified the fantastic inner life of a child in *The Curse of the Cat People*.

Webb's score for *The Body Snatcher* forces a shift in emphasis almost exclusively to Gorbman's referential/narrative principle. Here the presence of a horror star and all the stylistic differences necessitated by his presence impacted Webb's work. With few exceptions, Webb's score for the film, and the diegetic music within the film, serve to either stretch the film's meager budget by generating a sense of time and place for the audience or intensifying scenes of overt violence that were largely absent in the earlier films.

Edinburgh, Scotland, 1831

The shift from the domestic present to the foreign past placed a familiar burden on RKO's Art Department. They had to craft a faraway time and place on a shoestring budget. Roy Webb's writings on film scoring indicate that he first and foremost looked to see what the production needed him to do.[21] In this case, he needed to produce music that assisted the Art Department in transporting the audience to Edinburgh, Scotland, in 1831. To accomplish the task, Webb littered his score with quotations of Scottish folksongs while the film's narrative found Scottish folksongs sung frequently within the diegesis. In his remarkable discussion of ethnic signposts in Hollywood films, K. J. Donnelly rightly points out that "the use of music to provide conventional ethnic associations is unremarkable, yet powerful."[22] He further argues that Scotland and Ireland require musical signposts of ethnicity in an American-made film, while America does not. He compares an American use of a musical signpost for Scotland to establishing shots. He may as well be describing the opening of *The Body Snatcher*.

These folksong quotations could be seen as a Scottish "topic" even though one of these folksongs is actually an English parlor song. Here all the criticisms of colonialism in film music cited by James Buhler might prove useful in an alternate reading of the film's soundtrack.[23] In defense of Webb and the film's diegetic music, the film itself does not appear nearly so dangerous to Scottish agency as Hollywood's more common use of national and ethnic "topics," which is not the same as saying the film transcends such a critique.

The opening of the film illustrates the efforts of Webb and the Music Department to aid the image track in leading the American audience back in time and far away. The film's shooting script opens with instructions that the main and title credits are to appear superimposed "on a mezzotint of Edinburgh castle viewed from the Causeway."[24] Using a still image in the form of a mezzotint was certainly an inexpensive initial image. Next the shooting script calls for a dissolve to stock footage of the castle, again, a low-cost solution establishing the action in Edinburgh. While the script asks for this second image to come to life, it doesn't. Instead, stock footage of sheep being herded in front of the castle appears. From there the shooting script moves to images of Gray's cab rolling past Greyfriar's kirkyard. But the film parts ways with the script at this point and cuts to the street singer (Donna Lee) receiving alms from a man bearing a shepherd's crook. Then we see two stock shots of sheep before rejoining the shooting script for an establishing shot of Greyfriar's kirkyard. That the street singer does not sing at this point in the script, but does in the film, suggests that the filmmakers expanded her role during the shoot. RKO records show that actress Donna Lee joined Val Lewton, Robert Wise, and Roy Webb for an additional day's shooting and another day in a recording studio after the film had wrapped.[25]

The music during the main titles and in the first moments of the film drips with Scottish folksongs. After a melodically uncertain opening in F minor, Webb arranges a Scottish tune he identified throughout his score as "Edinburgh." This tune, with its characteristically Scottish "snap" rhythms, reappears frequently throughout the film to come, making its prominence in the Main Title cue typical and reinforcing Donnelly's point that these musical ethnic signifiers function like an establishing shot. As the Main Title cue elides into the film's opening, and the static images of Edinburgh Castle and the Castle Rock give way to sheep being herded, Webb deploys a snatch of the Scottish folksong called "The Caledonian Hunts Delight" made popular in the late eighteenth century when Robert Burns wrote his poem "Ye Banks and Braes" to be sung to it.

The first image shot for the film features a lad with a drum marching with a soldier in kilt and bearskin, the regalia of the Royal Scots Guards. His drumming rather efficiently reinforces the title card "Edinburgh 1831" seen moments before for transporting the audience through a bygone sound.

Eventually sharing the soundtrack with the drum is the voice of the street singer giving throat to the song "We'd Better Bide a Wee." This song is not a true Scottish folksong, although many Scottish musicians have adopted it, and its presence in the film's diegesis constitutes the sort of anachronism Lewton strived to avoid. Both words and music were originally written by Charlotte Alington Barnard, an Englishwoman who lived from 1830–1869 and insufficiently precocious to have composed it in her first year. She published it in 1859 under the pseudonym Claribel. Disappointingly, Lewton's ersatz Scotland was established using an ersatz Scottish tune. Webb's orchestra eventually joins the street singer with a sweet accompaniment, lodging the film's opening in rapport with the logic governing the soundtracks of musicals.

By uniting the nondiegetic underscore with the singer in the diegesis and a "Scottish" topic, Webb's orchestra becomes more prominent for straddling the boundary of diegetic sound and nondiegetic sound. This moment gestures toward Ben Winters's work on the soundtrack in which he argues that framing film music as nondiegetic makes little sense. He writes:

> It is not whether or not the character can 'hear' the music that dictates whether the music is part of the fictional world . . . but whether the

music appears to exist in the time and narrative space of the diegesis, or whether it appears to 'narrate' at a temporal distance from that space.[26]

Illustrating Winters's point, the music here clearly exists "in the time and narrative space of the diegesis" for uniting underscore with onscreen singing.

This decision to accompany the street singer in this way connects the street singer intimately with the film's orchestral underscore. Her relationship with the orchestral music on the soundtrack differs from that of any other character. Why? Perhaps the answer exists within the narrative itself. Fettes identifies her as a Highlander and elsewhere in the film Meg also identifies as a Highlander. Meg possesses "the second sight" and prophesies the events of the film with keen accuracy. Her talent is something unknown to Fettes and all other Lowland Scots. Similarly, the street singer seems otherworldly, a person apart from her surroundings, which she knows differently for being blind. Fettes asks her for directions to Gray's home, but she never breaks her song, simply shaking her head "no." That she should enjoy an intimacy with the orchestral underscore lends her a measure of the magical the film bestows on its women from the Highlands. The orchestral underscore has not so much joined her song as she has joined the orchestral underscore, a being almost yet not quite apart from the film's fictional world using Winters' approach, and capable of drawing Webb's score into the time and place of the film.

The street singer's next song, "When Ye Gang Awa, Jamie" occurs as Fettes searches for Gray to order a fresh subject for MacFarlane. Here Webb's orchestra joins the singer as she nears the song's conclusion. Webb wrote accompaniments for the street singer's next two performances as well, but neither found its way into the film. As Fettes departs Gray's home, we hear the street singer performing "Will He Nah Come Back Again" offscreen and without the orchestra. Gray's thoughtful look and his dialogue to his horse about going out again clearly indicate his plan to murder the street singer and clarify that he can hear this music of invisible source.

The subsequent murder sequence ranks among the best in the RKO horror series. That Webb's underscore was cut from the scene is grounds for celebration, as the soundtrack is exquisite at this point in the film. As the street singer returns to "When Ye Gang Awa Jamie," Gray follows her in his cab. Both proceed up the otherwise vacant street and out of view. The clopping of Gray's horse halts, and soon after, as she reaches the top note of the song, her song abruptly stops as a hand cups over her mouth. One important continuity in style between the early Lewton output and *The Body Snatcher* remains the inventive use of sound to suggest scenes of horror.

Despite her death, the street singer's voice will return to the soundtrack. In the cue immediately after her murder, "The Second Body," Webb provides a faint echo of the tune "When Ye Gang Awa Jamie" in violins as Gray dumps the street singer's body onto a table with Fettes standing by. Later, as Fettes and MacFarlane discuss what to do now that Fettes has become party to a murder for having requested a subject from Gray, the street singer's voice, distorted slightly to sound ghostly, merges on the soundtrack with the opening of Webb's substantial cue "The Child's Operation" as a dissonant chord (pitch classes E-flat, B-flat, F, and B natural) thrums beneath the haunting voice.

K. J. Donnelly has argued that music on film soundtracks resembles ghosts by constituting "a repository of reminders, half-memories and outbursts of emotion and the illogical . . . these 'ghosts' and 'memories' that can haunt a film."[27] In this particular case, Donnelly's figurative description of film music becomes literal as a dead voice joins the film's music. Neither MacFarlane nor Fettes indicates that he hears the voice. It has become ghostly nondiegetic film music of the sort elegantly theorized by Donnelly.

This moment of sonic brilliance allows music to haunt the guilty conscience of Fettes whose interiority the music clearly serves at this point. But it also anticipates the film's climax when MacFarlane's guilty conscience prompts him to hear the dead Gray's voice first calling out "Toddy" (Gray's mocking nickname for MacFarlane) and later repeating the rhythmic phrase "never get rid of me" in concert with Webb's music and the rhythmic hoofbeats of MacFarlane's horse. In a ghost story in which the climax involves the return of a corpse, the street singer's voice in this scene serves multiple purposes, looking simultaneously back as a pique to Fettes's conscience and forward to Gray's voice haunting MacFarlane during the film's climax.

Identifying a rationale for choosing folksongs for the film proves difficult. In the case of "When Ye Gang Awa Jamie," a rationale presents itself. The choice of song is odd insofar as the text offers a courtship song in dialogue. The first stanzas clarify this as the text allocates dialogue to both Jamie, the lad set to move abroad, and Jeanie, the lass who wants to go with him.

> Jeanie:
> When ye gang awa, Jamie
> Far across the sea, laddie,
> When ye gang to Germanie,
> What will you send to me, laddie?
>
> Jamie:
> I'll send ye a braw new gown, Jeanie,
> I'll send ye a braw new gown, lassie,
> And it shall be o' silk and gowd,
> Wi' Valenciennes set round, lassie.

Jeanie:
That's nae gift ava, Jamie,
That's nae gift ava, laddie,
There's ne'er a gown in a' the land,
I'd like when ye're awa, laddie.

Jamie:
When I come back again, Jeanie,
When I come back again, lassie,
I'll bring wi' me o' gallant gay,
To be your ain gude man, lassie.

Jeanie:
Be my gudeman yoursel', Jamie,
Be my gudeman yoursel', laddie,
And take me ower to Germanie,
Wi' you at hame to dwell, laddie.[28]

The text offers no specific commentary on the action of the film; however, the fact that the song includes two people speaking yet sharing a single voice suggests that the street singer embodies two people as she sings this selection during her murder. The idea of two people inhabiting a single body is a recurring theme in the narrative.[29] Gray references this condition whenever he threatens MacFarlane. When two men share knowledge of a capital crime and one has lied for the other as Gray has for MacFarlane in the trial of William Burke, they share a common body, or so Gray's logic unfolds. With the death of the street singer, Gray places Fettes in his debt, a debt that unites their bodies for sharing knowledge of another capital crime. The text may not comment on the action, but its genre as a ballad for two lovers does by illustrating the unification of two persons in one.

Folksongs appear on the soundtrack at too many other points in the narrative to comment on all of them. Most serve the referential/narrative principle by assisting the image track in locating the film in a specific time and place. These include a carefully researched "Spit Song" sung by a "spit boy" (Jack Welch) in Hobbs Public House,[30] a song about Burke and Hare sung by Gray for Joseph, a spirited rendition of "Bonnets of Bonnie Dundee" sung at the Inn of the Fisherman's Tryst (a song interrupted when mourners enter), and numerous restatements of "Edinburgh" in Webb's score.

Yet with the selection of "When Ye Gang Awa, Jamie," the diegetic music exceeds the simple function of establishing time and place by adding luster to the film's theme of shared bodies. The song also happens to feature a long-held top note, perfect for interruption by Gray's cupped hand when he kills the singer.

Scoring the Grand Guignol

Webb's other key task in composing for *The Body Snatcher* involved intensifying the impact of scenes of suspense as well as those of actual violence. Webb acknowledged this later duty in his naming of cues. The film sees four bodies delivered to Dr. MacFarlane's school and another in transit as the film ends. For each of these five bodies, Webb provided a cue named as follows: "The First Body" (Gray delivers Mrs. McBride's son to MacFarlane), "The Second Body" (largely cut from the film, it offers an orchestral accompaniment for the street singer immediately prior to her murder), "Third Body" (Gray delivers Joseph's corpse to MacFarlane's home), "Fourth Body" (MacFarlane shows Fettes Gray's body), and "Last Body" (accompanies the film's horrific climax, the body belonging to an elderly woman).

The first indication in the score that something dreadful may unfold in this film occurs quite early in a cue innocuously titled "Introducing Meg" (Figure 7.1, "Introducing Meg"). Meg plays a dual role in the film as Dr. MacFarlane's housekeeper and secret wife, whom he dares not acknowledge for the sake of his standing in the community. Meg is a Highlander of low birth, and MacFarlane is clearly ashamed of loving her. The audience meets her before MacFarlane when Gray, performing half of his dual role of cabman and body snatcher, delivers the Marshes to MacFarlane's door. After a scene demonstrating Gray's thoughtfulness for the poor crippled Georgina, Mrs. Marsh raps at the door, and Meg opens it. Here Webb's cue "Introducing Meg" begins. A sinister chord (B-flat major with added sixth in first inversion over a B natural pedal) appears. A clarinet presents an atonal melody comprised of three interlocking 0-1-4 sets that descend as Gray looks guiltily at Meg. Clearly the music communicates that not all is as it seems at Dr. MacFarlane's door or with the kindly cabman.

Such moments of musical suspense in which a dissonant simultaneity grinds beneath an atonal melody pepper Webb's scores starting with *Stranger on the Third Floor* and continuing throughout the Lewton series and into his scores for RKO's films noirs. The only unusual element here is the absence of a larger connotative field at work. The descending melody in the clarinet is not a recurring motif in the score but a singular event designed to provide a suspenseful amplification of Gray's and Meg's guilty looks.

Webb composed no music that could reasonably be described as a motif, or leitmotif for that matter, with a stable connotative function for *The Body Snatcher*. While his earlier scores for Lewton offered liberal motifs with sharply defined functions, this score differs. The dual function of stretching the budget by suturing the audience to Edinburgh and intensifying action prevail through much of the film's underscore. The result is a greater presence of procedures typical of the genre.

Figure 7.1 Roy Webb, "Introducing Meg" from *The Body Snatcher*, mm. 15–27

One convention of suspenseful scores honored interestingly in Webb's score for *The Body Snatcher* concerns the presentation of stingers. These clichés of horror film scores are in notably short supply in the prior six horror films Lewton produced. The "bus" technique from *Cat People* whereby a sudden sound effect reinforces a sudden appearance on the screen supplanted the underscore stinger in the first six films. The instant Gray appears at MacFarlane's alley door delivering the corpse of Mrs. McBride's son robbed from its grave, Webb deploys a fine stinger in the form of two chords in iambic rhythm in his cue "First Body."

The next stinger occurs several reels later in Webb's cue "Danger Ahead." As Gray returns to his home at night, he lights a candle. Its illumination reveals a sour-looking MacFarlane seated in the corner waiting for a confrontation. The stinger occurs precisely as MacFarlane appears. The stinger itself is a heavily

Figure 7.2 Roy Webb, "Danger Ahead" from *The Body Snatcher*, m. 71

accented chord with a chromatic descent from B to B-flat in the uppermost voice (Figure 7.2, "Danger Ahead," m. 71). By deploying stingers, a standard practice in horror films, when both Gray and MacFarlane appear to one another, Webb draws subtle attention to their connectedness in the story. MacFarlane is every bit as much a "threat" in the film as Gray is, to use Andrew Tudor's parlance.

The loudest and most important stinger in Webb's score arrives predictably at the moment when the audience joins MacFarlane in his hallucination that Gray's body occupies the shroud in the carriage. MacFarlane insists that the body has changed. He demands that Fettes aims the carriage's lamp at the face of the corpse. A point-of-view shot looks down at Gray's face as flashes of lightning provide a macabre complement to the bright lamplight. Webb's score offers a terrific double hit that begins with a pedal A-flat in a timpani roll with low brass and strings marked "sfff" on beat one followed on beat two by a loud chord deployed throughout the orchestra including a large brass section. The chord compounds elements from a conventional horror topic by stacking a half-diminished F# seven chord over an A diminished chord over the lingering A-flat pedal heard on beat one, six pitch classes in all (Figure 7.3, "End Title," mm. 1–12). The result is a moment of visual and sonic terror worthy of the Grand Guignol.

In addition to generic conventions such as gloomy suspense reinforced with atonal materials, diminished harmonies, and dissonant stingers on unexpected appearances, Webb uses more partial chromatic scales in this score than all the others combined. Three scenes feature important physical struggles: Gray "Burking" Joseph, MacFarlane and Gray battling on the floor of Gray's house, and MacFarlane struggling with Gray's apparition in the carriage. All of them find generous use of partial chromatic scales often in ostinato patterns but always to intensify the action on the screen.

Figure 7.3 Roy Webb, "End Title" from *The Body Snatcher*, mm. 1–12

From a purely musical standpoint, I admire the cue supporting Gray's murder of Joseph the most, although all of them are effective. It features many fragmentary chromatic scales as the image of Gray reaching toward Joseph's drunken face with his outstretched hand opens the cue titled "Gray Kills Joseph." Webb anticipates rather than "mickey-mouses" Joseph's collapse to the floor with a huge chord in rapid downward glissando followed by a more energetic and spasmodic rhythm as Joseph struggles to breathe. Urgent three-note tone clusters on beat one followed by spasmodic partial chromatic scales on beat four of a 4/4 pattern follow in one of Webb's most vigorous and musically varied agitatos for any film he scored (Figure 7.4, "Gray Kills Joseph").

While Webb's score for *The Body Snatcher* does not analyze the film nor paint its subtexts consistently, it effectively supports the film's narrative. Returning to Gorbman's principles of "Classical Film Music," the connotative principle is not higher than the "referential/narrative" principle. Much as the film differs in style from the earlier Lewton output for accommodating the

Figure 7.4 Roy Webb, "Gray Kills Joseph" from *The Body Snatcher*, mm. 61–84

Figure 7.4 (*continued*)

presence of a movie star in Boris Karloff, so does its music by serving the needs of a period horror drama rife with explicit violence.

Rewriting Val Lewton

Next we might profitably examine other facets of the soundtrack upon which Karloff exerted some influence. The first involves his efforts to rewrite dialogue in the films in which he starred for Lewton.

In 1944, as Karloff began work with Lewton, he had become disillusioned with Hollywood. The quality of his roles had deteriorated notably after 1935 or certainly after 1936. The role of the Frankenstein Monster in *The Bride of Frankenstein* (1935) had been lively. The Monster has an agenda, he wants a friend, and later he specifically wants a female friend. He has also learned to talk since the first film and engages in scenes both comical and poignant including his famous visit to the blind hermit (O. P. Heggie). *Son of Frankenstein* (1939), by contrast, finds the Monster reduced in importance, serving as muscle for Ygor (Bela Lugosi) as he pursues an agenda of revenge. The Monster has lost all agency. The comical scenes all belong to Ygor, and the poignancy is reduced to a brief, wordless scene involving the Monster examining his own reflection.

Karloff's various roles as mad doctors dominated the period. In all, Karloff had played fifteen doctors displaying varying degrees of madness between 1936 and 1944. These roles range from the altruistic (Dr. Garth in 1940's *Before I Hang*) to the megalomaniacal (Dr. Janos Rukh in 1936's *The Invisible Ray*) to the entirely befuddled (Dr. Ernst Sovac in 1940's *Black Friday*). To some viewers Karloff appears bored in many of them.

Boris Karloff found his work with the Lewton unit energizing. Louis Berg of the *Los Angeles Times* interviewed Karloff in 1946 and summarized the actor's feelings about his career and his work with Lewton in an article titled "Farewell to Monsters," writing: "Mr. Karloff has great love and respect for Mr. Lewton as the man who rescued him from the living dead and restored, so to speak, his soul."[31]

Contemporaneous evidence for Karloff's energized state can be seen in his collection of scripts for the three films he made with Lewton.[32] In them, he made copious notes including dozens of suggestions for changes in the dialogue, not only for his character, but even for scenes in which he did not appear. Karloff collated some of his notes in typed pages, which are tucked into the scripts he donated to the University of Southern California Library.

By way of illustrating how the star modified the film's dialogue, here are a few examples of changes from *The Body Snatcher* that made it into the final film, and a few that did not. The script Karloff annotated is marked "Final 10/16/44." But this is not in any sense the final script issued prior to shooting. Another script dated October 23, 1944 and containing at least a dozen of Karloff's marginal amendments was issued by RKO.

Karloff's first changes involve a thorough rewrite of his opening scene with Georgina. The dialogue he delivered in the film is recorded in his handwriting in the margins of a much longer scene originally written by MacDonald.[33]

More efficient for documentation here are Karloff's smaller amendments to some of his later dialogue. For example, the brief speech beginning with, "Look at yourself, Toddy. Could you be a doctor [Karloff here inserts "a healing man"] with the things those eyes have seen? There's a look of knowing [Karloff crossed out "knowing" and wrote "knowledge"] in those eyes but there's no kindness" [Karloff crossed out "kindness" and substituted "understanding"].[34]

In Robert Wise's shooting script dated October 25, 1944, all of Karloff's handwritten amendments to this speech and many others are included.[35]

While Karloff rewrote many other lines and speeches leading to amendments to the script itself and therefore the finished film, some of his suggestions made no impact. On page 19 he writes a note questioning the logic of Gray's line, "You're the new assistant." Karloff muses, "What happened to the old one?"[36] The film never answers this reasonable question. On page 44 of his script, he writes a note to suggest that Lewton change the word "kirkyard" to "churchyard."[37] Kirkyard remained.

Karloff also donated a very early copy of the script to the University of Southern California. That one is marked with "July 20, 1944 REVISED FIRST DRAFT CONTINUITY."[38] This script differs from the finished film quite dramatically. In this early copy of the screenplay, Karloff's annotations deal less in improving individual lines of dialogue and more with his perception of the flaws in the story's larger structure. This early draft opens with a long scene between the Marshes and Mrs. MacBride in which we learn that Mrs. MacBride was Georgina's mother's nanny. Later Gray nearly runs over Jamie's wee doggie, Robbie, with his cab. This rigmarole drags on for eight pages. On page 11 Karloff wrote his first marginalia: "Too much Ann [Mrs. Marsh] and Georgianna?"[39] Whether he shared this criticism with Lewton or MacDonald, we cannot say, but subsequent rewrites ditched all of this material.

Karloff's marginalia supports the thesis of this chapter, that Boris Karloff's presence in Lewton's last three horror films made an important impact on the soundtrack leading to a stylistic disjunction. The actor literally rewrote a significant portion of the dialogue.

Karloff's Voice

Stan Link, in a foundational text on music in horror films, concludes his discussion with an overview of how voices serve the genre.[40] While his examples all post-date *The Exorcist* (1973), his point in concluding a chapter on horror film music with a meditation on the voice is well taken and informs all that follows.

As for Boris Karloff's direct impact on the music of the film, we have his musical voice. Easily mimicked for his accent, his lisp, his musical line readings full of carefully measured hesitations and emphases, Karloff's voice was perhaps more clearly a marker of the horror genre than his face, which was so frequently pasted over with make-up.

At one point, Karloff deploys his tuneful voice to sing in *The Body Snatcher*. As he explains the resurrection business to Joseph, Gray makes a reference to William Burke. Joseph, a recent émigré to Edinburgh by way of Lisbon, fails to apprehend the reference. To clarify, Gray sings lyrics first published in 1829 as a broadsheet titled *Alas! Jamie's Pickled: Elegiac Lines on the Tragical Murder of Poor Daft Jamie*.[41] The screenplay does not acknowledge this source and offers a much-edited version of the poem.

In Karloff's copy of the screenplay next to the text of the song, the actor wrote "Cheers, my laddies." Clearly, he is reminding himself what tune to use when singing these broadsheet lyrics. The published version of the broadsheet indicates no suggested tune or tunes. Oddly, no musical material concerning this song appears within RKO's Music Department files while "The Spit Song" is there. This may indicate a degree of independence on Karloff's part in choosing a tune suitable to his talents and fitting the simple poetic rhythm of the broadsheet lyrics.

Every bit as important as Karloff's singing voice to the film is the musical nature of his speaking voice. Claudia Gorbman has discussed the recognizable voices of several movie stars. While Boris Karloff did not enter into her discussion, he fits her description and invites application of the same attention she grants Philip Seymour Hoffman's performance in *The Master* to Boris Karloff in *The Body Snatcher*.[42] The film takes full advantage of Karloff's stylized and musical line deliveries. For example, his unceasing mockery through tuneful utterances of his nickname "Toddy" provides an aural hallucination as MacFarlane drives his carriage through the storm. An actor less inclined to milk the music out of his dialogue would not set up this hallucination half so well.

Even more musical than the ghostly "Toddy" is the rhythm of Karloff's reading of the line "never get rid of me." As mentioned above, this line becomes an ostinato uniting with Webb's climactic underscore and the sound effect of hoofbeats. The Lewton unit had repurposed prominently rhythmic line readings earlier in the series with Dr. Judd's "the, uh, key" heard during Irena's nightmare in *Cat People* and Julia Farrin's "and ride with the headless horseman" returning in Amy's nightmare in *The Curse of the Cat People*. The deranged Captain Stone hears his crew suggesting that "maybe the boy is right" over and over just prior to entering Tom's cabin to murder him in *The Ghost Ship*. The consistency with which the Lewton unit presented quoted dialogue enmeshed within aural collages at key moments within their horror films is notable and consistent stylistically from the early films to the Karloff vehicles.

The repetitious use of "never get rid of me" serves as a reasonable place to end this discussion of Boris Karloff's impact on *The Body Snatcher*'s soundtrack. His presence impacted every facet of the film from the decision to film a Victorian ghost story to editing of dialogue into aural collages. Music's overall function within the film toward the connotative/narrative results from the selection of a period costume piece suitable to the actor's onscreen persona. With the "never get rid of me" ostinato, his voice goes on haunting the film even after his death. Karloff's mere presence and his memorable performance transformed the sonic style of the Lewton unit and marked the soundtrack in ways obvious and obscure. As the film did superb business, the Lewton unit would never rid itself of Karloff. Instead, a fruitful collaboration blossomed between Lewton and the star he argued against employing.

The Body Snatcher lived up to Jack Gross's hopes for commercial success. Among Lewton's horror films, only *Cat People* and *I Walked with a Zombie* outperformed *The Body Snatcher* in generating profits.[43] Gratifying for both Lewton and his arch-enemy, Gross, the film made more money than Universal's *House of Frankenstein*,[44] the picture Universal hoped would reassert their dominance in horror production and Boris Karloff's last film for Universal during the 1940s. RKO offered Karloff a contract extension for three more films, an extension he happily signed.[45]

NOTES

1. Gregory Mank, *Bela Lugosi and Boris Karloff: The Expanded Story of a Haunting Collaboration* (Jefferson, NC: McFarland & Company, 2009), p. 483.
2. Louis Berg, "Farewell to Monsters," *Los Angeles Times* (May 12, 1946), p. F12.
3. Douglas Gomery, *The Hollywood Studio System: A History* (London: British Film Institute, 2005), p. 150.
4. This figure may be nearly accurate insofar as Lewton rewrote the film's ending after it had wrapped, forcing the picture to go back into production. The ending of the film constitutes a drastic improvement over the scripted ending; however, it added US$52,000 in additional costs.
5. Edmund Bansak, *Fearing the Dark: The Val Lewton Career* (Jefferson, NC: MacFarland & Company, 1995), p. 252.
6. Mank, *Bela Lugosi and Boris Karloff*, pp. 498–500.
7. Jack Gross produced *The Wolf Man* (1941), *The Phantom of the Opera* (1943), and *Son of Dracula* (1943).
8. Val Lewton, Letter to Nina and Lucy Lewton (August 20, 1944). Lewton Papers, Library of Congress.
9. Mank, *Bela Lugosi and Boris Karloff*, p. 490.
10. Budget materials for *The Body Snatcher*, RKO Radio Pictures Studio Records (Collection PASC 3). UCLA Library Special Collections, Charles E. Young Research Library, University of California, Los Angeles. The music in the film cost US$5,499. Compare this to *Cat People* with its overall cost of US$119,000 and music costing US$5,308.50. Clearly the presence of Boris Karloff mattered more to RKO than the music.
11. Mank, *Bela Lugosi and Boris Karloff*, p. 483.
12. Cynthia Lindsay, *Dear Boris* (New York: Knopf, 1975), pp. 108–110.
13. Joel Siegel, *Val Lewton: The Reality of Terror* (New York: Viking Press, 1973), p. 72.
14. The story's name isn't exactly the same. Stevenson hyphenated "The Body-Snatcher."
15. Lewton's script violated several of the suggested guidelines provided for Hollywood producers by the Motion Picture Alliance for the Preservation of American Ideals

(MPA) in their 1947 pamphlet, "Screen Guides for Americans." Specifically, Hollywood's leading anti-communists (both Walt Disney and Ayn Rand contributed to the pamphlet's writing) believed that "smearing the profit motive" and "glorifying the common man" were "subtle communist touches" that infiltrators placed within films.

16. Mank, *Bela Lugosi and Boris Karloff*, p. 495.
17. Office of Joseph Breen, Letter to Val Lewton (September 27, 1944). MPAA Files, "*The Body Snatcher*," Margaret Herrick Library, Academy of Motion Pictures Arts and Sciences, Beverly Hills, California.
18. Bansak, p. 284.
19. James Agee, "Films," *The Nation* (March 23, 1946), pp. 354–355.
20. Claudia Gorbman, *Unheard Melodies: Narrative Film Music* (Bloomington: Indiana University Press, 1987), p. 73.
21. See for example the opening of Roy Webb, "Things a Motion Picture Composer Has to Think About," *Film Music Notes* (October 4, 1941), p. 2, or his discussion of the needs of Lewton's early films in Roy Webb, "Pattern for Mystery," *Film Music Notes* (March 1945).
22. K. J. Donnelly, *The Spectre of Sound: Music in Film and Television* (London: BFI, 2005), pp. 57–58.
23. James Buhler, *Theories of the Soundtrack* (Oxford: Oxford University Press, 2019), pp. 197–198.
24. Philip MacDonald, shooting script for *The Body Snatcher*. RKO Radio Pictures Studio Records (Collection PASC 3). UCLA Library Special Collections, Charles E. Young Research Library, University of California, Los Angeles.
25. Production logs for *The Body Snatcher*. RKO Radio Pictures Studio Records (Collection PASC 3). UCLA Library Special Collections, Charles E. Young Research Library, University of California, Los Angeles.
26. Ben Winters, "The Non-Diegetic Fallacy: Film, Music, and Narrative Space," *Music and Letters*, Volume 91, Number 2, p. 236. Cited in Buhler, p. 172.
27. Donnelly, p. 21.
28. The version of the lyrics heard in the film appears in *Our National Songs*, ed. Alfred H. Miles (London: Hutchinson & Co., 1890), pp. 170–173.
29. This theme in the film receives excellent scholarly analysis in J. P. Telotte, *Dreams of Darkness: Fantasy and the Films of Val Lewton* (Urbana: University of Illinois Press, 1985), pp. 159–160.
30. At this point in the shooting script, MacDonald (or Lewton) wrote, "A huge fire is roaring in the fireplace and before it is a rack spit turned by a spit boy who sings as he turns. (Song to be supplied.)" The RKO Music Department supplied the song. It exists in the RKO Music Files at UCLA in handwriting that is neither Webb's nor his orchestrator Leonid Raab's. This may be the fruit of research done by the Music Department as the language is antique and the tune is simple.
31. Berg, p. F12.
32. Boris Karloff's personal scripts for *The Body Snatcher*, *Isle of the Dead*, and *Bedlam* are in the Cinematic Arts Library, University of Southern California.

33. Philip MacDonald, script for *The Body Snatcher* with Boris Karloff's marginalia, p. 5. Cinematic Arts Library, University of Southern California.
34. Philip MacDonald, script for *The Body Snatcher* with Boris Karloff's marginalia, p. 61. Cinematic Arts Library, University of Southern California.
35. Philip MacDonald, script for *The Body Snatcher*, Robert Wise's copy with handwritten marginalia. The Robert Wise Papers, Cinematic Arts Library, University of Southern California.
36. Philip MacDonald, script for *The Body Snatcher* with Boris Karloff's marginalia, p. 19. Cinematic Arts Library, University of Southern California.
37. Philip MacDonald, script for *The Body Snatcher* with Boris Karloff's marginalia, p. 44. Cinematic Arts Library, University of Southern California.
38. Philip MacDonald, script for *The Body Snatcher* (revised first draft) with Boris Karloff's marginalia. Cinematic Arts Library, University of Southern California.
39. Philip MacDonald, script for *The Body Snatcher* (revised first draft) with Boris Karloff's marginalia, p. 11. Cinematic Arts Library, University of Southern California.
40. Stan Link, "Horror and Science Fiction," in *The Cambridge Companion to Film Music*, eds. Mervyn Cooke and Fiona Ford (Cambridge: Cambridge University Press, 2016), pp. 213–215.
41. "J. P.," *Alas! Jamie's Pickled: Elegiac Lines on the Tragical Murder of Poor Daft Jamie* (Edinburgh: W. Smith, 1829).
42. See Claudia Gorbman, "The Master's Voice," *Film Quarterly* (January 12, 2015).
43. Mank, *Bela Lugosi and Boris Karloff*, p. 316.
44. Gregory Mank, *The Hollywood Cauldron* (Jefferson, NC: McFarland & Company, 1994), p. 358.
45. Ibid. When Val Lewton left RKO after producing *Bedlam*, the first of three films RKO planned for Karloff's second contract with the studio, RKO and the star agreed to suspend the contract for the last two films he owed them. This is a shame, as Lewton never thrived after leaving RKO. Their next project was planned to be "Blackbeard" and told the tale of the aging pirate captain seeking a calmer life. I would have paid to see that unrealized Lewton/Karloff collaboration.

8 VALIDATING UNCERTAINTY ON THE *ISLE OF THE DEAD*

Shooting *Isle of the Dead* proved frustrating for the members of the Lewton unit. On July 22, 1944, the ninth day of shooting, Boris Karloff's old back injury flared up so badly that the star needed surgery.[1] The film went into an indefinite hiatus. When Karloff was ready for work again, key cast members Skelton Knaggs and Rose Hobart were busy on other projects.[2] The entire film *The Body Snatcher* was scripted and shot before the cast for *Isle of the Dead* reassembled to resume shooting on December 1, 1944.

During the long hiatus, Lewton rewrote the entire script.[3] Among other changes, he shifted relationships among major characters. Originally General Pherides (Boris Karloff) was estranged father to Thea (Ellen Drew), Mrs. St. Aubyn (Katherine Emery) was Mr. St. Aubyn's (Alan Napier) daughter rather than wife, and Oliver (Marc Cramer) had a different love interest named Cathy (Rose Hobart) instead of Thea. Lewton streamlined the cast in his rewrite, eliminating the role of Cathy even though some of her scenes had already been shot.[4] These changes complicated everything as some material shot before Karloff's injury no longer made sense owing to various script revisions. Editor Lyle Boyer probably deserves more credit for the film's effectiveness than he gets in the critical literature for patching the pieces together, especially when considering that this was Boyer's first feature film as editor.

Lewton shared his despairing views on the production in letters to his mother and sister in New York. As reshooting began, he wrote: "*Isle of the Dead*, which we are shooting now, is a complete mess. I'm thankful that it is my last horror picture and, at the same time, sorry that I couldn't depart that field with a final success." Later, he wrote: "*Isle of the Dead*, which we just finished shooting, looks pretty hopeless." Then he offered his last words on the film after post-production concluded:

> It started out as a rather poetic and quite beautiful story of how people, fleeing from the battles of the Greek War of 1912, are caught on this island by plague and through their sufferings come to an acceptance of death as being good – the fitting end – Shakespeare's 'little sleep.' It ended up as a hodge-podge of horror ... This has been a horrible and unfortunate film from the beginning – largely my stupid supervisor's fault – but it has turned out so that it won't be too bad.[5]

Lewton blamed his "stupid supervisor," Jack Gross, but Lewton himself insisted on rewriting the script after shooting had begun, and Gross could scarcely be blamed for Karloff's injury. As for his claim that the film endorses death as good, even an imaginative reading of the divergent versions of the script makes this thematic conclusion impossible to justify.

The first aim of this chapter is a rebuttal of Lewton's harsh assessment of *Isle of the Dead*. The film is one of the most thematically coherent of his entire horror output. Uncertainty, a crucial stylistic and thematic element of all his horror productions, rises in this film to a position of validation. *Isle of the Dead* does not argue for "death as being good." The film aims higher, arguing without becoming didactic that uncertainty is the ideal human condition. That this theme was not what Lewton intended changes the facts of the film not at all.

Disputing Lewton's low opinion of the film runs counter to the views of both of Lewton's biographers. Joel Siegel opens his commentary on the film writing: "*Isle of the Dead* is not Lewton's worst RKO production but it is probably his most confused and surely his most disappointing."[6] Edmund Bansak echoes Lewton's view, calling the film "more a horror 'grab bag' than a coherent, unified whole."[7] While I am not entirely comfortable offering valuations of films, I will emphatically dispute that the film is "confused" or anything other than "a coherent, unified whole" by demonstrating how the film deals with both certainty and uncertainty in a way enfolding virtually the entire narrative and bleeding into the film's style.

The second aim of this chapter is an examination of how Leigh Harline's orchestral underscore complements the film's thematic validation of uncertainty. He accomplishes this through stylistic uncertainty rooted in his choice to emulate Greek epic vocal genres with their parlando melodies and tempo-rubato along with parallel harmonies denying a conventional harmonic grammar. But first we must try to unpack how Harline came to compose the score for this picture.

Enter Leigh Harline

Like Roy Webb, Leigh Harline remains one of the less-well-known major figures in Hollywood film scoring. Most similarities between the two men end there. While Webb enjoyed a patrician background with summers on Nantucket Island,[8] season tickets to the Metropolitan Opera, and an Ivy League education,[9] Harline was the thirteenth child of Swedish immigrants who moved to Salt Lake City in 1891 after converting to Mormonism.[10] Harline attended public schools, culminating with a Degree in Music from the University of Utah. In 1928, the twenty-one-year-old Harline relocated to Los Angeles, where he composed and conducted for various radio stations. His work on the first transcontinental radio broadcast emanating from the West Coast attracted the attention of Walt Disney, who signed Harline to join his musical staff.

Harline served Disney as composer and arranger from 1932 until 1941. He composed scores for dozens of Disney one-reel cartoons along with the first two Disney animated features, *Snow White and the Seven Dwarfs* (1937) and *Pinocchio* (1940). These feature scores included songs and underscore by Frank Churchill and Paul Smith, Harline's colleagues at Disney.[11]

Harline's work on both Disney features earned him Academy Award nominations. He won Oscars for Best Score for *Pinocchio* and Best Song for "When You Wish upon a Star" from the same film. Not long after winning these important industry accolades, Harline quit Disney. His last work for Disney was the score for the short subject *Pluto Junior*, released into theaters on February 28, 1942, but scored in early 1941.

Precisely why Leigh Harline abandoned Walt Disney for the uncertain business of freelancing in Hollywood is unknown. For a realistic basis for speculation, one only need look at the history of labor relations at Disney's studio during the early 1940s.

Snow White and the Seven Dwarfs was produced by RKO. It grossed an astronomical eight million dollars. But it cost a robust one million dollars to make. RKO took all the risk of that lavish capital outlay and realized most of the film's handsome profits. The healthy profit margin of his first feature prompted Walt Disney to turn his company into a publicly traded corporation. RKO would distribute Disney's pictures, but the production costs and most of the receipts would go to Disney. His next two animated features, *Pinocchio* and *Fantasia* (1941), performed well at the box office but generated very little profit.[12]

In order to maintain his stock prices and please his investors, Walt Disney began slashing the salaries of his workers. This led to a strike by his cartoonists, which halted all production for much of 1941.[13]

Just as Leigh Harline harvested industry accolades in the form of two Oscar statuettes, he saw his salary cut and then all work halt. While it would be helpful if Harline had penned a note stating the reasons why he left Disney, the story seems plain enough.

Harline's odyssey as a freelance composer working for most of the large Hollywood studios at some point between 1942 and 1944 differentiates him again from Roy Webb, who toiled for one studio for his entire career. From quitting at Disney until he began work for Val Lewton, Leigh Harline received screen credit for composing original scores for ten feature films, listed here in chronological order: *The Lady Has Plans* (Paramount), *Whispering Ghost* (20th- Century Fox), *Careful, Soft Shoulders* (20th-Century Fox), *Margin for Error* (20th-Century Fox), *They Got Me Covered* (MGM), *Pride of the Yankees* (RKO), *The More the Merrier* (Columbia), *Government Girl* (RKO), *Tender Comrade* (RKO), and *A Night of Adventure* (RKO). The most prestigious of these (*Pride of the Yankees*, for which Harline was nominated for another Academy Award), the most numerous, and the most recent were all composed for RKO.

Coming to an answer as to how Leigh Harline came to work with the Lewton unit may prove more difficult than answering why he left Disney. He had composed the scores for several RKO features. Jack Gross invested considerable money in signing Boris Karloff, so he naturally felt tremendous pressure for the first production starring his expensive signee to succeed. We might see Gross hiring Harline instead of Webb as an attempt to add luster to the production by contracting an award-winning composer to write the score.

Or, we might see Gross simply trying to shake up the Lewton unit, something he did regularly during 1944. A new composer might result in a more discernible stylistic rupture with what the Lewton unit had produced recently, an outcome Gross actively pursued. That may be a stretch, though, as Harline had no experience scoring horror pictures whereas several composers with Universal Pictures horror credits were also working freelance. Among these Paul Sawtell springs to mind. He did extensive work composing at RKO – including scoring Lewton's *Youth Runs Wild*[14] – while simultaneously shuttling to Universal to score five horror films during 1943 and 1944 including some Jack Gross had a hand in producing.[15] Of course speculation on which freelance composer could have worked on a particular film runs into the inevitable objection: was he available at the time the executive producer needed him?

This objection extends to the question of why replace Roy Webb at all. Webb's filmography indicates that he was only normally busy as *Isle of the Dead* entered post-production. Perhaps he had another project at that exact moment, Leigh Harline was on the lot recording *A Night of Adventure*'s score, so why not ask him to step in? Perhaps the stylistic ruptures chronicled in the previous chapter left Webb less interested in working with Lewton.

We might also consider money. Roy Webb was RKO's senior composer on staff. His weekly salary would be counted toward the budget of any film that enjoyed his services. Expenses on *Isle of the Dead* had run far over budget by the time the film entered post-production owing to the long hiatus. The film wound up costing RKO US$246,000 to make, by far Lewton's most expensive film to date. Perhaps cost-cutting during post-production necessitated hiring a freelance composer rather than using the well-salaried Webb. This might also explain why first-time feature editor Lyle Boyer cut the film. His weekly salary would realize a savings compared to a more senior employee.

We will return to Leigh Harline and consider his music for *Isle of the Dead* in some detail. First, we need to examine the film's narrative and its central thematic concern with the dichotomy of certainty and uncertainty.

Uncertainty in the Style and Narrative of Lewton's Horror Films

Confusion in studio-era Hollywood filmmaking held the status of *bête noir*. From mise-en-scène to editing grammar to the organization of soundtracks, indeed within all facets of motion picture production, the studios sought the banishment of confusion and the uncertainty it awakens.[16]

The Lewton unit, however, courted uncertainty from their earliest meetings onward. In an interview with the *Los Angeles Times*, Lewton explained his stylistic aims: "I'll tell you a secret: if you make the screen dark enough, the mind's eye will read anything into it you want! We're great ones for dark patches."[17]

This visual approach adheres closely to the narrative approach of banishing overt monsters. J. P. Telotte stated the positive case for Lewton's stylistic use of uncertainty and his avoiding monsters:

> Films that emphasize an external threat to our normal way of life attempt to expose our human weaknesses and fears, reminding us almost therapeutically of our natural vulnerability to the abnormal. By vacating that otherness, though, the RKO films could reveal that, in essence, we are 'they,' that the otherness we fear actually resides within, although it goes denied or unperceived in the welter of daily life. Our real fears, consequently, are shown to be of this hidden portion of the self that threatens the 'nomal' being which we show to the world in our efforts to remain in harmony with its formidable appearance of normalcy. The portentous shadows, strange sounds, and eerie low-key lighting that characterize these films add an ominous coloring that helps undercut their sense of the commonplace and marks a path which leads back within – in that vesperal motion described by [James] Hillman – to the darker regions of the self.[18]

The seven films discussed in the previous chapters all feature examples of the "portentous shadows, strange sounds, and eerie low-key lighting" Telotte mentions. They also emphasize a certain value within the narrative in characters who remain uncertain in this context. For example, in *Cat People*, Dr. Judd asks Irena, "Do you sincerely believe that if your husband were to kiss you, to take you into his embrace, you would change into a cat and rend him to bits?" Irena replies, "I don't know. I'm only afraid."

That not knowing more than any victimization of Irena by the "tyranny of the normal" clarifies her as a sympathetic figure within the film. To be uncertain in Lewton's films is to enjoy a measure of humanity that his relentlessly "normal" characters never enjoy.

Surveying a few uncertain characters may illustrate the point. *I Walked with a Zombie* finds Paul Holland sure that his wife suffered a fever, but the more sympathetic Betsy explores alternatives with an open mind. *The Leopard Man* features a speech from the film's killer about life. He claims that it resembles a glass ball mounted at the apex of a fountain, unaware of the forces that toss and catch it. The more sympathetic Jerry at the film's close cites this endorsement of uncertainty as an optimistic path forward for he and Kiki. Mary abandons her search for her sister, content not to know in *The Seventh Victim*. Burdened by guilt over the "resurrection" trade's darker impacts, the vacillating protagonist, Fettes, balks and reverses course three times over his decision to study medicine in *The Body Snatcher*.

Valorizing uncertainty, whether stylistic or narrative or thematic, grinds against the grain of America in the 1940s as usually depicted by Hollywood. A world war demanding myriad sacrifices and nearly unbearable compromises provides an unlikely context for a celebration of uncertainty. As *Isle of the Dead* entered production, the FBI had already concluded that Val Lewton was a subversive.[19] But his subversion is global rather than specifically ideological. He wasn't advocating communism by subverting American institutions, so much as celebrating the sort of hesitancies that resist the very fascistic ideologies America spilled its blood to help smash, ideologies promoting nothing if not certitude.

The Apotheosis of Uncertainty

In *Isle of the Dead*, two dichotomies govern the structure of the narrative. One resides on the film's surface and concerns the clash of Western Reason and Folk Superstition. The context is an outbreak of septicemic plague on a tiny island off the coast of Greece during the First Balkan War. In this case, "Reason" is code for viewing the plague through the lens of modern medicine. Whether this rises to the ideals of Reason not only can be debated, it is debated within the film itself. Superstition here concerns belief that the plague is a punishment from the ancient Greek gods for the island harboring a *Vorvolaka*, a sort of vampire from Greek legend that preys on the life energies of its victims.

The surface dichotomy plays out in the film interestingly. General Pherides begins the film a stern and certain commander who places all his faith in what he can sense and in what his military training expects of him. But as the story unfolds, he drifts to the side of superstition and views the plague as the product of unpunished evil. Often in horror films an authority figure moves from perfect skepticism to rueful certainty as regards a supernatural threat. General Pherides scoffs at the *Vorvoloka* initially, and firmly believes in one later. More important than his drift toward belief, the General – fully invested in superstition near the end – has become a monster himself.

This unusual treatment of the surface dichotomy points toward a more important though less obvious dichotomy at the heart of the film, the dichotomy of certainty and uncertainty. In the film, certainty exacerbates fear and proves a dangerous mental condition. By contrast, the film's uncertain characters, those who shy away from the film's surface dichotomy, or in the case of Albrecht (Jason Robards Sr.) mock it, all survive and enjoy sympathetic treatment. An overview of the film's action with the dichotomy of certainty and uncertainty in the foreground could illuminate my claim that the film is the apotheosis of Lewton's fascination with uncertainty. A synopsis may also set up a more detailed discussion of Harline's score to follow.

A Synopsis Emphasizing the Role of Uncertainty

General Pherides has just won a victory over the Ottomans, but one company lagged behind. While washing his hands in a basin, Pherides silently insists that the colonel responsible for this unit (Sherry Hall) shoot himself. Oliver, a reporter for a Boston newspaper, witnesses this scene and criticizes the General's approach as too harsh. Pherides insists on the rectitude of his actions, and the two men discuss briefly how the General came by the nickname "the watchdog." Already, the film establishes General Pherides as a cold man entirely certain of his singular truth rooted in nationalism and military discipline. During their conversation, the General reveals that he had a wife who is buried on a small island just off the coast. He and Oliver head out to visit the island. Along the way, they meet the army's medical officer, Dr. Drossos (Ernst Deutsch), who is supervising the burying of corpses after the battle. Oliver objects to the use of exhausted soldiers as draft animals. Pherides explains that horses cannot be made to understand why they must work beyond endurance for their country, while the men can. Drossos explains that the burials must take place immediately lest plague undo the army's victories.

The approach to the island justifies the film's title for featuring a matte painting strongly resembling Arnold Böcklin's painting of the same name. The island features several ruins and a fine statue of Cerberus guarding a stony cemetery. Oliver notes the similarity between Cerberus, guardian of the dead, and Pherides, the watchdog of his country. Pherides discovers that his wife's grave has been despoiled. He and Oliver hear a young woman singing and follow her voice to the home of Albrecht, a Swiss archaeologist who lives on the island with his Greek housekeeper, Kyra (Helene Thimig).

Albrecht and Kyra shelter a small band of travelers who took refuge on the island during the fighting. They are a tin merchant from England named Robbins (Skelton Knaggs); Mr. St. Aubyn, an English diplomatic attaché; Mrs. St. Aubyn, who is sickly; and Thea, the young Greek woman employed as Mrs. St. Aubyn's caretaker. Albrecht convinces General Pherides and Oliver to spend the night.

The film's first death belongs to Robbins. In his only scene, Robbins pines to return to England right away. He excuses himself for not feeling well and stumbles on the stairs as Thea passes him. "Horrible stairs," Robbins moans. Mr. St. Aubyn sternly remarks, "A strange way to describe plain drunkenness." The certain Mr. St. Aubyn is entirely wrong about the cause of Robbins's stumble. Robbins dies of the plague during the night. One of its early symptoms is a wavering gate. While not a participant in the film's dichotomy of certainty and uncertainty for dying so early, Robbins does realize his worst fears by failing to return to England.

Kyra uses the stumble and the presence of the healthy Thea in close proximity to her sickly mistress as evidence that a *Vorvolaka* is present on the island. General Pherides serves as audience for Kyra's conjecture, but he dismisses her worries as nonsense.

When Robbins's death alerts General Pherides to the potential for plague reaching the mainland and infecting his army, he summons Dr. Drossos to the island. Drossos concludes that Robbins died of septicemic plague. He provides the islanders with a short list of sanitary precautions including much hand-washing, and General Pherides forbids anyone from leaving the island, even ordering everyone to follow the doctor's sanitary regimen. The doctor holds out this piece of hope rooted in his scientific expertise: "The contagion is spread by fleas. With a 90% moisture content, these fleas will burn away if the hot Sirocco blows. Then all danger will pass in twenty-four hours."

No one protests the General's injunction against leaving the island more vociferously than Mr. St. Aubyn. He points out that he performs an important function for his government and must return to London on urgent business. Pherides is unmoved. St. Aubyn next points out that his wife is an invalid in need of care. Pherides remains steadfast. Mr. St. Aubyn accepts the doctor's diagnosis without hesitation and, like Robbins, fears the consequences of failing to return to England. He becomes the plague's next victim and dies certain that the logic of Western medicine is wholly true.

Mrs. St. Aubyn initially refuses Dr. Drossos's pronouncement of her husband's death. Drossos tries several tests for her all indicating that her husband is dead. She persists in her conviction that her husband is alive. Later Mrs. St. Aubyn apologizes to the doctor for her outburst and offers an explanation. Since childhood she has suffered from cataleptic trances sometimes lasting for days. She holds an all-consuming fear of premature burial. Drossos promises to make every known test should she fall victim to the plague.

With two victims felled by the plague, superstition rears up afresh. Kyra tries to persuade General Pherides that the plague is a punishment for the island harboring a *Vorvolaka*. Kyra believes that Mrs. St. Aubyn's handmaid, Thea, a healthy young woman, is the monster in question. She cites circumstantial evidence such as Thea's quiet walking at night and the fact that Mrs. St. Aubyn dwindles while Thea is "rose cheeked and full of blood." Her overtures to the General fall on deaf ears initially, but as his fears grow, her diagnosis gains traction.

Contrasting Kyra's credulity is Albrecht's mocking of Dr. Drossos's medical expertise. Pherides and Albrecht make a bet. Albrecht will pray to Hermes, physician to the gods, for protection while Dr. Drossos will apply his medical expertise. "We will see who lives or dies," Albrecht jokes.

In one of the film's visually most arresting scenes, Albrecht lights a votive to Hermes before a ruined arch from antiquity. Drossos – feeling the first symptoms of the plague in himself – stands within the arch, framed by the columns of a foundational Western civilization, and admits his defeat by feeding the votive flames. The reverse shots capture Albrecht standing before a background of uncivilized nature as a chaos of tree limbs frames the uncertain archaeologist. Visually linking the doctor's certainties to the ruins of an ancient civilization and Albrecht's playful uncertainty to nature offers a useful touchstone for the film's dichotomous structure.

Dr. Drossos's death finds this man of science mysteriously immersed in his failure. His farewell includes this telling dialogue directed to Mrs. St. Aubyn as she praises his courage for refusing palliative care: "A fool's courage. Fight Death all your days, then die knowing you know nothing." Pherides overhears Drossos's concession to the limitations of his knowledge, and the General's own certainty wavers, then transforms into an equal certainty in the efficacy of Kyra's supernatural perspective. Like Mr. St. Aubyn, Drossos dies certain that the plague has killed him, and in that way he shares the fate of all the dead on the island for dying sure.

Facing death, Oliver elects to ignore some of Drossos's regimen and makes romantic advances to Thea. While the doctor told everyone to avoid close contact and congregating in groups, Oliver and Thea prefer amorous clinches on the rocky island's shore. Mrs. St. Aubyn approves of this course, but General Pherides does not.

Saddened by Drossos's death, Albrecht admits that he has been mocking prayer with his votive fires to Hermes. He invites Mrs. St. Aubyn to lead the group in a prayer. He then offers a strangely ambivalent endorsement of prayer: "To pray, to believe – even in some Pagan god – it gives one comfort. That's true, isn't it?" Albrecht directs this question to Pherides, now without his medical officer, who replies, "I did not pray." Pherides's certainty leaves him unwilling to explore alternatives.

As the General's suspicions about Thea mount, Kyra begins a campaign of persecution. While Thea tends Mrs. St. Aubyn by night, Kyra takes up a post outside the door and lengthily insinuates that Thea is a monster draining away her companion's life. Uncertain, Thea queries Mrs. St. Aubyn about the nature of her illness and whether she believes that Thea causes her ailment. Mrs. St. Aubyn attempts to reassure her caretaker. Thea's doubts, even about her own nature, clarify her sympathetic role within the film.

Mrs. St. Aubyn finally succumbs to a cataleptic trance while alone in her room with Thea. Thea locks the doors, exacerbating Kyra's suspicions, and remains hidden away. Kyra works on General Pherides's flagging resolve and convinces him to break down the door. The group discovers Mrs. St. Aubyn on the floor, apparently dead, with the healthy Thea standing over her. Thea insists that Mrs. St. Aubyn was not like the others and did not die of plague. Several tests are made to see if she lives, and when they reveal that she does not, the group creates a makeshift coffin for her. During that activity, Mrs. St. Aubyn's face twitches, revealing to the audience that she is not dead, but in a trance.

Mrs. St. Aubyn feared premature burial, and fate delivers her one. Her coffin rests in a small stone passage. Before long, we hear her scrabbling and muttering incoherently within.

Pherides sides with Kyra. He plans to watch Thea closely and makes no secret that he will destroy her following legendary practices should he become sure of her nature as a *Vorvolaka*. Oliver, now romantically attached to Thea, warns the General, but mostly he tries to keep Thea away from the General first by leaving the island together. The General destroys the only boat on the island to keep the couple from spreading the plague to the army.

A Scirocco blows, but too late for General Pherides, who succumbs to the plague. His illness sends him to bed. Kyra, terrified, comes to his bedside and begs him to hear the sounds from the crypt. "Whoever is killed by a *Vorvolaka* becomes a *Vorvolaka*," she explains.

Mrs. St. Aubyn breaks out of her coffin. Thea, outdoors to stay away from Pherides, hears her and investigates. In a magnificent scene in the small stone crypt and using one lovely double-exposed shot that leaves audiences wondering whether Mrs. St. Aubyn is there or not, Thea sees Mrs. St. Aubyn in her flowing burial gown moving about the crypt. Thea informs Albrecht and Oliver of this, and they rush out to find Mrs. St. Aubyn while leaving Thea in the house with the delirious General who is now convinced that not one but two *Vorvolaki* threaten him.

Mrs. St. Aubyn kills Kyra by stabbing her throat with a trident from Albrecht's collection of antiquities. Pherides discovers Kyra's body, her throat bloody. He turns on Thea, crawling toward her threateningly. Mrs. St. Aubyn then kills Pherides before rushing out to the cliffs where she falls to her death. Both Kyra and General Pherides die certain that the *Vorvolaka* form of Mrs. St. Aubyn, a dead woman they entombed themselves, killed them. Mrs. St. Aubyn too dies as a result of what she feared most.

The wind having changed, danger passes with it. The three survivors are Albrecht, Oliver, and Thea. Albrecht, established as being from neutral Switzerland, never aligns with any certainty. Some he mocks only to regret his mockery later. Other certainties he undermines with ambivalence, as was the case with his commentary on prayer. By harboring no particular fears and distancing himself from the poison of certainty, he lives.

As for Thea, by doubting even herself, she survives the plague. Oliver too offers criticism of the wildly changeable certainties of the General and lives to leave the island.

For the others, fear and certainty inextricably intertwine in this film. Each character dies certain and dies as a result of precisely what they feared most. The resulting contrast of the film's dead and its survivors offers a rare and interesting validation of uncertainty's superiority over certainty, and an interesting alternative to the horror genre's usual preoccupation with Normal vs. Other.

Harline's Vaguely Greek Topic

Leigh Harline's approach to film scoring differs from Roy Webb's in how each composer managed coordinating the musical performance to the images on the screen. The RKO Music Department pioneered the use of a click track during Max Steiner's tenure as Music Director (1929–1937). Roy Webb was an early adopter. His work for the Lewton films provides evidence of the click track through the metrical consistency of execution as precise correspondences between image and music abound.[20] For *Isle of the Dead*, Harline's methods differ. A large number of measures in his score commence with a downbeat coordinated to an event on the image track. His autograph score contains his handwritten indication of the event meant to coordinate with the arrival of many measures.[21] The click track manages such precise coordination so that it can fall anywhere in the music's meter.

Harline's temporal practice facilitates tempo-rubato, something alien to click track use. Harline's score for *Isle of the Dead* takes full advantage of tempo-rubato to the point of inviting comparison to genres of Greek epic song in a parlando-rubato tempo and even pointing back to ancient practices.[22] While Harline's fluid tempi lack a singer and therefore the execution of a true parlando, something akin to a Greek topic emerges through Harline's approach to tempo and his oddly declamatory melodies.

Extending an examination of Harline's Greek topic, his score is often monophonic with solo instruments emerging whenever prominent melodies appear. When harmony exists, parallelism governs most harmonic motion suggesting something akin to heterophony achieved not through simultaneous presentation of a melody with differing embellishments, but through consistent parallel motion distancing the harmony from a conventionally achieved tonal syntax. Other times, Harline's harmonies repose as static block chords behaving similarly to a drone typical of much Balkan folk music.

How Greek any of this may be is likely not very. As with Webb's Scottish topic in *The Body Snatcher*, Harline's Greek topic may capture nothing authentically born of Greece, ancient or otherwise. Yet the score is effectively suited to an American picture laden with references to ancient Greek deities, monsters, and architecture for conjuring the temporal style and harmonic procedures of epic song. Harline's music trades in no cheap or easy methods like folksong quotations to achieve whatever Greek-ness may inform it. Like Webb in *The Body Snatcher*, Harline intuited a need to transport his audience in time and place. But Greece in 1912 complicates the problem for much of his American audience likely having scarcely any frame of reference.

To illustrate Harline's measure-by-measure approach to time, his parlando-rubato tempo, his coordination of image and downbeat, and his unorthodox harmonic practices, we might profitably examine the opening of the film. The outcome will point to the film's validation of uncertainty by emphasizing Harline's presentation of uncertain meter, rhythm, and mode. All this compliments the film's validation of uncertainty indicating that the "great care" Webb discussed in scoring Lewton's films was contagious, touching the entire RKO Music Department.

Main Title Cue

The spotting sheets for *Isle of the Dead* are mostly extant.[23] The one for the "Main Title" cue indicates the exact timing when each title card dissolves into the next. Harline received instructions about all the title cards and the exact timing of their appearance onscreen, but he honors these instructions in a selective manner. He indicated in his autograph short score where downbeats in his music coincide with title card dissolves (Figure 8.1, "Main Title"). The one card that receives no musical coordination belonged to Jack Gross, the film's executive producer and Lewton's enemy. The producer's, director's, and writer's cards all receive changes of texture in Harline's measure devoted to them, making the neglect of Gross's card all the more tangible.

Figure 8.1 Leigh Harline, "Main Title" from *Isle of the Dead*

Figure 8.1 (*continued*)

Figure 8.1 (*continued*)

The title card that receives the most special musical treatment was designated in the spotting sheet as "second technicians card (music)."[24] Here, Harline places the change to the new title card featuring his name listed first on beat four of a 4/4 measure. A solo muted trumpet enters with a melancholy melody that will haunt his first two cues and return periodically over roughly the first half of the film.

The last card features a brief foreword to the film: "Under conquest and oppression the people of Greece allowed their legends to degenerate into superstition; the goddess Aphrodite giving way to the *Vorvolaka*. This nightmare figure was very much alive in the minds of the peasants when Greece fought the victorious War of 1912." With this title card, Harline places a prominent melody in the English horn.

Both Harline's solo muted trumpet and solo English horn return with some consistency. The muted trumpet always draws attention to the sacrifices demanded by war. The English horn appears whenever the film makes reference to suffering. The English horn in the "Main Title" cue fits nicely with the film's foreword for the text drawing attention to the oppression of the Greek people. The muted trumpet coinciding with Harline's name might simply be a case of deploying one of his score's most memorable sonorities with his name, a practice first developed by Max Steiner in the early 1930s.

Throughout the brief scene supported by the last half of Harline's "Main Title" cue, he places muted trumpet and stopped horn ascents of a perfect fourth at every pause in the dialogue. These quiet brass solos continually reinforce the scene's martial setting and the General's grim authority.

As the foreword dissolves into the film's first image – General Pherides washing his hands as he silently prepares to sentence Colonel Kobestes to death – Harline places a low drum roll prominently in his underscore. Low drum rolls and drum cadences appear in Harline's score everywhere we find evidence on the image track and in the dialogue of Pherides using his authority. The next low drum roll occurs as Colonel Kobestes tries to explain. Harline pens his line, "They didn't rest," evidence from Kobestes that he followed Pherides's orders, in his score precisely as the low drum sounds for the second time. The Colonel's protests have fallen on deaf ears. The third low drum cadence coincides with the image of Kobestes picking up the pistol Pherides has placed on the table before the doomed man.

Harline remains quite faithful throughout the film to his linking of the trumpet, English horn, and low drum solos to events in the narrative. He consistently connects each one to an event or idea. In this one parameter of Harline's music, certainty prevails. In other parameters of his approach, he promotes uncertainty in the listener. These parameters include his approach to tempo, meter, and harmony throughout his score. We see this even in the "Main Title" cue.

The tempo marking he chose is "Broadly + rubato." By its nature, rubato troubles the listener's certainties about time.

Harline's constant changes of meter invite further uncertainty. Without seeing the score of the "Main Title" there is no way to know what meter or meters are operative in the cue. The meters appear to have been chosen to facilitate coordination of musical events with events on the image track or within the dialogue such as dissolves to new title cards, appearances of key images including hand-washing or the placement of a gun on a table, and dialogue motivated by applications of Pherides's authority.

Harmonically, Harline's approach in his "Main Title" cue invites uncertainty. Almost every chord in the harmony is minor, although a few major chords appear on beat four of some measures in a brass choir functioning more as melody than harmony. The nearly exclusive use of minor creates a situation inevitably rendering tonic uncertain for no diatonic pitch collection prevailing for long. Interestingly, the "Main Title" cue features almost no counterpoint. In keeping with Harline's vaguely Greek topic, the tendency of Western music to facilitate harmonic progress through interior, contrapuntal voices does not operate here. The one notable harmonic move in measure 32 is achieved entirely by parallel motion up a half-step. Harline's decision to accompany his score's slender melodic content essentially with block chords helps by transporting the American audience to a place far away not through an ethnic topic precisely, but through a musical craft very different from Roy Webb's scoring,[25] and possibly from norms throughout Hollywood. The following diagram charts the harmonic progression through the "Main Title":

Measure(s)	Harmony
1–2	cm
3	dm/EM
4	cm/DM
5–9	B-flat minor
10–12	cm
13	dm
14–15	cm
16	B-Flat major/dm
17–21	f#m
22	bm/c#m
23–24	c#m
25	bm
26	f#m7
27–29	f#m
30–31	a-flat m7 (enharmonic spelling)
32	C-F-B-flat/C#-F#-B both over E-flat pedal

33–35	previous collection held
36	e-flat m
37	b-flat m/e-flat m
38–40	bm

The abundance of minor chords creates one sort of harmonic uncertainty, but the overall progression creates another. C minor offers the harmonic point of departure with B minor serving as its at best unusual destination. This larger move echoes the motion from chord to chord, which are also unusual for the individual chords rarely occupying the same diatonic array. The weird sonorities in measures 32–35 coincide with the cut to the revolver on the table. They introduce some suspense into the music by posing the possibility that the music may abandon all reference to a modal center.

The final cadence contributes no closure. Harline's last two harmonies do not serve as the cadence for the cue. Instead, his last B minor chord sets up the sound effect of Colonel Kobestes firing the revolver offscreen. Its report brings the cue to a sudden close.

"The Battlefield"

Harline's next cue, "The Battlefield," accompanies Oliver and General Pherides crossing the battlefield strewn with dead and dying men. The groans of the injured and dying coincide with Harline's quiet cue to provide the film with one of its most arresting audiovisual moments. Much has been made in the literature on the film about the effectiveness of the image track with its cheap backdrops used in this sequence to create the illusion of a large space.[26] More should be made of the soundtrack. Here Harline's trumpet and low drums enjoy relative freedom for the entire scene pointing toward the narrative elements Harline chose to reinforce with these martial sonorities.

Unusual for this score, Harline deploys counterpoint in this cue (Figure 8.2, "The Battlefield"). An unusual descending scale appears in pizzicato in the low strings. The key signature indicates four flats suggesting F minor, but the bass line commences on G-flat lending the scale a Phrygian flavor suggestive of Harline's vaguely Greek topic.

The middle layer offers a contrapuntal line that lands on Fs and B-flats. In this line, Gs – of which there are four – are always natural, even when deployed in close proximity to G-flats in the bass line as happens in measures 12 and 17. This material is in minor, not Phrygian. A situation of quite unusual uncertainty arises, an uncertainty not between major and minor, but minor and a mode associated with ancient Greece.

The melody belongs to the muted trumpet as Harline references wartime sacrifice. As Oliver and Pherides cross the battlefield, its melancholy fanfares provide the score's most memorable moment. The second and third fanfare motif allocated to the trumpet ascend to G naturals, again creating modal uncertainty but now drawing special attention to it by placing the Gs at the apex of the cue's melodic contour while Phrygian scalar figures marked with G-flats unfold in the bass line. Again, Harline shuns harmonic closure (typical for a film score). His final sonority places a G in the trumpet supported by B-flats in the low strings and the middle line. This dyad gestures toward G minor, but in the measure prior the cellos and basses played G-flats.

While this cue is the most easily heard and memorable of the film, it offers a novel sort of musical uncertainty. It fails to commit to a mode by allocating Gs and G-flats to the respective strata of the contrapuntal texture. Like the "Main Title" cue, "The Battlefield" also offers an uncertain meter for switching

Figure 8.2 Leigh Harline, "The Battlefield" from *Isle of the Dead*, mm. 12–29

Figure 8.2 (*continued*)

between 3/4, 4/4, and 5/4 now without the image track justification of hitting the title card changes. Moreover, within these meters, Harline resists any metric emphasis. In the first measure, for example, the understated middle layers enter surreptitiously on beat one, the cellos and basses on beat two, and the low drum on beat three. Listeners would be wise to withhold judgment on the music's meter for having no frame of reference and no consistent sense of where beat one might be. All the trumpet entrances occur on off beats.

Overview of Harline's Contribution

Rather than complete this blow-by-blow description of Harline's score for the entire film, we might take a step back and summarize the key issues so far and see how several of them play out later in the film. So far, four elements of Harline's score received attention: connections of timbres to narrative elements, uncertainty in tempo, uncertainty in meter, and uncertainty in mode.

The muted trumpet and the low drum bear a burden of signification in the film that play out quite precisely in the film's opening scene, then more broadly in the battlefield sequence. But somewhere near the middle of the film, they both disappear from Harline's score. The trumpet fanfare sounds for the last time at the opening of the montage showing the people on the island bathing their hands. In this case, however, a solo clarinet, not the more martial trumpet, sounds the fanfare. That the figure is there reminds us that General Pherides gave this order, but the change in instrumentation indicates that his martial authority is dwindling as he orders civilians who face the plague with him.

The low drum rolls and drum cadence figures also disappear for long stretches of the film as General Pherides loses control of the situation. It drops out of the score even before the montage sequence where we hear the fanfare figure for the last time. But unlike the fanfare figure, it returns briefly just as General Pherides dies, perhaps reinforcing Albrecht's dialogue reminding us that Pherides died a watchdog trying to protect the others.

The English horn solos, by contrast, return many times, all coinciding with moments of human suffering and the compassion suffering prompts in others. Notable examples include the cue "Night Encounter" as Thea moves silently to alleviate her mistress's suffering, in the cue "Catalepsy" as Thea stands vigil over her mistress, and in the cue "Voice in the Coffin" as Oliver patiently assists the stricken General Pherides in getting into bed.

One sonority not heard in the opening cues discussed above but important later in the film is Harline's fantastical harp glissandi whenever the image of Cerberus appears. As the statue of Cerberus serves as the film's "familiar image," returning at moments of temporal ellipses, these glissandi proliferate later in the film, after the trumpet and drums have mostly fallen silent.

Uncertainty in Harline's tempi occurs in almost every cue. Many cues feature no tempo indication in Harline's autograph short score, and those that do often contain the word "rubato" within the tempo indication. The cue "Montage" is typical with its indication "Moderato and Rubato." If Harline's point in his temporal approach in this score is an evocation of epic parlando-rubato song from Greece, as I argue above, then the style needs to run through the entire score. Fortunately, temporal fluctuations haunt every cue, reinforcing it as a reference to a Greek topic rather than a convenience for lining up events in the score with events on the image track without recourse to a click track.

A similar uncertainty stems from Harline's approach to meter. There are several key moments later in the film that make champion use of metric instability. During the sequence when Mrs. St. Aubyn lies on the floor of her room in a cataleptic trance with Thea watching over her, Harline introduces a five quarter-note ostinato in the low strings in the context of 4/4 meter. This music supports Kyra's verbal persecution of Thea as a *Vorvolaka* (Figure 8.3).

Figure 8.3 Leigh Harline, "Vorvolaka" from *Isle of the Dead*, mm. 15–19

While the polymeter of the cue "*Vorvolaka*" provides one sort of metric uncertainty, Harline's next cue offers a kind of *augenmusik* typical of certain Renaissance madrigals, as it requires the score to see the connection to the text. Another bass ostinato – now in three – contradicts the printed 4/4 meter, but without the printed score, this moment of uncertainty would be imperceptible as very little in the music suggests the printed meter (Figure 8.4, "The Coffin") This music unfolds on the soundtrack as cinematographer Jack MacKenzie's camera draws nearer the makeshift coffin in which Mrs. St. Aubyn has been prematurely interred. Why would Harline deploy this music in the wrong meter unless he was exploring a theme of metric uncertainty in his score?

In addition to its unusual metric notation, "The Coffin" also features no modal or tonal center. This condition prevails in most cues. Even though Harline's harmonies are almost always tertian chords, as we saw in his "Main

Figure 8.4 Leigh Harline, "The Coffin" from *Isle of the Dead*, mm. 63–66

Title," they are almost never deployed in a way that promotes hearing a tonal or modal center. His first and only perfect authentic cadence arrives at the very end of the "End Title" cue where an A-flat major chord with an F# in the melody, easily heard as an enharmonic spelling of an A-flat7 chord, resolves to D-flat major. With the title card reading "The End" on the image track, this lonely instance of tonal closure in the score feels conventional yet necessary.

An Uncertain Conclusion

Harline's approach to scoring for Lewton differs notably from Webb's. For example, Harline does not create motifs that consistently function as signifiers of narrative elements. He lets instrumentation bear the weight of signification. There are a handful of recurrent motifs almost relentlessly present in his score, but the two most readily discernible of them do not consistently appear in clear reference to any particular person, place, or thing. The first appears in the opening measure of the "Main Title," an ascending triplet figure that repeats and holds the note or notes of the last triplet. The other is the parlando-style melody heard first in measures 5–9 of the "Main Title" cue. This latter motif serves as the basis for the understated trumpet fanfares that begin identically with this figure. Both of these melodic ideas appear frequently in the film, especially in transitions when no dialogue competes with them on the soundtrack. They suggest the melancholy mood that prevails throughout the film, but they do not function as specific signifiers in the Steiner-Webb mold.

The consistent presence of Harline's two motifs appearing as they do in most of the film's cues suggests that they serve Harline's desire to perform the functions Claudia Gorbman identifies as "Continuity" and "Unity."[27] These motifs help the film transition through its many temporal ellipses, maintaining the film's continuity while also uniting the film's content. Gorbman argues, "The major unifying force in Hollywood scoring is the use of musical themes."[28]

While Roy Webb consistently has his motifs perform double duty by associating them with some task of signification, Harline's approach allows his themes to appear in most scene changes without adding uncertainty through inconsistent signification.

And there Harline's commitment to avoid uncertainty ends. As Lewton's film offers a conclusion that "uncertainty is good," Harline's promotion of musical uncertainty through his management of time and harmony feels entirely fitting.

Up until *Isle of the Dead* and even within certain scenes in it, the Lewton unit exploited uncertainty as key to their approach to horror. With *Isle of the Dead*, they argue that uncertainty is the ideal human condition. Harline's score with its parlando-rubato style and ambivalent harmony provides a most fitting accompaniment to this singular film. It emphasizes the film's deeper, more important dichotomy of uncertainty vs. certainty in ways that it never addresses the surface dichotomy of Reason vs. Superstition.

Harline's score for *Isle of the Dead* received rare favorable notice from journalistic critics. The review in *Variety* offered that, "Leigh Harline's musical score, conducted by C. Bakaleinikoff, is particularly effective."[29] *The Hollywood Reporter* was more expansive: "And Leigh Harline comes up with another good score. In fact his music accounts for a large part of the entertainment value of the picture and it is certainly a good substitute for what might have been forced dialogue."[30] Ideally this chapter amplifies these good notices, just as it contradicts the low opinions this film prompted in its producer and his biographers.

Notes

1. Joel Siegel, *Val Lewton: The Reality of Terror* (New York: Viking Press, 1973), p. 72.
2. Clive Dawson, "Ardel Wray: Val Lewton's Forgotten Screenwriter," *Bright Lights Film Journal* (December 26, 2018).
3. Some of these rewrites were certainly done by Ardel Wray and Josef Mischel. All contemporary informants agree that Lewton wrote the final drafts for his productions, but how drastically these differ from those of his credited writers is unknown. As there are essentially two "final" versions of the script for *Isle of the Dead*, we can assume that all three writers worked on each version.
4. Ardel Wray and Josef Mischel, "The Isle of the Dead," screenplay. RKO Radio Pictures Studio Records (Collection PASC 3). UCLA Library Special Collections, Charles E. Young Research Library, University of California, Los Angeles. With *Isle of the Dead*, Lewton returned to his habit of not taking credit for screenplays; however, he rewrote Wray's and Mischel's work for the final drafts. Rose Hobart was originally slated to play Cathy. She was on the call sheets during the film's first nine days of shooting.

5. Val Lewton, Letters to Nina and Lucy Lewton, two undated and one dated "December, 1944." Val Lewton Papers, 1924–1982. Library of Congress, Washington, DC.
6. Siegel, p. 150.
7. Edmund Bansak, *Fearing the Dark: The Val Lewton Career* (Jefferson, NC: MacFarland & Company, 1995), p. 277.
8. Memo from Publicity Department, RKO Radio Pictures, Inc. Hollywood, California titled "Roy Webb Biography," Margaret Herrick Library, Academy of Motion Picture Arts and Sciences, Beverly Hills, California.
9. Christopher Palmer, *The Composer in Hollywood* (London: Marion Boyars, 1990), p. 162.
10. This and the biographical information that follows on Harline is found in Ross Care, "The Film Music of Leigh Harline," *Film Music Notebook*, Volume 2, Number 2 (1978), p. 32.
11. Most of Disney's early features were made under a team concept. *Snow White and the Seven Dwarfs*'s three composers were outnumbered by its six directors and eight screenwriters. This approach differs from any other studio in Hollywood and may illustrate how Walt Disney distributed creative control so widely as to render all creative personnel invisible save himself.
12. Douglas Gomery, *The Hollywood Studio System: A History* (London: British Film Institute, 2005), p. 153.
13. Ibid.
14. For readers curious why this book deals with Lewton's horror films only and not his two dramas produced at RKO, one answer lies in Sawtell's score for *Youth Runs Wild*. I share James Agee's high opinion of that film. He named it co-best picture of 1944 along with *The Curse of the Cat People*. The film offers a foretaste of Italian neo-realism with its understated faux documentary style and lower-class characters dealing with mundane problems. But Sawtell's score is nothing if not overwrought as he tries to compensate for the film's drab content with loud cues striving to wring every ounce of melodrama out of the proceedings. My celebratory approach has little to offer.
15. Sawtell scored or collaborated in scoring *The Mummy's Curse* (1943), *Dead Man's Eyes* (1943), *Jungle Woman* (1943), *Weird Woman* (1944), and *Calling Dr. Death* (1943) at Universal, all while remaining a freelance composer.
16. David Bordwell, Janet Staiger, and Kristin Thompson, *The Classical Hollywood Cinema: Film Style and Mode of Production to 1960* (New York: Columbia University Press, 1985), p. 265.
17. Cited in Siegel, p. 32.
18. J. P. Telotte, *Dreams of Darkness: Fantasy and the Films of Val Lewton* (Urbana: University of Illinois Press, 1985), pp. 13–14.
19. "Val Lewton File" from "Michael Ravnitzky Papers," National Security Archive at George Washington University.
20. The relentless mickey-mousing in Webb's score for *My Favorite Wife* (1940) with its comically exaggerated correspondences between image and music provides a much clearer use of a click track to facilitate minute coordination than anything produced for the Lewton unit.

21. Leigh Harline, autograph score, *Isle of the Dead*. RKO Radio Pictures Studio Records (Collection PASC 3). UCLA Library Special Collections, Charles E. Young Research Library, University of California, Los Angeles.
22. M. L. West, *Ancient Greek Music* (Oxford: Clarendon Press, 1992), p. 154.
23. Spotting sheets for *Isle of the Dead*. RKO Radio Pictures Studio Records (Collection PASC 3). UCLA Library Special Collections, Charles E. Young Research Library, University of California, Los Angeles.
24. Main Title spotting sheet for *Isle of the Dead*. RKO Radio Pictures Studio Records (Collection PASC 3). UCLA Library Special Collections, Charles E. Young Research Library, University of California, Los Angeles.
25. Roy Webb's music tends toward modern harmonies outside the tonal system and generous contrapuntal interest. In a letter to Christopher Palmer, he attributed this tendency toward contrapuntal textures to his education at Columbia University where he learned his craft studying the music of J. S. Bach. See Palmer, p. 162.
26. See the lengthy quote from director Mark Robson about this sequence quoted in Siegel, pp. 72–74. That quote is echoed in Bansak, p. 269, and the scene's visuals are briefly analyzed in Telotte, p. 135.
27. Claudia Gorbman, *Unheard Melodies: Narrative Film Music* (Bloomington: Indiana University Press, 1987), p. 73.
28. Ibid., p. 90.
29. "Isle of the Dead," *Variety* (September 7, 1945).
30. "Isle of the Dead," *The Hollywood Reporter* (September 7, 1945).

9 "DAINTY LITTLE NOTES, AIN'T THEY?": ROY WEBB'S AGE OF REASON IN *BEDLAM*

On May 25, 1945, *The Body Snatcher* opened at the two most famous theaters specializing in showing horror films, the Rialto in New York City and the Hawaii in Los Angeles. The reviews were uniformly positive and the opening weekend box office receipts smashed records at the Hawaii and approached doing so at the Rialto.[1]

RKO rewarded Lewton with a vastly increased budget of US$350,000 for his next horror vehicle for Boris Karloff. This budget represents a considerable increase over his earlier films, which ranged in budget from *The Seventh Victim*'s punitive US$116,000 to *Isle of the Dead*'s inflated US$246,000. To place these figures in context, consider RKO's "A" budget pictures from the same period. *Bedlam* went into production at the same time as *The Bells of St. Mary's*, a vehicle for star Bing Crosby. That film's budget of US$1.3 million provides a sense of scale. RKO produced fourteen films in 1945 with budgets greater than a million dollars.[2] *Bedlam* is not an "A" picture by any stretch of the imagination, although it did benefit from getting to recycle the church set from *The Bells of St. Mary's* for its titular asylum.

The film's core story concerns the efforts of a young woman, Nell Bowen (Anna Lee), to reform the treatment of the mentally ill at St. Mary's of Bethlehem Hospital, known colloquially as "Bedlam." But first she must journey from cynical entertainer, to injured party seeking revenge, to inmate at Bedlam wrongfully interred, and only then to reformer.

Nell's antagonists are Lord Mortimer (Billy House) and Master Sims (Boris Karloff), members of the upper classes who seek to thwart her reforms. These hypocrites congratulate themselves for residing within an Age of Reason, but they defend an inhuman order that makes sport of the afflicted. Unusual within the series, Roy Webb devotes considerable musical attention to the film's antagonists. He accomplishes this through a vivid conjuration of eighteenth-century musical manners that led his orchestrator, Gilbert Grau, to comment to his copyist in marginalia in the orchestral score "Dainty little notes, ain't they."[3] Yet generic demands pull at Webb as topics of suspense and horror rooted in modern musical procedures unlike anything produced in the eighteenth century upend his stylistic evocation of the past. His modernist material draws the film into the present of 1940s America, a move necessary to the message picture for bringing the injustice of the past into comparison with contemporary injustice. In so doing, we will see Webb's music providing its own comment on how similar our times are to those depicted in the film.

WILLIAM HOGARTH, ART DIRECTOR AND MORE

For his final horror film, Lewton crafted a tale that, like *Isle of the Dead*, began with a painting as its inspiration. Lewton chose William Hogarth's Plate VIII from his series *The Rake's Progress* (1732–1735). This final image of the series is titled "Bedlam." Founded in the thirteenth century, "Bedlam" is Europe's oldest institution for the care of the mentally ill. The painting depicts Tom Rakewell – now penniless, diseased, and disgraced – half naked and surrounded by lunatics. Rakewell serves as the unwilling object of curiosity for two genteel upper-class ladies. The practice of allowing "persons of quality" to enter the hospital to satisfy their curiosity began in approximately 1598 and only ceased in 1770.[4]

Val Lewton wrote the script, although he again took credit under the pseudonym Carlos Keith. Also credited on the script is the film's director, Mark Robson. Insofar as many notes to the director appear within the script, we can assume that Lewton did the lion's share of the work.[5] Many of these notes to the director concern blocking particular scenes so that they recreate the mise-en-page of several of Hogarth's illustrations. For example, Lewton wanted the blocking in Hogarth's "Bedlam" recreated when the film's heroine, Nell Bowen, pays a visit to Master Sims, Apothecary General to St. Mary's of Bethlehem Hospital, to "see the loonies in their cages." The script reads: "This set up should approximate the picture of Bedlam by Hogarth, with Sims and Nell in the places of the mistress and the maid, visitors to the institution who can be seen in the left middle of the painting."[6]

Other Hogarth paintings used to inform the blocking of the film include *Industry and Idleness* Plate XI "The idle 'prentice executed at Tyburn"; *A Harlot's Progress* Plate I "Moll Hackabout arrives in London at the Bell Inn, Cheapside"; and *Hudibras* Plate IX "The Committee." When recalling the film, Mark Robson boasted that, "we virtually used Hogarth as our art director."[7] The artworks themselves also appear in the film in brief flashes throughout the credit sequence and at each scene change.

A Mixed-Message Picture

Like Hogarth's paintings, which careen between satirical caricature and moralizing instruction, often revealing themselves to be both, Lewton's script struggles to be multiple things. Lewton surely meant the script to be the blueprint for a commercially successful horror film, although ironically Jack Gross complicated this ambition by forcing cuts to save money, cuts that diminish the horrific potentials within the story. His excisions include several situations in which Nell is menaced inside Bedlam and the removal of a harrowing chase across the rooftops of London at the film's climax.[8]

Lewton also wanted to create a historical drama, escalating his attention to period detail first revealed in *Mademoiselle Fifi* and refined in *The Body Snatcher*. He further enmeshed a message into his film by allocating several speeches about the need for more humane treatment of the mentally ill to his characters.

Some of these aims work at cross purposes. Much of the film's horrific content flows from "othering" the inmates, resulting in conflicts with the humanitarian messaging. Lewton's screenplay participates in this "othering." A passage describing Bedlam's inmates during Nell's (and the audience's) first visit typifies Lewton's conflicted relationship with the inmates as simultaneously the objects of a horrified gaze and deserving humane treatment:

> . . . strange aimless human beings can be dimly seen. At the same moment that this curious room reveals itself to the eye the horrid SOUND of Bedlam bursts upon the ear; the moans, the shrieks, the maniacal laughter, and the bird-like twitter of idiocy. At the far end of the room, Sims leads Nell from the dark doorway to a blazing square of sunshine. . .
>
> MED. CLOSE SHOT – Nell and Sims are seen through the weaving ribbons in the fumbling hands of an idiot who is amusing himself at "Cat's Cradle."[9]

In this moment, Lewton situates his audience along with Nell in the position of observing the lunatics in the asylum in a manner recreating Hogarth's moralizing image by effectively implicating his audience in the very abuse the film and the painting it is based upon criticize.

Lewton's tale of reform and horror offers a conflicted reading of the era wherein he set it. The film's foreword places the conflict in the foreground.

Presented with Hogarth's Plate XI from *Industry and Idleness*, "The idle 'prentice executed at Tyburn," behind it,[10] Lewton's foreword reads: "London–1761 The people of the Eighteenth Century called their Period 'The Age of Reason–". Here Lewton conjures the "hermeneutics of suspicion" with its roots in the Enlightenment by suggesting that what people call themselves may not be what they are.[11] His failure to close his own scare quotes begs the reader to manufacture a "however" even before the film can supply one. Here again Lewton implicates his audience in his project by inviting them to a knowing relationship with his foreword by assuming that they too have a criticism of the Age of Reason already unfolding in their heads.

The film's conflicted tone – often humorous, other times frightening, and frequently moved to moral outrage – marries with the tone of William Hogarth's output. A supremely funny caricaturist and a master of sensitive portraiture, Hogarth simultaneously mocked and lamented, cajoled and amused his large English clientele. Hogarth's output contributed more than virtual art direction, as Robson claimed later. It provided the model for the film's conflicted tone.

Lewton's Age of Reason

In his sterling analysis of the film, J. P. Telotte described *Bedlam*'s depiction of eighteenth-century England this way: "In this Age of Reason man has enthroned his rational capacities and set about imposing an artificial order on his world, and he has begun by casting out those whose claims to reason are suspect."[12]

Bedlam houses many figures who appear quite unable to reason. Dan the Dog (Robert Clarke) provides one of the most likable examples of this group. He imagines himself a dog whose enthusiasm in gentle human company registers effortlessly on his face. When Sims addresses him, Dan cringes pitifully, offering one of the film's many poignant moments for Bedlam's sufferers. Yet the cages in Bedlam contain frightful personages whose bare, white arms reach out to claw at passersby. They too occupy this category of inmates unable to reason.

Some of Bedlam's residents teeter between lucidity and delusion, like Sydney Long (Ian Wolfe), who imagines himself a lawyer who has been blocked from practicing for having many enemies. Still others, like Oliver Todd (Jason Robards Sr.), have been interred not due to insanity but for other reasons. Nell eventually falls into this latter category. As Telotte explains, "Anyone can be declared mad in this society, although especially vulnerable are those who threaten to disturb its normal appearance."[13]

Evidence of the artificial order appears everywhere in the film. We see it in the bizarre make-up and costuming including the wigs, powders, pomades, applied beauty marks, and layers upon layers of clothing worn by the characters. These measures are often revealed to be disguising an ugly reality, such as the scene early on when Master Sims unsuccessfully attempts to extract a bribe from the

Quaker mason, Hannay (Richard Fraser). Nell bursts into the scene unexpectedly, causing Sims to hurriedly don his wig to hide his unkempt and graying hair. The immediacy of Sims's action underscores how automatic, how conditioned he is to the dictates of the artificial order of his age. Master Sims strives to deploy exquisite manners when interacting with his social betters including Lord Mortimer and Mortimer's protégée Nell. Yet among those he perceives as lower caste, his refined manners vanish. Earlier in that same scene, Sims contents himself to keep Hannay waiting to discuss the Institute's business indefinitely while growling orders to his manservant Podge (Larry Wheat) without the least hint of a "please" or "thank you."

Beyond costuming and manners, the film depicts an Age of Reason in which a corrupt social order allocates positions of authority based on favor rather than merit. Sims holds his position of responsibility entirely owing to Lord Mortimer's favor. Sims abuses this favor first in his own interest by interring a rival poet named Colby in Bedlam. We see Colby murdered in the film's first scene. Later Sims abuses his position of trust in favor of both his and his patron's interests by contriving to have Nell locked up in Bedlam to silence her calls for reform.

Worse even than the corruption of the film's titular institution is the indifference the powerful feel for the afflicted among them. The death of a young inmate as he performs for an audience of the influential at Sims's insistence prompts laughter and jesting from the witnesses to a crime. This scene and others provide ample evidence of a society gone mad.

Nell the Reluctant Reformer, an Analytical Synopsis

The film centers on young Nell Bowen. She is an actress now employed as protégée to Lord Mortimer whose lone responsibility is making her employer laugh. Quick-witted and cynical, Nell performs this duty well. The film follows her journey from calloused indifference to a more sympathetic posture toward those less fortunate than herself. Nell is a reluctant reformer, however, and her calls for reform in Bedlam flow initially from her hatred of Sims and not from any reservoir of kind feelings.

After seeing Colby fall to his death trying to escape Bedlam, Lord Mortimer commands Master Sims to come and account for this tragedy. During that interview, Nell reveals that Lord Mortimer was concerned for Colby owing to his having "paid in advance for poetry promised in future." Colby was to write a rhymed comedy for a party Lord Mortimer planned for the Vauxhall Gardens in one week's time. Colby's death matters only insofar as it cost Lord Mortimer "a night of laughter." Sims suggests that he might be employed to write the masque in Colby's place and sells Lord Mortimer on the idea by promising to have "his company of wits, the Bedlamites" perform the play.

In this scene, the first of many shared between Nell and Sims, Nell's contempt for Sims begins to manifest itself. As the cause for this encounter was the consequence of a rivalry between poets capable of amusing Lord Mortimer, we might reasonably conclude that Nell feels some rivalry of her own for Sims, who seems intent on insinuating himself into Lord Mortimer's company as a self-styled wit. Validating this surmise, later in the film, when Nell has disqualified herself as Lord Mortimer's protégée, Sims will supply his niece (Elizabeth Russell) as a substitute for his fallen rival just as he nominated himself as substitute for the literally fallen Colby.

From here, Nell's opinion of Sims worsens, although her commitment to reform has not fully materialized. She takes Lord Mortimer's advice and pays her admission to see Bedlam's inmates. Sims strives to amuse her with his showman's banter about the animality of the inmates. The film strongly implies that Sims takes sexual advantage of one young female inmate, Dorothea the Dove (Joan Newton). Seeing Sims tenderly touch the young woman's face prompts Nell to depart the asylum in anger. Outside, she strikes Sims out of disgust for his glib way of talking about his charges. Hannay witnesses this blow and chides Nell for delivering it. In their first interaction of many in the film, Nell presents Hannay with a hard facade as she denies having any feelings of pity for the inmates. She concludes the scene saying, "Come a week hence to Vauxhall in the evening and you will see me laughing at those same loonies you think I pity."

Sims's masque at the Vauxhall opens with a speech delivered by a young inmate credited as "The Gilded Boy" (Glenn Vernon). An allegorical figure for Reason, the Gilded Boy haltingly recites a speech praising Lord Mortimer that Sims readily admits having beaten into the lad that morning. The spectacle serves only to set up Sims's punch line, "You see, Milord, Reason is overcome with emotion when it must speak of you." After straining to utter a few more words of Sims's speech, the Gilded Boy collapses dead, the heavy coating of gilt having blocked his pores.

Lord Mortimer and his guests display no dismay at this cruel spectacle. On the contrary, they laugh uproariously at Sims's jests over the youth's death. Among the party, two figures do not join in the merriment at the dead boy's fate: Nell, whose own position remains threatened by Sims, and the historical figure, John Wilkes (Leland Hodgson). The historical Wilkes was, among other things, a ferocious critic of William Hogarth whose flippant satires Wilkes – an inveterate reformer – detested. Hogarth retaliated with a famous engraving of Wilkes looking demonic and holding on a staff a miter with "Liberty" printed upon it. In the film, Wilkes is a member of the opposition Whig Party while Lord Mortimer is an enthusiastic Tory.[14] Nell storms out of the performance, but Wilkes remains to take playful jabs at his Tory host.

Nell takes her concern for the maltreatment of Sims's inmates to Hannay. She begins to describe the sad events at the Vauxhall, but Hannay cuts her off:

"Thou need not tell me. It is a bad time for the poor – and people suffer, the ones with wit and the ones without." He suggests that she use her influence with Lord Mortimer to effect needed change.

All goes well with Nell's efforts to improve Bedlam until Master Sims points out that the reforms Nell wants will cost Lord Mortimer an additional 500 guineas in taxes. Lord Mortimer promptly withdraws his support for Nell's cause, claiming that keeping up appearances at court is a costly matter for a gentleman. Nell loses her temper and insults Lord Mortimer, effectively ending their comradeship.

At this point, one should still doubt the sincerity of Nell's commitments. She takes her cause to Wilkes. In a marginal note in his script for the film, Boris Karloff objects to the scene in which Nell makes a pact with Wilkes to force reforms on Bedlam without Lord Mortimer's or Sims's approval. In the margins of his script, Karloff wrote: "I think this rather overstates the case. Nell wants first to get at Sims, then Mortimer, and then more or less incidentally Bedlam. Don't make Nell a crusader."[15]

Karloff's insight here is keen. Nell works for reforms out of personal spite rather than sincere desire for a better world. In a maneuver designed to thwart Nell's efforts to enlist Wilkes in her cause, Sims and Lord Mortimer contrive to have Nell adjudged insane and committed to Bedlam. At that point, Nell begins her true journey toward reformer.

Initially Nell tries to find a means of protection from her fellow inmates. She convinces Hannay, who by coincidence is aiding in erecting masonry in Bedlam, to give her his trowel. Hannay balks initially but succumbs to Nell's superior skills of persuasion. Nell then introduces herself to Sydney Long, Oliver Todd, and Dan the Dog – the most reasonable of Bedlam's inmates – with whom she plays cards. During the game, she hears the groaning of another of Sims's prisoners who is being tormented with "a dose of iron."[16] Nell aids the poor man by placing strips of cloth torn from her petticoats between the man's flesh and the iron. During her act of kindness, Dorothea the Dove steals Nell's trowel. Its disappearance bears symbolic significance, for here Nell switches from self-interested figure to actual reformer.

Master Sims mocks Nell's former life as a reformer only to have her admit that she would like to minister to the needs of her fellow inmates with clean straw, improved food, and soap and water. Sims obliges her, and Nell makes good. Returning later to mock her progress, Sims wonders at what good Nell will do with a lifetime of such Augean labors. Sims's sneering reminder of Nell's lifelong commitment underscores her terrifying predicament in a horror film notably short on shudders.

Meanwhile, Wilkes manages to gain Nell a fresh hearing. Sims strives to forestall Nell's restoration to society by prescribing for her a "remedy." On hearing of Sims's intention, the other inmates recoil in horror at its mention. Nell refuses, but Sims insists.

The inmates seize Sims to defend their benefactress in a maneuver Sims believed impossible. Nell escapes to the rooftop, as the inmates put Sims on trial. In a magnificent scene, Sims pleads his case to Sydney Long and Oliver Todd, claiming that he had to do all that he did so that he might keep his place in the great world. The speech resembles Galbraith's at the close of *The Leopard Man* among others and rehearses a favored trope of Lewton's; evil acts stem from the unjust pressures of the larger world. Sims's trial offers a lovely rhyme for Nell's trial earlier in the film. Todd concludes that Sims is sane. The inmates, having convicted Sims of sanity, determine that he has no place among them and send him out to the great world in a deft rebuke to the larger society of eighteenth-century London.

As Sims backs toward the door, Dorothea the Dove stabs him with Hannay's trowel. Fearful of retribution for killing the Apothecary General, the inmates bury Sims behind a wall they create with the bricks and mortar remaining at the construction site at which Hannay previously worked. Just as the last brick covers Sims, his eyes open indicating that he has been buried alive. This echo of Edgar Allan Poe aids in positioning the film within the horror genre.

The film concludes with Nell, Hannay, Wilkes, and the Chief Commissioner (John Goldsworthy) touring Bedlam, mystified by Sims's disappearance. Hannay notes the moist mortar on the wall where Sims is buried. He looks as if he will speak, but Nell talks him out of it. Dialogue announces that better treatment shall commence at Bedlam, Nell's reforms finally poised for implementation.

Roy Webb's Age of Reason

Roy Webb's task on *Bedlam* involved reinforcing the threads of the film's conflicting narrative tones as historical drama, message picture, and horror film. In this first task, he received good help from the film's carefully researched diegetic music and selective borrowing from his own work on the soundtrack for the film *Quality Street* (1937). In many ways, his labors on *Bedlam* resemble those on *The Body Snatcher*, when he had to provide period music designed to suture the audience with nineteenth-century Edinburgh and intensify scenes of overt violence. The scenes of violence in *Bedlam* are few, however, so now his music needed to manufacture the ominous potential of horrific events in a film featuring few of them. Composing suspenseful music rather than music intensifying violence put *Bedlam* more in Webb's wheelhouse.

Several scenes in *Bedlam* take place on the streets of London. In an effort to stretch the film's budget and reinforce the sense of time and place, the filmmakers called upon diegetic music of the sort presented by the street singer in *The*

Body Snatcher. Here the RKO Music Department ran into a problem. Establishing Scotland through Scottish folksongs proves relatively easy. London, however, is harder to capture in a simple musical topic. Perhaps Hollywood, itself an offshoot from "the colonies," owes too much to London for an English musical topic to emerge easily. K. J. Donnelly claims that "there is a little piece of a Hollywood sound stage that is forever England" as he unpacks English and other ethnic signifiers in Hollywood films.[17] Here I am informed by Mary Ann Doane's observation that musical topics stem from "the nineteenth-century colonist imperative to conquer other times, other spaces."[18] London is not a colony. The film's solution can be found in Lewton's screenplay. The first scene on the street, in addition to recreating the mise-en-page of Plate I of *A Harlot's Progress*, asks for street hawkers to perform "street cries" – a genre of song announcing wares comprised of a few snatches of memorable melody. Street cries filled the air of London in the eighteenth century.

Interestingly, Donna Lee, who played the sweet-voiced street singer in *The Body Snatcher*, appears in *Bedlam* hawking lavender, the first street cry Lewton mentions. Lewton strived to invest his films with as much historical accuracy as his budgets allowed. The text Donna Lee sings can be found in *A History of the Cries of London, Ancient and Modern* published in 1881.[19] Whether this was the source consulted is unknown, but at least it confirms an antique provenance for the film's first street cry and evidence that someone executed some research to locate historically accurate materials. The text is not in the screenplay, so the person responsible was likely an unknown figure from RKO's Music Department of the sort celebrated in Catherine Haworth's research.

Roy Webb's work focused less on evoking London in the audience's mind than 1761 when the cosmopolitan gallant style had recently emerged. Additionally, Webb devoted energy shoring up the film's thin horrific content by deploying ample doses of suspenseful music. Examining Webb's Main Title cue provides a good summary of his approach for the film as a whole.

Measures 1–9 (Figure 9.1, "Main Title"] are entirely borrowed from Webb's Oscar-nominated score for *Quality Street*, a comedy set in London in 1805 and then surging ahead to 1815. The film lost a quarter of a million dollars for RKO and prompted the studio to allow its star's contract to expire at the year's end.[20] That the star was Katharine Hepburn reminds us how RKO managed to lose money through most of its years of operation. As music introducing a comedy, the genre is all wrong. But then *Bedlam* is based on the images of a satirist and is full of characters who live on their wits, so perhaps not quite so wrong as it seems. These measures are full of diatonic bustle with nary an accidental to be found, quite unlike Webb's usual, modernistic approach. With its cheerful prattling, the opening of the "Main Title" might be heard as the music of the world of appearances. Like the pomade and artificial beauty marks, this music offers a pleasing surface with no hidden depths to plumb.

Figure 9.1 Roy Webb, "Main Title" from Bedlam, mm. 1–9

Measures 10–18 (Figure 9.2, "Main Title") are original and witness a sudden modal shift from the opening's bubbly C major to a stern A minor presented in the low brasses. The running sixteenth notes also vanish as the entire rhythmic pace slows. Here Webb conjures a darker side of the great world. He deploys the music of its rules and walls, and its pitiless maltreatment of the unfortunate.

Measures 19–29 largely reprise the stern A minor material, but now in the full string orchestra rather than just the low brasses. While warmer in timbre, Webb's music here takes on a strict quality as contrapuntal interior voices thicken the texture in an evocation of a "learned" topic.

Measures 30–37 (Figure 9.3, "Main Title") remain in A minor, but Webb's marking of "scherzando" and thinning of the texture to homophony lighten the mood. Insofar as the marking "scherzando" indicates that the performers should approach the music playfully, or in the manner of a joke, Webb clearly wants to evoke the tone of the film's opening. The minor mode and the playful tone remind of the film's rival wits as they conjure amusement from suffering.

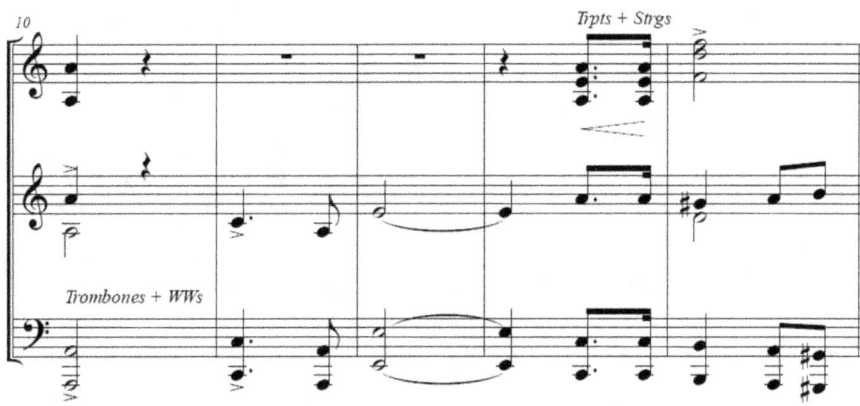

Figure 9.2 Roy Webb, "Main Title" from Bedlam, mm. 10–18

Measures 38–52 witness a switch to E major. The tune remains the same as the "scherzando" melody just heard, albeit in a new mode. The texture thickens over the course of these measures almost as though all society laughs at the bleak humor referenced in the previous section.

Measures 53–58 witness a truncated return of the stark material in A minor, now performed by the entire orchestra. Webb departs his joking music of artificial amusement to refresh his listener's memory of his music of the great world's terrors.

Measures 59–62 (Figure 9.4, "Main Title") provide the accompaniment for Lewton's foreword for the film. The melody is diatonic and in A minor, even moving up an A minor triad at its close. The underlying harmony drops all pretense of resulting from an eighteenth-century topic for moving always in

Figure 9.3 Roy Webb, "Main Title" from *Bedlam*, mm. 30–37

Figure 9.4 Roy Webb, "Main Title" from *Bedlam*, mm. 59–62

root position from am to FM (with major seventh) to dm to B-flat major and ending on A major. Webb abandons his period topic and turns to something more modern with the melody's clash of minor against the harmony's major. The harmony itself offers a progression entirely outside the harmonic practices of the eighteenth century.

Figure 9.5 Roy Webb, "Main Title" from *Bedlam*, mm. 63–70

Measures 63 to the end (Figure 9.5, "Main Title") of the cue commence with the dissolve onscreen from the foreword title card to the image of Colby dangling from the gutter of Bedlam. The film opens on a note of the horrific, so Webb's music abandons a tonal center and deploys partial ascending chromatic scales drawn from a suspense topic similar to his scenes of violence in *The Body Snatcher* for his reliance on partial chromatic scales. As the warder begins crushing Colby's hand with his boot, Webb presents loud outbursts in the muted brasses comprised of a tritone with two minor second dyads above. The man's scream (borrowed from recordings used in *King Kong*)[21] coincides with a great blast of the dissonant chord in muted brass. The cue concludes with a melody in a solo horn outlining a fully diminished C# minor seventh chord. This last sonority, an unmistakable element from a horror topic, drags the cue far from where it began in sunny C major.

Reviewing the "Main Title" cue's contents, a topic representing the bustling society appears prominently at the open. A powerful musical evocation of mid-eighteenth-century grandeur follows in the stern A minor material, which paints the rigidity of the era's institutions. The "scherzando" calls forth the blithe indifference of the times. Then Webb presented a sudden stylistic rupture. The ending ceases the cue's efforts to transport the audience back in time by presenting material suitable for suspense and horror. In the "Main Title" cue, Webb has managed to foreshadow all the music he will write for the film by addressing each of his diverse tasks. In addition to history and horror, there is even a dash of messaging consistent with the film to follow in the laughing minor-mode "scherzando." Central to my claim is Webb's presentation of stylistically conflicting materials far beyond the juxtaposition of the opening's cheerful C major music and the stern A minor material.

Interestingly, nothing of the musical material heard in the "Main Title" returns at any point in the subsequent cues. These are not motifs linked to events in the narrative, but representations of the conflicted and conflicting forces at work in the film. Ascribing meanings to them is partially an imaginative act as the autograph score, where I found Webb's previous labels cited in other chapters, is not present in UCLA's archive of RKO film scores. It is also not included among the scores Webb shared with Christopher Palmer, now housed at the University of Syracuse Library where Palmer worked. As the material does not return within the film, we must discover its meaning through associations within earlier music. My hearing of mid-eighteenth-century music informs my imagination here. As the "Main Title" of *Bedlam* is one of the more discussed cues in the literature, having other writers draw similar conclusions helps. Scott MacQueen, for example, claims that the "Main Title" "employs contradictory styles to reduce the themes of the film to a perfect miniature."[22]

Rather than discuss one by one each of these potentialities found in the "Main Title" as they find their echo and amplification in later cues, I will look in some detail at several cues or points within cues that demonstrate the excellence of Webb's contribution in offering a musical mirror for the conflicts within the film's structure. This exploration reinforces that other points in Webb's score gesture toward hybridization of eighteenth-century musical manners representing the Age of Reason quickly juxtaposed with modernist material typical of Webb's approach to scenes of suspense and horror.

Music and Madness

Roy Webb's cue "Nell's Visit to the Asylum" (Figure 9.6) supports the scene cited from Lewton's screenplay in which Nell Bowen visits Bedlam for the first time. Lewton's script explains that at this point, "the horrid SOUND of Bedlam burst upon the ear." The cue begins with Master Sims reciting his preparatory pitch for the amusement to come including his quote from a speech found in *The Honest Whore* (1604) by Thomas Dekker, which includes a scene in Bedlam.

Figure 9.6 Roy Webb, "Nell's Visit to the Asylum" from *Bedlam*, mm. 31–41

Webb's music for this cue begins with music appropriate to the period as a melody in parallel thirds in G minor unfolds over a D pedal, culminating in an exciting E-flat minor seven chord. Under the dialogue including the Dekker quotation, Webb switches to a subtle two-part invention that leaves the period harmonically through the lower voice offering broken augmented triads as the upper voice eventually takes up a partial chromatic scale ascending, Webb's favored mechanism for introducing suspense. As Nell enters Bedlam, Webb abandons triadic references. The melody here mostly presents an ascending chromatic scale, although it begins and ends with 0-1-4 sets before ending on an ascending diminished triad over a chord made up of seven pitch classes.

To simplify Webb's approach, what begins tonally and "in period" turns by the cue's end to an atonal suspense topic impossible prior to the twentieth century. The climax of the cue finds Webb's music overwhelmed on the soundtrack by the cacophonous sound effects of Bedlam. This transformation of the soundtrack from locus of orchestral underscore to sound effects is called for in the script. The moment ranks among the most effective in Lewton's entire output at providing a jolt to the audience.

Webb's next two cues support Sims's Masque of Madness. The first cue is entirely borrowed from a ball scene from Webb's score for *Quality Street*. The simplistic tonal progression of this period-sounding confection speaks volumes to Webb's low opinion of antique dance music. The piece is in G major. The chord changes each measure, rocking back and forth between tonic and dominant-seventh until the final cadence where Webb adds one submediant chord before the final dominant-seventh chord.

Next Webb presents a sprightly gavotte. The dance unfolds in many short sections, each one in a stable major key. Indeed, the material is so stable that only one short section features any accidentals at all.

The Masque of Madness presents the reasonable veneer of the era as Lord Mortimer's guests delight in observing the patients from Bedlam displayed for their amusement. The RKO Music Department could have easily supplied any number of actual works from the period to accompany Lord Mortimer's party. Webb elected instead to recycle and compose music of brutal harmonic simplicity and slavish diatonicism. His neo-classicist approach is less an intervention into modern music than a negative comment on the Age of Reason.

Sims's Masque of Madness and the depiction of Lord Mortimer and his guests function as the film's most pointed negative comment on the age as well. This is also the scene in which Nell's hostility toward Sims passes the breaking point. "I've seen enough," she announces as her patron's eyes twinkle at the merriment he has purchased for himself and his friends. The music of the scene, entirely diegetic, provides a simplistic and grinning accompaniment to the sad spectacle.

A cue from much later in the film, "Hannay Finds Nell," again juxtaposes the glib music of the period as Webb imagines it with the music of horror. The scene opens with Hannay's frightening walk into Bedlam's main chamber, includes his drawing Nell's attention over the din of her fellow inmates, and concludes with their conversation regarding first Wilkes and then the trowel. Webb's score responds with prompt changes in tone and style to suit the narrative. Nell recourses to manipulating the Quaker into giving her his trowel, a gift he does not wish to give for knowing she means to use it as a weapon. When she asks him, "Look at my face. Would you have me maimed, scarred," Webb's music switches to suit this strange seduction by introducing material marked "tenderly" in stable E major. The music Webb composed to support Nell's dishonest reference to a pleasing surface hiding a violent intent could easily be from the period. Immediately before and after this switch, however, Webb's modernist style evoking suspense and horror prevails. Webb's music misses no opportunity to careen into a period style whenever commenting negatively on the times and its fixation on surfaces.

This might raise an interesting question. Musicians of the eighteenth century supplied ample models for a music of horror and suspense within the theatrical works of the age. Christoph Willibald Gluck's *Orfeo ed Euridice* (1762) – a hugely popular and influential work – presents ample topical music concerning horror in the Act II dances of the furies, for example. Webb, an inveterate enthusiast of the opera since his youth, had to know that scene and others like it in the theatrical music of Wolfgang Amadeus Mozart or the terrifying "Sturm und Drang" symphonies of Franz Joseph Haydn. Why did Webb supply modernistic music for the scenes of suspense and horror while reserving his eighteenth-century topic for scenes of "the great world" Sims feared and its moral indifference to the suffering of others?

Perhaps Webb's modern style serves to link the horrors hidden beneath the superficial beauty of the Age of Reason more effectively for drawing the messaging of the film into the present context. A lack of good treatment for the less fortunate was not a unique problem of the distant past or faraway places, but a pressing and contemporary problem in the aftermath of a world war that saw millions displaced, hungry, and shattered. As much of the film's horror stems rather ironically from the film's "othering" of Bedlam's inmates, Webb's modern music reinforces scenes when injustice is revealed for what it is in the film. Here, perhaps, Webb wanted his audience to hear how contemporary the film's messaging really is. To illustrate this point, I turn to the musical depiction of Hannay, the Quaker.

A Quaker Chorale

Nell Bowen is the film's protagonist and one of the more dynamic heroines in the entire horror output of the 1930s and 1940s. Hannay, the Quaker, by contrast, enjoys the unenviable position of hero. Andrew Tudor offers this general characterization of the type:

> Although in strict story terms they may be their movie's protagonists, and although their capacity for autonomous action is an essential constituent of the genre's narrative progress through disorder to order, they are rarely afforded the same kind of attention routinely paid to heroic figures in other narrative forms. That is particularly the case where the movie's monster invites some degree of anthropomorphic sympathy, displacing audience involvement away from the official hero and onto the apparent 'villain.'[23]

Hannay definitely participates in containing the film's threat, Master Sims. He uses the information supplied him by Varney (Skelton Knaggs) that Nell is imprisoned in Bedlam to alert Wilkes. He reluctantly delivers Nell the trowel that Dorothea uses to strike Sims down. But his "capacity for autonomous action" is slight at best.

The film, meanwhile, heaps sympathy upon its "villain." Master Sims enjoys much of the film's most amusing dialogue. Moreover, Sims delivers a memorable and somewhat persuasive justification for his actions while on trial. His look of terror as the inmates wall him in while still alive is played for horror and shock both on the screen and in Webb's effectively frightening orchestral underscore. This expenditure of energy leaves scant left for the film's "hero."

Conversely, near the end, the film presents its "hero" Hannay as a potential threat. As Wilkes and the Chief Commissioner tour Bedlam with Hannay and Nell in the aftermath of Sims's murder, Hannay notices the moist mortar in the wall where the inmates encased Sims. He immediately knows that these bricks were newly laid, and not by the masons hired for the work. Webb's music turns decidedly suspenseful as Nell looks on in fear that Hannay will speak of it and the criminality of the inmates will be punished. For a brief moment, Hannay provides the film's last suspenseful threat.

Yet Hannay is the film's most consistent reformer, the closest thing the film depicts as a moral voice. In examining the scores for the earlier films, I often noted that Webb links his orchestral underscore to female characters, albeit with a few notable exceptions. In *Bedlam*, one cue primarily references Hannay; Webb titled it fittingly enough as "The Quaker." Webb provides the cue the marking "Religioso." As it is heard inside the Quaker meeting house during a service, an audience member might be within her or his rights to hear it as diegetic. But Quakers of the eighteenth century performed no music in their services, preferring to limit expression in meetings to heartfelt utterances only. Group singing of chorales would undermine their core tenets of worship by formalizing expressions of faith.

The cue is Webb's musical comment on Hannay and his beliefs including his instinct to advance reforms in the treatment of the afflicted. While sounding "in period," the instrumental Quaker Chorale is not stylistically possible in the Age of Reason for the harmony being entirely too strange. It progresses up a tritone in its lone phrase, an unthinkable trajectory prior to the twentieth century.

The key signature of Webb's cue is E-flat minor, an improbable key for the era. Hugh MacDonald's famous essay titled with symbols for the key signature of six flats and the meter 9/8 argues that the placement of musical works in keys remote from C major with large numbers of flats imparted "attributes of sensuousness and mysterious ecstasy" upon them.[24] MacDonald further observes that "puritanical" composers avoided them.[25]

Webb's harmonic progression for his E-flat minor chorale unfolds as follows: i VI III IV VII III i iv #IV. The A-flat of the penultimate iv chord serves as the leading tone of the cadence to the final chord built on A. The string of major sonorities in the chorale's middle, including a chromatically altered subdominant chord, lends the music an odd normalcy. But the beginning and ending are disqualifying as music from the period of the film. Webb, who bragged about his careful study of Bach's chorales in his first letter to Christopher Palmer,[26] surely knew exactly how "wrong" his Quaker Chorale is. Webb's choices invest Hannay's Quaker beliefs not only with modernity in terms of the chorale's musical language, but with a modern and sensual moral sensibility to echo MacDonald's argument on the signification of its key.

Unlike the dance music heard at the Vauxhall, the Quaker Chorale is not a simplification of eighteenth-century music, but a modernist enhancement of it. In this regard, it serves more typically as an example of neo-classicism. Webb's period music is sly. It simplifies and renders brutal the music of the times, pricking their self-satisfaction while his music associated with Quakers and social uplift feature modernist traits. The character Hannay offers an unusual figure for being as relentlessly "othered" as anyone in the film, yet also the person articulating the most forward-looking sensibility in terms of criticizing the Age of Reason. That sensibility stems from his Quaker faith. Webb's musical motif for Hannay's faith including its modern call for greater kindness toward the unfortunate is a chorale that gestures toward but emphatically violates the musical ideals of the film's period setting in a single chord progression.

Hannay, the film's "hero," does not receive much music associated with him. The little he does receive turns out to be quite significant for revealing Webb pointing toward a future beyond the film's period setting where Hannay's ideals are still urgently needed.

The Last Words

The film closes, as many Lewton films do, with an onscreen Afterword, which Lewton called an "end title." With Hogarth's painting "Bedlam" behind it, this optimistic text appears: "Reforms were begun in 1773 – a new hospital was erected shortly afterward – and since that time Bedlam – once a by-word for terror and mistreatment – has led the way to enlightened and sensible treatment of the mentally ill." In his memo to Jack Gross, Lewton promised that his rewrites would eliminate the necessity of this card. Lewton wrote, "We hope in this way to get enough tension and finality in the final scene to let us dispense with the end title."[27] It disappeared from the shooting script, but clearly Lewton could not present the film without it.

Lewton's end title card is not accurate on many accounts. A reading of Bedlam's history finds no rebuilding in 1773. The building in use in 1761 when the film was set was completed in 1676 with a major expansion in 1739. That building had fallen into disrepair by 1780 but was still used until a new building was erected in 1815. As for reforms in treatment, the practice of allowing visitors to gawp at the inmates ended in 1770, ushering in a period of terrible mistreatment at the hospital owing to the total lack of outside supervision. This period of worsened abuse only ceased after Quakers erected a rival institution in York and unfavorable comparison of Bedlam to that rival institution forced a full parliamentary inquiry into the treatment of the mentally ill at Bedlam in 1816.[28] As a presentation of history, *Bedlam* leaves much to be desired. One fear the film posed for RKO's overseas distributors concerned the reaction the British would have to a film presenting an extant national institution in such an unflattering light. This end title with its myriad inaccuracies may be Lewton's attempt to assuage British censors. It made no impact; the film was banned in Great Britain for decades.

Despite its inaccuracies, Lewton's end title points toward the producer's ambition for the film. Lewton wanted to embrace the message picture, which was becoming quite popular in Hollywood as the war ended. But his end title feels weirdly out of tune. Why congratulate the past in a message picture, a quasi-genre inviting action from its audience?

Here Webb parts ways with Lewton. His messaging is clearer despite his artistic medium lacking the precision of the written word. Through his Quaker Chorale, Webb points to Hannay as a bridge from the "in-period" bustle and facade of the Age of Reason to the urgency of action in modern times.

Notes

1. Joel Siegel, *Val Lewton: The Reality of Terror* (New York: Viking Press, 1973), p. 77.
2. "14 RKO Pictures to Exceed Million in Prod. Cost in Coming 'Year of Years,'" *Variety* (September 12, 1945), p. 12.
3. Gilbert Grau, orchestral score for "Vengeance" from *Bedlam*. RKO Radio Pictures Studio Records (Collection PASC 3). UCLA Library Special Collections, Charles E. Young Research Library, University of California, Los Angeles.
4. Jonathan Andrews, Asa Briggs, Roy Porter, Penny Tucker, and Keir Waddington, *The History of Bethlem* (New York: Routledge Press, 1997), p. 14.
5. Carlos Keith [Val Lewton] and Mark Robson, "Chamber of Horrors: A Tale of Bedlam" script dated June 30, 1945. RKO Radio Pictures Studio Records (Collection PASC 3). UCLA Library Special Collections, Charles E. Young Research Library, University of California, Los Angeles.
6. Ibid.
7. Charles Higham and Joel Greenberg, *The Celluloid Muse: Hollywood Directors Speak* (Chicago: Henry Regnery Company, 1969), p. 211.
8. Evidence of Jack Gross's insistence on cuts can be found in a memo from Lewton to Gross dated June 26, 1945 with the subject line, "'Bedlam Rewrite Notes." In it Lewton writes, "While the trial of Sims commences in the general room, Tom the Tiger and Nell make their escape. Once they are safely on the roof it is the intention to dissolve and avoid further chases across the roof tops and corridors, thus saving many expensive sets and time." Val Lewton, memo to Jack Gross housed in RKO Radio Pictures Studio Records (Collection PASC 3). UCLA

Library Special Collections, Charles E. Young Research Library, University of California, Los Angeles.
9. Carlos Keith [Val Lewton] and Mark Robson, "Chamber of Horrors: A Tale of Bedlam" script dated June 30, 1945. RKO Radio Pictures Studio Records (Collection PASC 3). UCLA Library Special Collections, Charles E. Young Research Library, University of California, Los Angeles.
10. In keeping with Hogarth's tendency to provide text in his paintings, this one features two verses (27 and 28) from Chapter One of *Proverbs*: "When fear cometh as desolation and their destruction cometh as a Whirlwind: When distress cometh upon them, then they shall call upon God, but He will not answer." The foreword's tone of judgment upon the times receives amplification through this choice of images and the text Hogarth used to contextualize his image.
11. The term comes from Paul Ricouer, *Freud and Philosophy*, Denis Savage, translator (New Haven, CT: Yale University Press, 1970), p. 32.
12. J. P. Telotte, *Dreams of Darkness: Fantasy and the Films of Val Lewton* (Urbana: University of Illinois Press, 1985), p. 173.
13. Ibid., p. 175.
14. The film's presentation of the Whigs as the opposition and the Tories in power in 1761 when the film is set is an anachronism. The Whigs ceased to function as a cohesive political party in 1760 with the ascent of King George III for their permanently dividing into factions. The Tories had expired as an important political force during the year depicted in the film and never recovered. The modern colloquialism of calling the Conservative Party the Tories is just that, a colloquialism.
15. Carlos Keith [Val Lewton] and Mark Robson, "Chamber of Horrors: A Tale of Bedlam" script with Boris Karloff's marginalia. Cinematic Arts Library, University of Southern California, p. 54.
16. Lewton defines "a dose of iron" in his screenplay: "This is a curious and frightening contraption of steel plate and chain, a terrifying travesty of chivalrous armor."
17. K. J. Donnelly, *The Spectre of Sound: Music in Film and Television* (London: BFI, 2005), p. 55.
18. Mary Ann Doane, *The Emergence of Cinematic Time: Modernity, Contingency, the Archive* (Cambridge, MA: Harvard University Press, 2002), pp. 2–3.
19. Charles Hindley, *A History of the Cries of London, Ancient and Modern* (London: Reeves and Turner, 1881), p. 131.
20. Richard Jewell and Vernon Harbin, *The RKO Story* (New York City: Arlington House, 1982), pp. 104 and 116.
21. Edmund Bansak, *Fearing the Dark: The Val Lewton Career* (Jefferson, NC: MacFarland & Company, 1995), p. 309.
22. Scott MacQueen, "Roy Webb: The Forgotten Man." CD liner notes for *Roy Webb: Music for the Val Lewton Films* (Munich: Marco Polo, 2000), p. 20.
23. Andrew Tudor, *Monsters and Mad Scientists: A Cultural History of the Horror Movie* (Oxford: Basil Blackwell, 1989), p. 113.
24. Hugh Macdonald, "[G-Flat Major]," *19th-Century Music*, Volume 11, Number 3 (1988), p. 226.
25. Ibid.

26. Christopher Palmer, *The Composer in Hollywood* (London: Marion Boyars, 1990), p. 162.
27. Val Lewton, Memo to Jack Gross dated June 26th, 1945, p. 2. RKO Radio Pictures Studio Records (Collection PASC 3). UCLA Library Special Collections, Charles E. Young Research Library, University of California, Los Angeles.
28. Andrews et al., pp. 99 and 415–417.

10 A CLOSING ARGUMENT

By way of closing these nine stories of how music operates within the horror films of Val Lewton, I want to remind the reader of elements of the introduction that resonate throughout the book and justify its approach. These few echoes set the stage for a discussion of the origins of the project and its methods.

Echoes

This book benefits enormously from Val Lewton Jr.'s revelation of his father's tone deafness. "[My father] must have understood the importance of music to film but didn't have the facility to really appreciate the nuances of a film score."[1] By severing the auteur from a key parameter of an audiovisual medium, space opens for examining that parameter's independent voice.

One could easily conjecture that few studio-era producers really understood music's inner workings, so this observation about Val Lewton is not itself wholly explanatory. But how many producers do we know from first-hand testimony were actually tone deaf?

Next, I want to sound an echo not of Roy Webb's music but of his words by way of explaining why treating the music of these films as a gateway to understanding them makes sense. His interview with *Film Music Notes*, includes this key passage, "I was lucky to be working on the artistic melodramas of producer Val Lewton, and felt that they deserved a deeper and more thoughtful treatment than the usual picture of this category."[2]

This echo from the introduction prompts an echo of K. J. Donnelly's claim that the films themselves prompted Roy Webb to a high degree of subtlety in his musical treatment.[3] What Webb claimed about his work, Donnelly heard decades later. This book explores the contours of what Webb called "a deeper and more thoughtful treatment."

My aim has been an effort to supply the contours not only of Webb's "deeper treatment," but also of the entire RKO Music Department's. A different scholar looking at the same films, scores, scripts, memos, letters, and source material would surely tell a different story. My claim is not that I know what Webb meant, but that I can imagine what I believe to be one version of this story.

The Origin of this Project

This project finds its origin rooted in my love for these texts. The nine horror films discussed in this book offer a distinct, alternate vision of how a cinematic genre might operate. The Lewton unit's intervention touched on both the intrinsic and extrinsic qualities of the horror genre. In terms of the intrinsic, we find the genre's conventional dichotomy of "normal and other" upset in every film. This upset troubles the film cycle's relationship with society by accentuating the "other" within the "normal" and the "normal" within the "other."

By way of examples, *Cat People* humanizes Irena while underscoring how callow her "normal" husband proves. Similarly, *I Walked with a Zombie* examines the irrational embedded in the thinking of the supposedly reasonable characters and the rationality in the perspective of the superstitious ones. While the zombie Carrefour provides a figure easily rendered "other" for his imposing black body, the film shows him walking calmly with the film's female lead in its opening shot. RKO's original one-sheet poster for the film features Jessica's imposing figure, not Carrefour's. Even in selling the film, RKO's marketing department declined to trade on this potential "other" so central to the horror genre.

Universal Pictures' horror cycle also humanizes its monsters now and then. Karloff's sad-eyed monster may not be the noble personage of Mary Shelley's novel, but he invites sympathy, especially in the sequel *The Bride of Frankenstein* (1935). A difference in degree divides the films discussed in this book and those of their rival studio. The Monster abducts Elizabeth under the instructions of the fiendish Dr. Pretorius (Ernest Thesiger), who holds him in thrall. Like all the films in Universal's Frankenstein franchise, *The Bride of Frankenstein* is in every sense a monster movie.

More important than the occasional scene of sympathy for the devils of the genre is the depiction of their adversaries. Some Universal horror "pursuers" look pretty bad. Dr. Garth (Otto Kruger) in *Dracula's Daughter* (1936) springs to mind with his unthinking use of Lili (Nan Grey) in order to extract knowledge from her for his purposes, not her salvation. But make no mistake, Lili is in this doomed position for being the victim of the film's monster, not Garth's recklessness.

Where Lewton's approach wholly parts company with genre norms is at the extrinsic level. Lewton's approach banishes the physical manifestations of monstrosity that mark Universal's legendary "others." Similarly banished are the vague middle European settings, the unclear historical contexts, the angry villagers, the hunchbacked minions, the mad scientists and their laboratory lairs, castles, fog-bound moors, bats, electrical storms, and full moons.

In place of the genre's more typical settings, props, and personages of the 1930s, Lewton locates his films – until the advent of Karloff at RKO – in everyday settings associated with contemporary America. Attending this stylistic change, he further locates monstrousness in ordinary people who clearly view their actions as wholly justified, even inevitable given their circumstances. Given the films' intervention into the intrinsic elements of the genre, this leads from time to time to the "pursuers" becoming the monster and vice versa. Irena, for example, even becomes her own pursuer as the tyranny of normalcy hounds her to suicide.

The result of Lewton's interventions is a cinema outlining a surprisingly humane agenda: one that humanizes figures easily cast as "other" (Irena or Carrefour or The Finn or Thea), explores the dehumanizing potentials of certitudes rooted in self-styled normalcy (Oliver or Paul or Pherides or Sims), and even offers atonement for trading in violent entertainment (*The Leopard Man*). Moreover, Lewton locates violence not in the action of an individual, monstrous transgressor, but in a larger communal context that failed the "other" and itself through economic injustice and a lack of compassion for everyone, from a young girl (Amy) to a madwoman (Dorothea, the dove).

More than recasting its monsters in a more sympathetic light, Lewton's films cast its pursuers, its leading men and women, its community under threat in an emphatically skeptical light. *Cat People* interrogates heteronormativity, psychiatry, and the reassurances Oliver finds in just being "a good plain Americano." *I Walked with a Zombie* sounds out misgivings about Western Reason. *The Leopard Man* hammers away at commercialism in art, eventually striking true against capitalism with its critique of the profit motive in a context of economic disequilibrium. *The Seventh Victim* doubts the potential for much human happiness, even rendering its leading man oddly "other." *The Ghost Ship* questions authority, but more importantly, questions whether the victims of authority can muster the courage to save themselves. *The Curse of the Cat People* offers an unhappy portrait of parenthood while casting doubt on the suitability of its adults to guide its lonely, damaged youngster into a stable future. *The Body Snatcher* looks at the economics of crime rooted in social convention. *Isle of the Dead* shows military duty and the certitudes it prompts in a negative light – surprising for a wartime film. And *Bedlam* is not convinced that The Enlightenment was at all enlightened. These are discordant films. They doubt their genre's logic, extending that doubt to social conditions often taken for granted by their intended audience.

After falling in love with these films, my admiration only grew with repeated viewings. Then, as a college student, I read J. P. Telotte's book *Dreams of Darkness*,[4] and his psychoanalytic reading of them opened my eyes to the possibilities not only of these films but to the vistas the Humanities might open. My problem evolved into the question of how can musicology, one of the Humanities, approach these texts with the same enthusiasm Telotte displayed in his work?

The Origins of an Ad Hoc Analytical Method

When I decided that I needed to write something about the music within Lewton's horror films, the project took me into the archives at UCLA, USC, the University of Syracuse, the Cincinnati Conservatory, the Library of Congress, George Washington University, and The Margaret Harreck Library. These many, lengthy visits revealed more and more evidence of the Lewton unit's attention to detail, but more specifically the RKO Music Department's attention to detail.

My first discovery of a clear path toward an argument of the Music Department moving beyond the instructions in spotting sheets came when reading a draft of the script for *Cat People*. Bodeen and Lewton call for the monkey organ in the opening scene to play *Aida*, yet the Music Department supplied *Martha* in its stead. This opened my eyes to the possibility that an argument about the music in the films might yield something fresh, something that the volumes of analysis by film scholars dealing with the film and with the larger Lewton cycle had missed.

After that, my path became clear. The music in each film may be offering an analytical path into the core of each film just as the *Martha* quote points toward the possibility that Irena is the victim of the self-styled normal people who literally intrude into her solitary life and finally into her home. To be sure, Irena clawed Dr. Judd to death. But remember that Judd assumed Irena would want him sexually and deceived Oliver in order to enter her home to facilitate an unwanted sexual encounter with his patient in violation of both law and professional codes of conduct. I am not alone in seeing Irena as the film's victim. Kim Newman spelled it out with clarity some years ago albeit without recourse to music,[5] while the RKO Music Department, with its canny substitution of *Martha* spelled it out in one of those carefully crafted details that make these films an enduring pleasure.

In UCLA's superbly managed archive of RKO's Music Department materials is Roy Webb's handwritten arrangement of a very particular moment in *Martha*.[6] I would not want to say he is the sole agent of this substitution. He may have arranged that moment at the suggestion of anyone in the Music Department. My goal is not to make Webb into a hero, only to illustrate that in films crafted with such creative care, the Music Department both participates in that care and reveals an early understanding of what these films might mean. "Might mean" because in the end the audience decides that, and almost everything I claim in this book about its music could be fairly charged as non-obvious to a lay audience.

That *Martha* moment in the archive transformed my vague desire to write about the music in these films into a systematic exploration of how the music within each of them benefitted from the same care and subtlety so frequently attributed to their hands-on producer. I do not think this diminishes Lewton's stature, but it does recast his collaborators not merely as able contributors to his vision, but as important interpreters of that vision who translated his vision into sound. In translating, meanings invariably take on fresh nuance.

A Concluding Overview Film by Film

The films are subtle and surprisingly diverse in their aims. Each requires its own analytical methodology. Insofar as Film Studies has generally argued for their unity of style and theme, I would like to point out the different conclusion I came to as a musicologist.

In brief, I argue that *Cat People* criticizes the tyranny of normalcy. To illustrate this musically, I rely on more than the *Martha* substitution. Peter Franklin provides a model in his discussion of *King Kong* by looking at the link of music to the fantastic and feminine.[7] In *Cat People*, these two concepts are both embodied in Irena, not in a woman and a giant ape. The film's music entirely illustrates the interiority of Irena, binding the audience to her, not to those she threatens. On the singular occasion when the film provides music for Oliver and Alice, all of it comes from Irena's record collection which they use to kill time waiting to fulfill their tyrannical agenda.

All of the music in *I Walked with a Zombie* participates in the film's organizational conceit of doublings first observed by Robin Wood and extended to the musical realm in this book.[8] By weakening the film's Western nondiegetic score through stylistic disunity and limiting it scope to one setting while favoring its diegetic music created by actual Caribbean musicians, the film's critique of Western Reason finds able musical support. Moreover, by linking the film's male lead along with his claims to Reason to Chopin, an entire hermeneutic field of subjectivity opens up to undermine the male lead's claim to the sort of objectivity essential to the brand of Reason he espoused.[9]

Robynn Stillwell's theoretical discussion of music from a fantastical gap allows for an examination of how music drifts into and out of the diegesis in *The Leopard Man*,[10] often existing only in the gap between them. This drift sutures the work of the Music Department to the film's larger project. As musical performance appears within the film's diegesis, it entertains within a film that criticizes the unintended consequences of entertaining. Among those unintended consequences is the realization that the root of violence can be found within the generation of violent imagery.

Three madrigalistic gestures appear often in the score of *The Seventh Victim*. Each is associated with aspects of the film's epigraph: "I runne to death and death meets me as fast, and all my pleasures are like yesterday." While I chose to use the older term "madrigalism" rather than the more contemporary "topic" or the vaguely pejorative "mickey-mousing," I did so because of the literalism of the music resembling the aristocratic musical practices of the Italian madrigal. Ascents illustrate the striving of the Donne quote. The Freudian "death impulse" and its attendant repetitious behaviors are represented by repeated ostinatos. An iambic rhythm akin to the last two strikes of a clock's chime come to illustrate death itself, the end of time.

Irwin Bazelon's understanding of a film's soundtrack as proto-*musique concrète* reached me first through Neil Lerner's work on the "sonic stew" of *Dr. Jekyll and Mr. Hyde*.[11] Sarah Kozloff's work on voices in film completed the theoretical underpinning of my argument about *The Ghost Ship*.[12] The possibility of hearing the entire soundtrack as musical makes my discussion of *The Ghost Ship* possible. The discrete elements of the film's soundtrack (sound effects, dialogue, diegetic music, and nondiegetic music) combine to reinforce the film's chilling proposition that authoritarianism finds support in the complacency of the many concerning the plight of the few.

Star studies and musicology may constitute strange bedfellows; however, my examination of music within *The Body Snatcher* suggested this odd hybrid. In truth, my work is not strictly a star study, but rather an examination of how Boris Karloff's presence altered the sonic style of Lewton's films. "B" budget period pieces necessitate help from the soundtrack in order to transport the audience to another place and another time. Roy Webb supplied ample such help for *The Body Snatcher*. I argue that Karloff's presence did more than force Webb to trot out a Scottish topic in his film or rehearse the conventions of the *agitato* or the "stinger," both in such short supply in his earlier films. By analyzing the music of Karloff's voice delivering lines of his own writing, the chapter lurches close enough to star study as to provide fans of Boris Karloff an insight into his methods that earlier fine studies of the star missed.

Isle of the Dead offers Lewton's most compact and thorough meditation on the value of uncertainty. The Lewton unit's emphasis on shadow and absence offers a visual stylistics prompting uncertainty in his audience. Leigh Harline provides a musical score also emphasizing uncertainty through its unusual approach to meter, tempo, and mode. While we can never know Harline's intentions, we can see him consistently serving the film's central theme with the same "deeper and more thoughtful treatment" Webb described in *Film Music Notes*.

Finally, we come to *Bedlam*, where a critique of Enlightenment-era practices and general self-satisfaction comes under fire from the Lewton unit. In making a hybrid message picture, period piece, and horror film, the RKO Music Department found itself pressed with the same burdens faced on *The Body Snatcher* but now with the added pressure of serving the film's messaging about compassionate care for the mentally ill. Webb's music depicting the age offers a brutally simplistic tonal language with pages passing by with scarcely an accidental to indicate tones outside the key. His music supporting the film's most steadfast reformer, the Quaker Hannay, offers an anachronistic chorale arranged for instruments replete with an urgent, modern tonal harmonic language disqualified as "in period." Message pictures of the postwar era generally call for some action or reform. They are almost always set in modern times, as that constitutes the only space where something can be done. Webb's Quaker Chorale links the film's period setting with a contemporary sound, effectively striving to bridge the odd gap between a past that cannot be saved and a present that desperately needs saving.

A Needed Concession

Here, at the end, I must confess a limitation of this book, one that has certainly been noted by readers long before now. I have treated music in the horror films of Val Lewton often as though it was an aristocratic art aimed at the edification of only those who perform a minute excavation into its hidden meaning. I am no aristocrat, but I enjoy the privilege of tenure that grants me the time a movie audience normally lacks. "B" budget horror movies of the 1940s were never created for such careful viewing, let alone listening. I doubt anyone ever heard Webb's music for the Quaker meeting in *Bedlam* as I have heard it here. Indeed, I did not hear it this way until well into the project of writing this book.

Readers may be similarly annoyed here and there by what may appear an overreach on my part, or as my students sometimes say, "my reading too much into it." Occasionally I have taken the reader to the fringes of what I think possible. After all, I began this project from the suspect posture of loving these films, of wanting to celebrate them through the means available within my profession of musicology. My defense for any overreach is simply this: care has been taken to consider every scene and every note, and even more than one scene scripted but never shot or shot but cut before release. Every draft of every screenplay, every extant memo not hidden away from view by its owner, every page of notated music, every word of literary sources, and certainly every published analysis of these films and their music has been considered. All this informs an argument designed to allow the RKO Music Department to take its full share of the admiration these films inspire.

My aim in approaching the music of Lewton's horror films has never been to expose what is readily and obviously there for all to see and hear. I have willfully bucked the tendency in film music scholarship to trade in the general and theoretical. In doing so, I wanted to set aside the assumption that we must consume this art as its corporate origins intended. Instead, we can celebrate the care undertaken in using music in and creating music for these films that seem to me still, even after spending far too much time with them, bursting with humane insight. These films are of their time in many ways, and are certainly available to all manner of critique. *Bedlam* most of all seems conflicted and on the verge of doing what it protests, of "othering" the mentally ill. If we only look for flaws, we surely miss something. Critique on its own is ill-equipped to discover the Lewton unit's exquisite striving toward a cinema of compassionate ideals expressed through a wealth of details that bear close scrutiny without wilting. Similarly, only by imagining for a time that the music within them might be painting the text with detail and imagination can we hear this bizarre, corporate, easily ignored music in a way that celebrates it and more importantly rewards it for the sheer pleasure it has caused, and I hope will persist in causing.

Notes

1. Correspondence between the author and Val Lewton, Jr., January 19, 2006.
2. Roy Webb, "Pattern for Mystery," *Film Music Notes* (March 1945).
3. K. J. Donnelly, *The Spectre of Sound: Music in Film and Television* (London: BFI, 2005), p. 98.
4. J. P. Telotte, *Dreams of Darkness: Fantasy and the Films of Val Lewton* (Urbana: University of Illinois Press, 1985).
5. Kim Newman, *Cat People* (London: BFI Publishing, 1999).
6. Music Department files for *Cat People*, RKO Radio Pictures Studio Records (Collection PASC 3). UCLA Library Special Collections, Charles E. Young Research Library, University of California, Los Angeles.
7. Peter Franklin, "*King Kong* and Film on Music: Out of the Fog," in *Film Music: Critical Approaches*, ed. K. J. Donnelly (Edinburgh: University of Edinburgh Press, 2001), pp. 88–102.
8. Robin Wood, *Hollywood from Vietnam to Reagan . . . and Beyond* (New York: Columbia University Press, 2003), pp. 133–134.
9. Rose Rosengard Subotnik, *Developing Variations: Style and Ideology in Western Music* (Minneapolis: University of Minnesota Press, 1991), p. 163.
10. Robynn Stilwell, "The Fantastical Gap between Diegetic and Nondiegetic," in *Beyond the Soundtrack: Representing Music in Cinema*, eds. Daniel Goldmark,

Lawrence Kramer, and Richard Leppert (Berkeley: University of California Press, 2007).
11. Irwin Bazelon, *Knowing the Score: Notes on Film Music* (New York: Van Nostren Reinhold, 1975), p. 147, and Neil Lerner, "The Strange Case of Rouben Mamoulian's Sonic Stew: The Uncanny Soundtrack in *Dr. Jekyll and Mr. Hyde* (1931)," in *Music in the Horror Film*, ed. Neil Lerner (New York: Routledge, 2010), pp. 66–72.
12. Sarah Kozloff, *Overhearing Film Dialogue* (Berkeley: University of California Press, 2000).

REFERENCES

Agee, James, *Agee on Film* (New York: Grosset & Dunlap, 1969).
Agee, James, "*Curse of the Cat People*," *The Nation* (April 1, 1944).
Agee, James, "Films," *The Nation* (March 23, 1946).
Agee, James, "Year in Review," *The Nation* (January 20, 1945).
Andrews, Jonathan, Asa Briggs, Roy Porter, Penny Tucker, and Keir Waddington, *The History of Bethlem* (New York: Routledge Press, 1997).
Anker, Elizabeth, and Rita Felski, *Critique and Postcritique* (Durham, NC: Duke University Press, 2017).
Austin, Bruce, "An Interview with Robert Wise," *Literature/Film Quarterly*, Volume 6, Number 4 (Fall, 1978).
Bansak, Edmund, *Fearing the Dark: The Val Lewton Career* (Jefferson, NC: MacFarland & Company, 1995).
Bazelon, Irwin, *Knowing the Score: Notes on Film Music* (New York: Van Nostren Reinhold, 1975).
Benshoff, Harry, *Monsters in the Closet: Homosexuality and the Horror Film* (Manchester: University of Manchester Press, 1997).
Berg, Louis, "Farewell to Monsters," *Los Angeles Times* (May 12, 1946).
Berks, John, "What Alice Does: Looking Otherwise at *The Cat People*," *Cinema Journal* (Fall, 1992).
Bodeen, DeWitt, "Val Lewton Proved that Even Low-Budget Films Can Have Artistic Integrity," *Films in Review* (Fall, 1963).
Bordwell, David, *Reinventing Hollywood: How 1940s Filmmakers Changed Movie Storytelling* (Chicago: University of Chicago Press, 2017).
Bordwell, David, Janet Staiger, and Kristin Thompson, *The Classical Hollywood Cinema: Film Style and Mode of Production to 1960* (New York: Columbia University Press, 1985).

Bowman, Laura, and LeRoy Antoine, *The Voice of Haiti* (New York: Clarence Williams Music, 1938).
Brosnan, John, *The Horror People* (London: St. Martin's Press, 1976).
Buhler, James, *Theories of the Soundtrack* (Oxford: Oxford University Press, 2019).
Care, Ross, "The Film Music of Leigh Harline," *Film Music Notebook*, Volume 2, Number 2 (1978).
Chion, Michel, *Audio-Vision: Sound on Screen*, Claudia Gorbman, translator (New York: Columbia University Press, 1994).
Chion, Michel, *Film, A Sound Art*, Claudia Gorbman, translator (New York: Columbia University Press, 2009).
Clarens, Carlos, *An Illustrated History of Horror and Science-Fiction Films* (New York: Putnam, 1967).
Crowther, Bosley, "Boo to You," *The New York Times* (May 20, 1943).
Crowther, Bosley, "The Screen," *The New York Times* (March 4, 1944).
Crowther, Bosley, "Who's Looney Again?" *The New York Times* (September 18, 1943).
Dawson, Clive, "Ardel Wray: Val Lewton's Forgotten Screenwriter," *Bright Lights Film Journal* (December 26, 2018).
Dennis, David B., *Beethoven in German Politics, 1870–1989* (New Haven, CT: Yale University Press, 1996).
Doane, Mary Ann, *The Emergence of Cinematic Time: Modernity, Contingency, the Archive* (Cambridge, MA: Harvard University Press, 2002).
Donnelly, K. J., *The Spectre of Sound: Music in Film and Television* (London: BFI, 2005).
Eggert, Brian, "The Definitives: Appreciations and Critical Essays about Great Films: *The Curse of the Cat People*," in *Deep Focus Review* (October 22, 2017).
Eisler, Hanns, and Theodor Adorno, *Composing for the Films* (New York: Oxford University Press, 1947).
Ellis, Sarah Reichardt, and Michael Lee, "Monsters, Meaning, and the Music of Chopin in American Horror Films of the 1930s and '40s," *Journal of Musicological Research*, Volume 39, Issue 1 (Winter, 2020).
Farber, Manny, "Against the Grain," *The New Republic* (September 11, 1944).
Franklin, Peter, "*King Kong* and Film on Music: Out of the Fog," in *Film Music: Critical Approaches*, ed. K. J. Donnelly (Edinburgh: Edinburgh University Press, 2001).
Franklin, Peter, *Seeing Through Music: Gender and Modernism in Classic Hollywood Film Scores* (Oxford: Oxford University Press, 2011).
Freud, Sigmund, *Beyond the Pleasure Principle (The Standard Edition)*, James Strachey, translator (New York: Liveright Publishing Corporation, 1961).
Fujiwara, Chris, *Jacques Tourneur: The Cinema of Nightfall* (Baltimore, MD: Johns Hopkins University Press, 1998).
Gomery, Douglas, *The Hollywood Studio System: A History* (London: British Film Institute, 2005).
Gorbman, Claudia, "The Master's Voice," *Film Quarterly* (January 12, 2015).
Gorbman, Claudia, *Unheard Melodies: Narrative Film Music* (Bloomington: University of Indiana Press, 1987).

Hanson, Helen, "Sound Affects: Post-Production Sound, Soundscapes, and Sound Design in Hollywood's Studio Era," *Music, Sound, and Moving Image*, Volume 1, Number 1 (2007).

Haworth, Catherine, "Dames, Darlings, and Detectives: Women, Agency, and the Soundtrack in RKO Radio Pictures Crime Films," PhD dissertation, University of Leeds, 2010.

Hayward, Philip, "Introduction," in *Terror Tracks: Music, Sound and Horror Cinema* (London: Equinox Publishing, 2009).

Higham, Charles, and Joel Greenberg, *The Celluloid Muse: Hollywood Directors Speak* (Chicago: Henry Regnery Company, 1969).

Hillman, James, *Re-Visioning Psychology* (New York: Harper & Row, 1975).

Hindley, Charles, *A History of the Cries of London, Ancient and Modern* (London: Reeves and Turner, 1881).

Hollinger, Karen, "The Monster as Woman: Two Generations of *Cat People*," in *Film Criticism*, Volume 13, Number 2 (Winter, 1989).

Hugill, Stan, *Shanties from the Seven Seas* (Mystic, CT: Mystic Seaport Press, 1994).

Jewell, Richard, and Vernon Harbin, *The RKO Story* (New York: Arlington House, 1982).

Klein, Michael, *Intertextuality in Western Art Music* (Bloomington: University of Indiana Press, 2005).

Kozloff, Sarah, *Overhearing Film Dialogue* (Berkeley: University of California Press, 2000).

Kramer, Lawrence, *Music as Cultural Practice, 1800–1900* (Berkeley: University of California Press, 1993).

Larson, Randall, *Musique Fantastique: A Survey of Film Music in the Fantastic Cinema* (Metuchen, NJ: The Scarecrow Press, 1985).

Larson, Randall, "The Quiet Horror Music of Roy Webb: Scoring Val Lewton (The Robert Wise Films)," *Midnight Marquee*, Issue 44 (Summer, 1992).

Lee, Michael, "Sound and Uncertainty in the Horror Films of the Lewton Unit," in *Music, Sound, and Filmmakers*, ed. James Wierzbicki (New York: Routledge Press, 2012).

Lee, Michael, "Subverting Horror Genre Conventions in Val Lewton's *The Leopard Man*," in "The Image of Violence in Literature, Media, and Society: 1995 SASSI Conference Proceedings" (Pueblo, CO: *Society for the Academic Study of Social Imagery*, University of Southern Colorado, 1995).

Lerner, Neil, "Preface" to *Music in the Horror Film: Listening to Fear* (New York: Routledge Press, 2010).

Lerner, Neil, "The Strange Case of Rouben Mamoulian's Sonic Stew: The Uncanny Soundtrack in *Dr. Jekyll and Mr. Hyde* (1931)," in *Music in the Horror Film*, ed. Neil Lerner (New York: Routledge, 2010).

Lindsay, Cynthia, *Dear Boris* (New York: Knopf, 1975).

Link, Stan, "Horror and Science Fiction," in *The Cambridge Companion to Film Music*, eds. Mervyn Cooke and Fiona Ford (Cambridge: Cambridge University Press, 2016).

McCarten, John, "The Current Cinema," *The New Yorker* (July 16, 1949).

Macdonald, Hugh, "[G-Flat Major]," *19th-Century Music*, Volume 11, Number 3 (1988).
MacQueen, Scott, "Roy Webb: The Forgotten Man." CD liner notes for *Roy Webb: Music for the Val Lewton Films* (Munich: Marco Polo, 2000).
MacQueen, Scott, "The Val Lewton Thrillers." CD liner notes for *Roy Webb Music for the Val Lewton Films* (Munich: Marco Polo, 2000).
Mank, Gregory, *Bela Lugosi and Boris Karloff: The Expanded Story of a Haunting Collaboration* (Jefferson, NC: McFarland & Company, 2009).
Mank, Gregory, *The Hollywood Cauldron* (Jefferson, NC: McFarland & Company, 1994).
Mulvey, Laura, "Visual Pleasure in Narrative Cinema," *Screen* (Autumn, 1975).
Nemerov, Alexander, *Icons of Grief: Val Lewton's Home Front Pictures* (Berkeley: University of California Press, 2005).
Neumeyer, David, and James Buhler, "Analytical and Interpretive Approaches (I)," in *Film Music: Critical Approaches*, ed. K. J. Donnelly (New York: Continuum, 2001).
Newman, Kim, *Cat People* (London: BFI Publishing, 1999).
Nugent, Frank, "The Grapes of Wrath," *The New York Times* (January 25, 1940).
Palmer, Christopher, *The Composer in Hollywood* (London: Marion Boyars, 1990).
Paul, William, "What Does Dr. Judd Want? Transformation, Transference, and Divided Selves in *Cat People*," in *Horror Film and Psychoanalysis: Freud's Worst Nightmare*, ed. Steven Jay Schneider (Cambridge: Cambridge University Press, 2004).
Platte, Nathan, *Making Music in Selznick's Hollywood* (New York: Oxford University Press, 2018).
Reisman, David, *The Lonely Crowd* (New Haven, CT: Yale University Press, 1950).
Ricoeur, Paul, *Freud and Philosophy*, Denis Savage, translator (New Haven, CT: Yale University Press, 1970).
Roeder, George, *The Censored War: American Visual Experience during World War II* (New Haven, CT: Yale University Press, 1993).
Rohrer Paige, Linda, „The Transformation of Woman: The ‚Curse' of the Cat Woman in Val Lewton/Jacques Tourneur's *Cat People*, its Sequel, and Remake," *Literature Film Quarterly* (Fall, 1997).
Rosar, William H., "Music of the Monsters: Universal Pictures' Horror Film Scores of the Thirties," *The Quarterly Journal of the Library of Congress*, Volume 40, Number 1 (Winter, 1983).
Rosengard Subotnik, Rose, *Developing Variations: Style and Ideology in Western Music* (Minneapolis: University of Minnesota Press, 1991).
Samson, Jim, "Chopin Reception: Theory, History, and Analysis," in *Chopin Studies 2*, eds. John Rink and Jim Samson (Cambridge: Cambridge University Press, 1994).
Siegel, Joel, "Tourneur Remembers," *Cinefantastique* (April 1973).
Siegel, Joel, *Val Lewton: The Reality of Terror* (New York: Viking Press, 1973).
Steiner, Max, "Notes to You," unpublished manuscript, Film Music Archives, Brigham Young University.
Stilwell, Robynn, "The Fantastical Gap between Diegetic and Nondiegetic," in *Beyond the Soundtrack: Representing Music in Cinema*, eds. Daniel Goldmark, Lawrence Kramer, and Richard Leppert (Berkeley: University of California Press, 2007).

Telotte, J. P., *Dreams of Darkness: Fantasy and the Films of Val Lewton* (Urbana: University of Illinois Press, 1985).

Tudor, Andrew, *Monsters and Mad Scientists: A Cultural History of the Horror Movie* (Oxford: Basil Blackwell, 1989).

van Elferen, Isabella, *Gothic Music: The Sounds of the Uncanny* (Cardiff: University Press of Wales, 2012).

Wallace, Inez, "I Walked with a Zombie," *American Weekly Magazine*.

Wallington, Nellie Urner, *American History by American Poets, Volume One* (New York: Duffield and Company, 1911).

Wang, Dan, "The Voice of Feeling: Liberal Subjects, Music, and Cinematic Speech," *The Oxford Handbook of Voice Studies*, eds. Nina Sun Eidsheim and Katherine Meizel (Oxford: Oxford University Press, 2019).

Weaver, Tom, Michael Brunas, and John Brunas, *Universal Horrors: The Studio's Classic Films, 1931–1946*, second edition (Jefferson, NC: McFarland & Company, 2007).

Webb, Roy, "Pattern for Mystery," *Film Music Notes* (March 1945).

Webb, Roy, "Things a Motion Picture Composer Has to Think About," *Film Music Notes* (October 4, 1941).

West, M. L., *Ancient Greek Music* (Oxford: Clarendon Press, 1992).

Winters, Ben, "The Non-Diegetic Fallacy: Film, Music, and Narrative Space," *Music and Letters*, Volume 91, Number 2.

Wood, Robin, *Hollywood from Vietnam to Reagan ... and Beyond* (New York: Columbia University Press, 2003).

Wood, Robin, "The Shadow Worlds of Jacques Tourneur: *Cat People* and *I Walked with a Zombie*," in *Personal Views: Explorations in Film, Revised Edition* (Detroit, MI: Wayne State University Press, 2006).

Woolrich, Cornell, *Black Alibi* (New York: Ballentine, 1982).

FILMS CITED

Apache Drums (1951), dir. Hugo Fregonese
Bedlam (1946), dir. Mark Robson
Before I Hang (1940), dir. Nick Grinde
Belle of the Yukon (1944), dir. William Seiter
The Bells of St. Mary's (1946), dir. Leo McCarey
Black Friday (1940), dir. Arthur Lubin
The Body Snatcher (1945), dir. Robert Wise
The Bride of Frankenstein (1935), dir. James Whale
Brute Force (1947), dir. Jules Dassin
Calling Dr. Death (1943), dir. Reginald Le Borg
Captive Wild Woman (1943), dir. Edward Dmytryk
Careful, Soft Shoulders (1942), dir. Oliver Garrett
Cat People (1942), dir. Jacques Tourneur
Cattle Queen of Montana (1954), dir. Allan Dwan
Citizen Kane (1941), dir. Orson Welles
The Climax (1944), dir. George Waggner
The Curse of the Cat People (1944), dir. Gunther Fritsch and Robert Wise
Dead Man's Eyes (1943), dir. Reginald Le Borg
The Devil and Daniel Webster (1941), dir. William Dieterle
Dr. Jekyll and Mr. Hyde (1931), dir. Rouben Mamoulian
Dracula's Daughter (1936), dir. Lambert Hillyer
The Exorcist (1973), dir. William Friedkin
The Falcon's Brother (1942), dir. Stanley Logan
The Falcon and the Co-eds (1943), dir. William Clemens
Fantasia (1941), dir. James Algar, Samuel Armstrong, and Ford Beebe Jr.

Frankenstein (1931), dir. James Whale
Frankenstein Meets the Wolf Man (1943), dir. Roy William Neill
The Ghost of Frankenstein (1942), dir. Erle C. Kenton
The Ghost Ship (1943), dir. Mark Robson
Government Girl (1943), dir. Dudley Nichols
The Grapes of Wrath (1940), dir. John Ford
Hitler's Children (1943), dir. Edward Dmytryk
Horror of Dracula (1957), dir. Terence Fisher
House of Frankenstein (1944), dir. Erle C. Kenton
The Hunchback of Notre Dame (1939), dir. William Dieterle
I Walked with a Zombie (1943), dir. Jacques Tourneur
The Invisible Ray (1936), dir. Lambert Hillyer
Isle of the Dead (1945), dir. Mark Robson
Journey into Fear (1943), dir. Norman Foster
Jungle Woman (1943), dir. Reginald Le Borg
King Kong (1933), dir. Merian C. Cooper and Ernest Schoedsack
The King's Speech (2010), dir. Tom Hooper
La última cena (1976), dir. Tomás Guttiérez Alea
Lady and the Tramp (1955), dir. Clyde Geronimi, Wilfred Jackson, and Hamilton Luske
The Lady Has Plans (1942), dir. Sidney Lanfield
The Leopard Man (1943), dir. Jacques Tourneur
Love Actually (2003), dir. Richard Curtis
Mademoiselle Fifi (1945), dir. Robert Wise
The Magnificent Ambersons (1942), dir. Orson Welles
Margin for Error (1943), dir. Otto Preminger
The Mask of Fu Manchu (1932), dir. Charles Brabin
The Master (2012), dir. Paul Thomas Anderson
A Midsummer Night's Dream (1935), dir. Max Reinhardt
The More the Merrier (1943), dir. George Stevens
The Most Dangerous Game (1932), dir. Irving Pichel and Ernest Schoedsack
The Mummy (1932), dir. Karl Freund
The Mummy's Curse (1943), dir. Leslie Goodwins
The Mummy's Hand (1940), dir. Christy Cabanne
The Mummy's Tomb (1942), dir. Harold Young
My Favorite Wife (1940), dir. Garson Kanin
A Night of Adventure (1944), dir. Gordon Douglas
The Old Dark House (1932), dir. James Whale
Pacific Liner (1939), dir. Lew Landers
The Phantom of the Opera (1943), dir. Arthur Lubin
Pinocchio (1940), dir. Ben Sharpsteen and Hamilton Luske
Pluto Junior (1942), dir. Clyde Geronimi
Pride of the Yankees (1942), dir. Sam Wood
Quality Street (1937), dir. George Stevens
Rhapsody in Blue (1945), dir. Irving Rapper
The Seventh Victim (1943), dir. Mark Robson

The Seventh Voyage of Sinbad (1958), dir. Nathan Juran
She (1935), dir. Lansing Holden and Irving Pichel
Snow White and the Seven Dwarfs (1937), dir. David Hand
Son of Dracula (1943), dir. Robert Siodmak
Son of Frankenstein (1939), dir. Rowland Lee
A Song to Remember (1945), dir. Charles Vidor
Stranger on the Third Floor (1940), dir. Boris Ingster
A Tale of Two Cities (1935), dir. Jack Conway
Tender Comrade (1943), dir. Edward Dmytryk
They Got Me Covered (1943), dir. David Butler
To Have and Have Not (1945), dir. Howard Hawks
Two Yanks in Trinidad (1941), dir. Gregory Ratoff
Weird Woman (1944), dir. Reginald Le Borg
Whispering Ghosts (1942), dir. Alfred Werker
White Zombie (1932), dir. Victor Halperin
The Wizard of Oz (1939), dir. Victor Fleming
The Wolf Man (1941), dir. George Waggner
Youth Runs Wild (1944), dir. Mark Robson
Zombies on Broadway (1945), dir. Gordon Douglas

INDEX

Academy Awards, 145, 146
Adorno, Theodor, 7
aeolian flute, 44
aeolian harp, 44
"Aeolian Harp" (poem), 55–6n
Agee, James, 109, 116, 124, 167n
Aida, 27, 34, 194
Alas! Jamie's Pickled: Elegiac Lines on the Tragical Murder of Poor Daft Jamie, 138–9
Alea, Thomás Gutiérrez, 56n
"The Amorous Ghost", 106, 117n
Anker, Elizabeth, 8
"Annie Laurie", 6
Antoine, LeRoy, 9, 13, 44–6, 49, 56n
Apache Drums, 56n
Arsenic and Old Lace (play), 120
atonality, 10–11, 131
auteur theory, 4–7, 124

Bach, Johann Sebastian, 53, 168n, 187
    Toccata and Fugue in D Minor, 53
Bakaleinikov, Constantin, 23, 166
Bansak, Edmund, 83n, 87, 144
Barnard, Charlotte Alington, 127
Bazelon, Irwin, 10, 91, 110, 196

BBC, 20
Bedlam, 16, 124, 169–88, 195, 197, 198
Beethoven, Ludwig van
    Piano Sonata No. 14 in C# Minor, 77–8
    Symphony No. 5 in C Minor, 12, 20–1
Before I Hang, 137
Belle of the Yukon, 45
The Bells of St. Mary's, 169
Bennet, Norman, 9, 14, 52, 77, 84n
Benshoff, Harry, 84n, 87
"Berceuse du chat", 29
Beyond the Pleasure Principle, 73
Billy Budd, 87
Black Alibi, 59–61
Black Friday, 137
"Blow the Man Down", 97–9, 101, 102, 104n
Böcklin, Arnold, 122, 148
Bodeen, DeWitt, 5, 6, 24, 26–7, 29, 71, 107, 109
The Body Snatcher (film), 11, 15, 121, 122–3, 125–40, 143, 148, 154, 169, 171, 176–7, 181, 193–4, 196, 197
"The Body-Snatcher" (short story), 122–3

INDEX

"The Bombardment of Bristol" (poem), 26–7
"The Bonnets of Bonnie Dundee", 130
Bordwell, David, 14, 41–2, 93, 105, 107, 110, 117n
Boyer, Lyle, 143, 147
Brahms, Johannes
  Waltz in A-flat Major, 77–8
Breen, Joseph, 123
The Bride of Frankenstein, 10, 136–7, 192
"The British Grenadiers", 51
Brontë, Charlotte, 40
Buhler, James, 10–11, 56n, 96–7, 126
Burke, William, 122, 130, 138
Burns, Robert, 127

"The Caledonian Hunts Delight", 127
Calling Dr. Death, 107, 167n
Captive Wild Woman, 71
Careful, Soft Shoulders, 146
Cass, John, 9
Cat People, 4, 6, 7, 8, 11, 12–13, 20–3, 24, 25–32, 33–6, 37n, 39–40, 49, 55, 56n, 59, 66, 71, 83n, 85n, 91, 105, 106, 108, 109, 110, 113–14, 115, 116, 124–5, 139, 140, 148, 192, 193, 194, 195
Cattle Queen of Montana, 103n
"The Chambered Nautilus", 80, 84n
"Cheers, My Laddies", 139
Chion, Michel, 3, 81–2, 93, 97
Chopin, Frédéric, 50, 52–5, 195
  E Major Étude, Op. 10, No. 3, 13, 51–5
Churchill, Frank, 145
Citizen Kane, 13, 41–2
Clarens, Carlos, 1–2
Claribel, 127
click track, 153
The Climax, 120
"Cobbler, Cobbler Mend My Shoe", 115
Coleridge, Samuel Taylor, 55–6n
Committee for the First Amendment, 71
Conrad, Joseph, 87
Cooper, Gary, 94

Cooper, Merian C., 23
Craig, Alec, 26–7
Crawford, F. Marion, 106
Crosby, Bing, 169
Crowther, Bosley, 61, 82, 105, 109
The Curse of the Cat People, 14–15, 72, 83n, 103n, 105–16, 117n, 120–1, 124–5, 139, 167n, 193

D'Agostino, Albert, 6
Dead Man's Eyes, 167n
Dean, Julia, 110
Dekker, Thomas, 182–3
De Packh, Maurice, 9, 14, 79
Derrida, Jacques, 57n
The Devil and Daniel Webster, 27
Dieterle, William, 22, 23
Disney Studios, 15, 145–6, 167n
Disney, Walt, 140–1n, 144, 167n
Dix, Richard, 92, 103n
Dmytryk, Edward, 71–2, 106
"Do, do l'enfant do", 29, 30–2, 114
Doane, Mary Ann, 177
Dr. Jekyll and Mr. Hyde (1931 film), 9, 10, 12, 53, 91, 123, 196
Dr. Jekyll and Mr. Hyde (novel), 123
Dr. Willowbird, 56n
Donne, John, 73, 74, 196
  Holy Sonnets, 73, 74, 83n
Donnelly, K. J., 10, 11–12, 15, 26, 126, 127, 129, 177, 192
Dracula's Daughter, 192–3

Eggert, Brian, 116–7n
Eisler, Hans, 7
Elferen, Isabella van, 53
Ellis, Sarah Reichardt, 13, 18n, 57n
The Exorcist, 138

The Falcon and the Co-Eds, 83n
The Falcon's Brother, 83n
Fantasia, 145
Farber, Manny, 6
Faulkner, Norbert, 103n
FBI, 71, 148
Fearing, Franklin, 111
Felski, Rita, 8

209

"The Fort Holland Song", 51–2, 57n, 96, 97
Foster, Susanna, 120
The Fountainhead (film), 94
The Fountainhead (novel), 93–4
Frankenstein (1931 film), 119
Frankenstein Meets the Wolf Man, 107, 120
Franklin, Peter, 2–3, 12–13, 19n, 32–3, 195
Freud, Sigmund, 73, 196
Fritsch, Gunther V., 117n
Fujiwara, Chris, 48–9

The Ghost of Frankenstein, 107, 120
The Ghost Ship, 14, 83n, 86–102, 104n, 106, 124–5, 139, 193, 196
Gluck, Christoph Wilibald, 185
Golding, Samuel, 103n
Gorbman, Claudia, 3, 12–13, 15, 29, 32, 33, 34, 49, 102, 106, 125–6, 135, 139, 165
Government Girl, 146
The Grapes of Wrath (film), 93
The Grapes of Wrath (novel), 93
Grau, Gilbert, 9, 170
Gross, Jack, 121, 123, 140, 144, 146, 154, 171, 187, 188n
Grubb, John C., 79–80

Hare, William, 122
Harline, Leigh, 9, 12, 15–16, 144–6, 149, 153–66, 196–7
A Harlot's Progress, 170, 177
Hartfield, Kathleen, 56n
Hawaii Theater (Los Angeles), 169
Haworth, Catherine, 7, 11, 13, 65, 68, 69, 83n, 177
Haydn, Franz Joseph, 185
Hayward, Philip, 9, 10–12
Hearst, William Randolph, 41
Hepburn, Katherine, 177
"Here We Come to San Sebastian", 97
Herrmann, Bernard, 27
Hillman, James, 112, 147
A History of the Cries of London, Ancient and Modern, 177

Hitchcock, Alfred, 6
Hitler's Children, 71
Hobart, Rose, 143, 166n
Hoffman, Philip Seymour, 139
Hogarth, William, 170–1, 172, 187, 189n
Hollywood Ten, 71
Holmes, Oliver Wendall, 80
The Honest Whore, 182–3
Horror of Dracula, 9
House of Frankenstein, 120, 121, 140
Hudibras, 170
The Hunchback of Notre Dame (1939 film), 23

"Ich ruf zu dir: Herr Jesu Christ", 53
"Il est né, le divin Enfant", 111
"I'm Billy Radd", 96–7
Industry and Idleness, 170
Invisible Ray, 137
Isle of the Dead (film), 15–16, 122, 143–4, 146–7, 148–66, 169, 170, 195, 196–7
Isle of the Dead (painting), 122
I Walked with a Zombie, 8, 13, 39, 40–1, 42–51, 54–5, 56n, 58, 59, 71, 85n, 86, 96, 100, 102n, 104n, 123, 124–5, 140, 148, 192, 193, 195

Jane Eyre (novel), 40
Jones, Darby, 50, 51
Journey into Fear, 87
jump scare, 9, 26
Jungle Woman, 167n

Karloff, Boris, 10, 15, 119–20, 121–2, 124, 125–6, 135, 136–40, 142n, 143, 144, 146, 169, 175, 192, 193, 196
Keller, Walter, 6
Kesselring, Joseph, 120
King George III, 189n
King Kong (1933), 9, 10, 12, 13, 19n, 23, 29, 32–3, 181, 195
The King's Speech, 104n
Klein, Michael, 35
Knaggs, Skelton, 104n, 143

Koerner, Charles, 20, 22–3, 39, 40, 55n, 59, 71, 83n, 103n, 106, 107, 120–1
Kozloff, Sarah, 103n, 196

Lady and the Tramp, 118n
The Lady Has Plans, 146
Larsen, Randall, 116
Lee, Donna, 127, 177
"The Legend of Sleepy Hollow", 110, 112, 116
Le Gon, Jeni, 56n
The Leopard Man, 11, 13–14, 58–70, 124–5, 148, 176, 193, 196
Lerner, Neil, 9, 10, 91, 196
LeRoy Antoine Haitian Dance Troupe, 45, 56n
"Levee Dumbala", 45
Lewton, Nina, 58, 121, 143–4
Lewton, Ruth, 6
Lewton, Val, 1–2, 3, 4, 5–7, 13, 14, 16, 22–5, 26–7, 29, 35–6, 39–40, 45, 50, 51, 52, 55–6n, 58, 59, 60, 61–5, 66, 71–2, 82, 83n, 87, 97–9, 103n, 104n, 106–8, 109, 118n, 119–23, 124–7, 136, 137, 138, 139–40, 141n, 142n, 143–4, 146, 147, 148, 149, 154, 166n, 169, 170, 171–2, 182, 187, 189n, 191, 193, 195, 196, 197, 198
Lewton, Jr., Val, 6–7, 191
Liebestraum, 52
Link, Stan, 9–10, 18n, 138
Liszt, Franz, 52
Lockert, John, 72, 83n
London, Jack, 87
The Lonely Crowd, 111
Lorentz, Pare, 22
Los Angeles Council of Social Agencies, 111
Love Actually, 104n
Lugosi, Bela, 123

McCarten, John, 94
McCarthy, Joseph, 71
MacDonald, Hugh, 186, 187
MacDonald, Philip, 123, 141n
MacQueen, Scott, 182

Mademoiselle Fifi, 103n, 121, 171
The Magnificent Ambersons, 24
Mamoulian, Rouben, 91
Margin for Error, 146
Martha, 27–8, 34, 83n, 194–5
The Mask of Fu Manchu, 119
The Master, 15, 139
Melville, Herman, 87
The Merry Wives of Windsor, 112
MGM, 22, 24
"mickey-mousing", 10, 167n, 196
A Midsummer Night's Dream (film), 118n
Mischel, Josef, 166n
The More the Merrier, 146
The Most Dangerous Game, 10, 23
Mozart, Wolfgang Amadeus, 185
MPA, 140–1n
The Mummy, 119
The Mummy's Curse, 167n
The Mummy's Hand, 117n
The Mummy's Tomb, 107, 117n
Musuraca, Nicholas, 6, 25, 110
musique-concrète, 2, 10, 79–80, 91, 110–11, 196
My Favorite Wife, 167n

Nazimova, Alla, 22, 108
Neal, Patricia, 94
Nemerov, Alexander, 2, 5–6, 87, 101, 102
Neumeyer, David, 10–11
Newman, Alfred, 23
Newman, Kim, 4, 34–5, 194
A Night of Adventure, 146
"Nothing Else to Do" (song), 27
novachord, 31, 38n, 66
Nugent, Frank, 93

Odeta, 57n
The Old Dark House, 119
"O Legba", 45
"O Marie Congo", 45, 46
O'Neal, Charles, 71
Orfeo ed Euridice, 185
Ostrow, Lew, 39–40

Pacific Liner, 103n
Palmer, Christopher, 18n, 168n, 182, 187

Pierce, Jack, 119, 120
Pinocchio, 145
Platte, Nathan, 3
Pluto Junior, 145
Poe, Edgar Allan, 176
Ponitz, Jessie, 24
Previn, Charles, 25
Pride of the Yankees, 146
Production Code, 64, 81, 85n, 97–8

Quality Street, 176, 177, 184

Raab, Leonid, 9, 14, 30–1, 66, 85n, 114–15
The Rake's Progress (painting), 170
Rand, Ayn, 93–4, 140–1n
Randolph, Jane, 105, 106–7
"Reuben Ranzo", 112
Rhapsody in Blue (film), 45
Rialto Theater (New York), 20, 169
Ricoeur, Paul, 8
Riesman, David, 111
Rimsky-Kosakov, Nikolai, 6
RKO Pictures, 1, 12, 18n, 22–3, 29, 40, 41, 45, 55n, 59, 71–2, 103n, 106, 107, 117n, 120, 121, 123, 124, 131, 140, 142n, 145, 146, 169, 177
  Art Department, 110, 126
  logo, 20–1
  Marketing Department, 192
  Music Department, 3–4, 7, 9, 13, 14, 15, 27, 31, 35, 45, 58, 77, 116, 119, 126, 139, 141n, 153, 154, 177, 184, 192, 194, 195, 196, 197, 198
  theater chain, 22
Robat, Ed, 39, 55n
Rogell, Sid, 120–1
Robson, Mark, 24, 25, 71, 72, 87, 168n, 170–1, 172
Rosar, William H., 19n

St. Mary's of Bethlehem Hospital, 169, 187–8
Salter, Hans, 25
Samson, Jim, 53
Sarver, Francis, 14, 90, 103n

Sawtell, Paul, 83n, 146, 167n
Schaefer, George, 22
Scheherazade, 6
The Sea Wolf, 87
"The Screaming Skull", 106, 117n
The Secret Sharer, 87
Selznick, David O., 3, 22
The Seventh Victim, 10, 14, 55–6n, 71–83, 87, 91, 125, 148, 169, 193, 196
The Seventh Voyage of Sinbad, 118n
Shakespeare, William, 112, 144
"Shame and Sorrow", 51–2, 57n, 96, 97
She, 23
Shelley, Mary, 192
"Shepherds Shake Off Your Drowsy Sleep", 111
Siegel, Joel, 5, 61, 105, 107, 144
Simon, Simone, 29, 105, 106–7, 108
Siodmak, Curt, 40, 106
Sir Lancelot, 9, 13, 14, 45, 50–2, 53, 57n, 96–7, 104n
Skinner, Hans, 25
Smith, Kent, 94, 105, 106–7
Smith, Paul, 145
Snow White and the Seven Dwarfs, 145, 167n
Soldi, Steve, 23, 27
A Song to Remember, 53
Son of Dracula, 107
Son of Frankenstein, 137
"Spit Song", 130, 139, 141n
Steinbeck, John, 93
Steiner, Max, 10, 11, 13, 18n, 23, 29, 32–3, 96–7, 153, 158, 165
Stevenson, Edward, 110
Stevenson, Robert Louis, 122–3
Stilwell, Robynn, 13–14, 68–9, 80, 83, 196
stingers, 10, 132–4, 196
Stranger on the Third Floor, 72, 83n, 131
Strauss, Richard, 10
Stravinsky, Igor, 29
Subotnik, Rose Rosengard, 53

A Tale of Two Cities, 24
Telotte, J. P., 13, 15, 41, 51, 78–9, 87, 104n, 111–12, 147–8, 172, 195

Tender Comrade, 146
"They Creep By Night", 107
They Got Me Covered, 146
topic theory, 15–16, 22, 126, 153–4, 159, 160, 164, 177, 178, 196
Tourneur, Jacques, 6, 24, 39–40, 48, 59, 61
Tristan und Isolde
  Liebestod, 52
Tudor, Andrew, 28–9, 33, 60, 68, 90, 94, 100, 185
Two Yanks in Trinidad, 51

La última cena, 56n
Universal Pictures, 9, 11, 15, 22, 24, 25, 26, 40, 71, 83n, 106, 107, 119, 120, 121, 123, 140, 146, 167n, 192, 193

Vidor, King, 94
The Voice of Haiti, 45
Von Flotow, Friedrich, 27

Wagner, Richard, 10, 52
Wallace, Inez, 40–1
"Wallee Nan Guinan", 45
Wang, Dan, 104n
Warner Brothers, 22
Waxman, Franz, 10, 11
Webb, Roy, 4, 6, 7, 9, 10, 11–14, 16, 18n, 20–2, 26, 27–8, 29–32, 33–4, 35–6, 44, 46, 47–50, 53–4, 58, 65–7, 69, 70, 72–3, 75–7, 78, 79, 80–3, 90, 91, 99–102, 110–1, 112–5, 116, 125–9, 131–6, 139, 145, 146–7, 153, 154, 159, 165, 166, 167n, 168n, 170, 176, 177–85, 186–7, 188, 191–2, 195, 196, 197
"We'd Better Bide a Wee", 127
Weird Woman, 167n
Welles, Orson, 6, 22
Whale, James, 119
"When Ye Gang Awa, Jamie", 128–30
"When You Wish upon a Star", 145
The Whispering Ghost, 146
"Will He Nah Come Back Again", 128
Winters, Ben, 127–8
Wise, Robert, 117n, 121–2, 127, 138
The Wizard of Oz, 118n
The Wolf Man, 24–5, 37n, 40, 60
Wood, Robin, 4, 43–4, 195
Woolrich, Cornell, 59–61, 69
Wray, Ardel, 40, 52, 60, 66, 166n
Wray, Fay, 32–3

Youth Runs Wild, 83n, 106, 109, 121, 146, 167n

Zombies on Broadway, 51, 123

EU representative:
Easy Access System Europe
Mustamäe tee 50, 10621 Tallinn, Estonia
Gpsr.requests@easproject.com